HANDBOOK OF INTERNATIONAL DISASTER PSYCHOLOGY

**Recent Titles in
Contemporary Psychology**

HANDBOOK OF INTERNATIONAL DISASTER PSYCHOLOGY

Volume 4
Interventions with Special Needs Populations

Edited by Gilbert Reyes and Gerard A. Jacobs

Preface by Charles D. Spielberger

Foreword by Benedetto Saraceno

Praeger Perspectives

Contemporary Psychology
Chris E. Stout, Series Editor

Westport, Connecticut
London

Library of Congress Cataloging-in-Publication Data

Handbook of international disaster psychology / edited by Gilbert Reyes and Gerard A.
Jacobs ; preface by Charles D. Spielberger ; foreword by Benedetto Saraceno.
     p. cm. — (Contemporary psychology, ISSN 1546–668X)
    Includes bibliographical references and index.
    ISBN 0-275-98315-3 ((set) : alk. paper) — ISBN 0-275-98316-1 ((vol. I) : alk.
paper) — ISBN 0-275-98317-X ((vol. II) : alk. paper) — ISBN 0-275-98318-8 ((vol. III) :
alk. paper) — ISBN 0-275-98319-6 ((vol. IV) : alk. paper) 1. Disaster victims—Mental
health. 2. Disaster victims—Mental health services. 3. Disasters—Psychological aspects.
4. Disaster relief—Psychological aspects. 5. Humanitarian assistance—Psychological
aspects. 6. Community psychology. I. Reyes, Gilbert. II. Jacobs, Gerard A. III. Contemporary
psychology (Praeger Publishers)
    RC451.4.D57H36   2006
    362.2'2—dc22   2005018786

British Library Cataloguing in Publication Data is available.

Library of Congress Catalog Card Number: 2005018786
ISBN: 0-275-98315-3 (set)
       0-275-98316-1 (vol. 1)
       0-275-98317-X (vol. 2)
       0-275-98318-8 (vol. 3)
       0-275-98319-6 (vol. 4)

ISSN: 1546–668X

First published in 2006

Praeger Publishers, 88 Post Road West, Westport, CT 06881
An imprint of the Greenwood Publishing Group, Inc.
www.praeger.com

Printed in the United States of America

The paper used in this book complies with the
Permanent Paper Standard issued by the National
Information Standards Organization (Z39.48–1984).

10   9   8   7   6   5   4   3   2   1

DEDICATION

The *Handbook of International Disaster Psychology* would not have been possible without the compassion and commitment of the international humanitarian community. In a world where millions are killed or harmed each year, either by natural hazards or because of the intentional and accidental actions of humankind, legions of caring people rise to these occasions, determined to relieve the suffering and protect the welfare of people who are in the most dire of circumstances.

The recent history of humanitarian operations has seen a surge of violence directed against these most charitable and nonpartisan individuals who have sacrificed the safety of their homes and families, and who have risked their lives to comfort distant neighbors and to promote peace in the face of force.

Those of us living in zones of relative safety, passing our days and nights in homes and workplaces equipped with modern conveniences, and having plentiful access to clean water, should feel humbled by the courage, dedication, and resilience of those who journey unarmed to enact the values and embody the virtues of our better nature.

In light of these things, it is a small thing indeed to dedicate this book to the international humanitarian personnel who are its inspiration.

Gilbert Reyes

CONTENTS

SET FOREWORD

As I write this, the media are filled with video footage and written accounts of survivors and relief workers in the aftermath of "The Tsunami." For many this is a word newly added to their vocabulary, along with words like "al Qaeda" or "anthrax" that were added a few years ago—formerly foreign and unknown, now sadly popular and common in use, as is "tsunami." But disasters—whether man-made or nature-born—share the common thread of victims in need. Historically the psychological and emotional impacts of disasters, regardless of genesis, on those impacted were largely left unconsidered. Thankfully, this has changed, and these books demonstrate another critical step in this evolving process and area of endeavor—a global consideration.

Too often, once psychological aspects of a phenomenon were considered, they were done so through a narrow lens of exclusively Western or Northern perspectives. Such work, while of definite merit, rigor, and additive benefit to knowledge, was limited in its generalizability. I very much enjoyed the turn of phrase that a reporter for the *Wall Street Journal* used in citing coeditor Gerard Jacobs: "Care for traumatic stress," he warns, "can't be delivered by Western experts parachuting into affected cultures without an appreciation of the cultures infused with strong Islamic, Hindu, and Buddhist beliefs." So true in so many additional ways, and yet so often unwittingly ignored—but thankfully changing.

At this point in time there is a growing appreciation, understanding, and grateful application of the adage that one size does not always fit all. Reyes and Jacobs have woven together a group of authors whose perspectives and work clearly demonstrate the differential aspects of dealing with the trauma of disasters from a global, diverse set of perspectives. Such is a major step forward, and I congratulate them.

For some reason still a mystery to me, it is very easy for most observers to consider post-disaster aid and relief efforts to exclusively include food, shelter, and medical attention. But what cameras cannot capture as well as food stations, vaccination lines, and pitched tent encampments are the psychological wounds that without intervention (when called for) can become scars at best, or risk the infection of apathy or stigma, and result in the deadly consequences of suicide, substance abuse, and other manifest ills. Perhaps this inability for many to "see" fosters a concomitant inability to understand. People can see grain being trucked in and food stations preparing and distributing it, but they cannot see those who cannot eat it for lack of will.

Still More to Do

Much of my work involves medication distribution and medical interventions in areas of need. And again, and thankfully, while there is still a massive amount to be done globally in the battle for treating HIV/AIDS and getting retrovirals distributed, it is equally important to distribute culturally based and relevant psychosocial support for those who need such care. Both are necessary to save their lives. Both.

It is said that there are often opportunities in crises. Perhaps we may see some as a result of the current worldwide focus on the region impacted by the tsunami. Many had never heard of or cared about Aceh prior to the disaster, but there had already been a 15-year-long "disaster" when the water hit that the world had ignored—an often brutal Indonesian military dominion that has resulted in deaths of over 10,000 in Aceh alone, resulting from guerrilla skirmishes with separatist rebels. Along with this loss of lives are comorbid human-rights abuse allegations of torture and rape at the hands of the troops. Now with Kofi Annan's pronouncement that "the UN is the lead in the coordination of the humanitarian effort," there is renewed hope that a side effect will have a kindling influence for the end of such political violence. Likewise, in Sri Lanka then U.S. Secretary of State Powell visited vis-à-vis relief efforts, and it is hoped that the tsunami will also be a catalyst for restarting the stalled peace talks between the government and the ethnic-based insurgency known as the Liberation Tigers of Tamil Eelam (ETTE), or Tamil Tigers.

Psychologically trained researchers and clinicians obviously have much to offer, as evidenced in this set of books. It is a positive evolution that such psychological professionals are now considered along with other colleagues when the proverbial yellow tape is strung in the aftermath of a catastrophe. It is also important to have like involvements in preparation—be it in conflict resolution, resilience training, or other related aspects.

Irony?

Perhaps it is the psychology of indifference or just irony, but last year the United Nations proclaimed that the world's "worst humanitarian disaster" was . . .? The tsunami? No, in fact they were referring to the mass killings in the Darfur region of Sudan by militias. This appears on few television screens or newspaper front pages, and thus is not on many people's minds or touching many people's hearts. Not that there is some morbid competition for compassion, response, and intervention between tsunami victims and the Sudanese, but it certainly is easier to offer relief to an area after a natural catastrophe than it is to intervene in an armed combat situation. The ghosts of Rwanda come to mind, however, and many mental health professionals are focusing efforts there a decade after the genocide, and it makes me wonder what the psychological aftermath will be in Sudan.

Most of the world has empathetically responded to those impacted by the tsunami—they have contributed, volunteered, prayed, and shed tears. And this is how it should be. But such is not so for Darfur today or Kigali a decade ago. Perhaps psychology and mental health professionals should add to their already overburdened to-do lists to work on how to move the world away from such indifference. I remain hopeful based on the work of those herein.

Chris E. Stout
Series Editor

FOREWORD

Every day millions of people in the world are affected by disasters. For many reasons, people in resource-poor countries tend to be hit especially hard by disasters. Data from Red Cross and Red Crescent societies suggest that resource-poor countries tend to be confronted with more conflict and more natural disasters compared to countries that are rich. Resource-poor countries tend to have weaker physical infrastructures that are less likely to withstand extreme conditions, such as earthquakes or cyclones. Also, resource-poor countries tend to have fewer financial resources to prepare for and respond to disaster. Most resource-poor countries often invest relative few resources in their health systems. Most resource -poor areas in the world hardly invest in mental health services and do not have well-functioning community-based mental health systems through which a post-disaster mental health response may be organized.

Disaster psychology is a complex field. Disaster psychology deals with psychological trauma (i.e., an extreme stressor that is likely to elicit a strong acute anxiety and/or dissociation reaction in most people) as a risk factor for mood and anxiety disorders and for nonpathological physical and emotional distress. Psychological trauma is an area that is generating rich research in the areas of anthropology and sociology, child protection and social work, epidemiology and health economics, history and philosophy, neuroscience and pharmacology, clinical and social psychology, psychiatry and psychotherapy, public health and health services research, political science and social policy, and alcohol and other substance abuse management. Thus, disaster psychology practitioners need to be able to think beyond their discipline. Disaster psychology deals not only with psychological trauma but also with enormous losses, which often tend to be forgotten. Affected persons may have lost family members, community support structures, employment and valued material possessions during the disaster. Like trauma, loss is a well-known risk factor for mood and anxiety disorders, for nonpathological distress as well as social problems. Thus, a disaster psychology practitioner needs to be not only an expert on psychological trauma but also an expert on loss and community change. Moreover, the practitioner needs to know how to work in and with communities in a culturally appropriate way. Also, the practitioner needs to know how to work in a collaborative and coordinated manner with others, because uncoordinated aid responses are not in the best interest of disaster survivors.

Concern for people's mental health after disasters is a relatively recent phenomenon. Disaster psychology is a young field; practitioners and researchers alike need to learn from one another. We all need to learn from one another on how to achieve meaningful objectives in a culturally appropriate and sustainable manner in order to reduce avoidable mental and social suffering without causing harm. This handbook provides a rich collection of writings by many of the world's experts on disasters. Reading these chapters will prepare both novice and experienced practitioners for a better response. This is an important book.

Benedetto Saraceno
Director
Department of Mental Health and Substance Abuse
World Health Organization

PREFACE

Catastrophic events causing great damage and destruction have been a part of human life since the beginning of world history. The earth-shaking, cataclysmic eruption of Mount Vesuvius in 79 AD, which wreaked terrible destruction and loss of life, and completely destroyed the Roman city of Pompeii, continues to be reflected in recent excavations. The devastation caused last year by four hurricanes in Florida during a period of less than six weeks and the great seawave produced by the tsunami in the Indian Ocean and Southeast Asia have received major recent attention. Hundreds of people in Florida are not yet back in their homes nearly a year after the fourth hurricane; victims who lost their lives in the tsunami disaster are still being identified and survivors are still searching for them months later.

Not so visible or readily recognized are the psychological effects of disasters for survivors, effects that can linger large and long in the minds of even those with no apparent physical injuries. Effects from the horrific and huge loss of life. Loss of home. Loss of identity. Loss of nearly all that was familiar. Sometimes, too, loss of dignity, faith, or even the will to live.

The development of theory, research, and professional practice by psychologists and other mental health specialists evaluating and helping the victims of such catastrophic events is relatively new, and much needed. This four-volume *Handbook of International Disaster Psychology* provides a solid foundation to facilitate understanding of the terrible effects of traumatic disasters. Vital information is also provided on assessment of disaster victims, and on interventions to help those who are directly affected to deal with their resulting emotional distress and physical injuries.

The general goals of these volumes are to provide information for furthering the assessment of the psychological impact of disasters, and to report procedures for developing, implementing, and evaluating the effectiveness of these programs. Many contributors to this set have been deeply involved in projects to reduce the suffering of disaster victims, and to help them adapt to life circumstances substantially and adversely altered. The editors here have remarkable experience in disaster psychology, reflected in the chapters that they have contributed. Professor Gilbert Reyes is a tireless activist and educator in the field and Professor Gerard Jacobs was recently appointed to coordinate the activities of the American Psychological Association in providing assistance for victims of the recent tsunami.

The chapters first focus on fundamental issues pertaining to international disasters. Significant political and philosophical issues are also examined, and the need for effective collaboration among culturally diverse groups providing assistance is emphasized. The critical importance of understanding the particular needs and interests of populations indigenous to a disaster site is also spotlighted, along with the necessity of assessing available resources. Several contributors show us community-based models for assessment and intervention, as opposed to Western-oriented clinical approaches. Clearly, providing effective, culturally appropriate psychosocial support requires a great deal of skill and flexibility in programs that are delivered under very difficult circumstances.

We also come to understand, with these volumes, programs and practices that have been carried out in diverse geographical and cultural settings in Europe, Latin America, and Africa. In most, the interventions have focused on small groups, along with individuals and families, as the basic targets of intervention. The critical impact of national disasters in parts of the world where poverty, disease, and civil strife have weakened the capacity for coping with adversity is especially difficult to navigate, due to a persistent sense of danger that interferes with the healing process. Yet excellent examples of interventions are described, demonstrating why organizations such as the International Red Cross and the Red Crescent are considered best suited for dealing with disasters.

Reading in these books of interventions with refugees and "special needs" populations, we see that cultural diversity compounds the difficulty of developing effective programs. A prevailing climate of hatred and violence in many refugee populations further impairs effectiveness. And special emphasis is given to interventions that address the psychosocial needs of women and children, and to crisis interventions with military and with emergency services personnel.

These four volumes on international disaster psychology will be of great interest to psychologists, mental health workers, and other professionals working with disaster victims and their families. Trauma researchers, those interested in topics such as post-traumatic stress disorder (PTSD) and related disorders, will also find a wealth of useful information here. Indeed, these books will also well serve all students, scholars, and general readers focused on understanding how the most horrific, trying, and torturous of events can tear at psychological health, and how we all might play a role in helping heal the wounds.

For the past 30 years, I have personally worked in collaborative cross-cultural research with colleagues from more than 50 countries, and in developing adaptations of our anxiety and anger measures. I have also enjoyed and greatly benefited from participation in international meetings and conferences. While international psychology has addressed a wide range of topics, including stress and emotions, which have been the major focus of my work, these volumes pioneer new directions in psychological research and professional practice. Tsunamis, earthquakes, and other worldwide disasters are frequently encountered in modern life. Effective clinical and community interventions are urgently needed to help people cope. These volumes provide both a solid foundation for the emerging field of international disaster psychology and important guidelines for future research.

Charles D. Spielberger, Ph.D., ABPP
Distinguished Research Professor
University of South Florida, Tampa
Past President, American Psychological Association

ACKNOWLEDGMENTS

It goes without saying that the writing and editing of such an extensive book as this takes a great deal of effort and patience on the part of all concerned. What is perhaps less evident is that it also takes a great deal of trust and respect. As first-time editors undertaking a project of this scope and complexity, we required the trust of our publisher that we could indeed complete what we started. In this regard, we were extremely fortunate to be working with Debbie Carvalko at Greenwood Publishing, who came at this project with such infectious enthusiasm and confidence that she inspired the same in us. She also gently but firmly guided us through the unfamiliar process of delivering an edited book in four volumes consisting of over 40 chapters by authors from around the world. Without her patience, persistence, and professionalism, it is doubtful that this project could have proceeded so successfully.

We also required a great deal of trust from our colleagues, the authors who toiled for months over these chapters, that their efforts would not be in vain and that our work as their editors would prove commensurate to their investment in us. Many of these humanitarians and scholars knew us personally, but several did not, and all had only our word that the project would be completed as promised. We thank them sincerely for their confidence in our ability to make worthy use of their contributions.

The editors also wish to acknowledge the work of Mary E. Long, Ric Monroe, Sandra Schatz, and Tina Waldron, graduate research assistants who helped us to organize and process an almost unmanageable amount of information. Particular gratitude is owed for the editorial assistance supplied by Sandra Schatz, who labored tirelessly and diligently over the final drafts to detect and correct any errors or omissions. The efforts of these assistants are greatly appreciated and are reflected in the quality of these volumes.

Overview of the International Disaster Psychology Volumes

Gilbert Reyes

The four volumes that constitute the *Handbook of International Disaster Psychology* are composed of chapters addressing most of the pressing issues being confronted in this relatively new and expanding area of research and practice. Each volume and the chapters it contains are designed to inform a diverse audience of readers about the activities that have been undertaken around the globe to improve the psychological and emotional well-being of people affected by disasters. Many of the authors are deeply involved in developing programs and projects designed to relieve the psychological suffering of people exposed to disasters. They are mostly citizens of the Western nations, though the editors have attempted to attract contributions from colleagues residing in Asia, Africa, and South America. The objectives pursued by these authors in their humanitarian roles include, among other things, the assessment of the psychosocial impacts of disasters, implementation of prevention and intervention programs, and the development of strategies for improving the effectiveness of their programs. This in turn requires a sophisticated appreciation of factors that exert influence on the success of these operations. The authors have drawn from their own experience and what they have learned from other sources to share the key ideas and practices with the greatest promise of succeeding under the least favorable conditions. Their dedication to serving the psychosocial needs of people coping with terrifying and debilitating circumstances is deserving of the highest respect and admiration. Each is a humanitarian in the truest sense.

Volume 1: Fundamentals and Overview

The first volume of the *Handbook of International Disaster Psychology* provides readers with an orientation to the field of international disaster psychology

(Reyes, 2006) and an overview of the fundamental issues that pertain across most disasters and humanitarian emergencies. Toward that aim, the contributors identify and discuss many of the political and philosophical issues and assumptions involved in the humanitarian "therapeutic" enterprise and the "psychosocial" lens that magnifies the existence and importance of trauma to suit Western expectations (Pupavac, 2006). These matters cannot be easily dismissed, disputed, or ignored and reflect a perception among some that an intentional or inadvertent cultural imperialism comparable to "White Man's Burden" is at work.

The recent blending of military operations with humanitarian relief services has further complicated these issues by blurring the boundaries between partisan use of force to coercively serve national interests and impartial initiatives compelled by empathy and compassion (Wessells, 2006). Sadly, at the same time that agents of humanitarianism are accused of having sacrificed their fundamental principles to political expediency (Rieff, 2002), the casualty rates among relief personnel have skyrocketed, leading even the most courageous of NGOs to withdraw in the face of mounting dangers (Burnett, 2004; Gall, 2004; Kelly, 2004). And while few question the benefits and necessity of providing the tradition "survival" supplies, the value of psychosocial support has been a more contentious issue than most and remains unresolved. As a matter of conscience and ethics, anyone involved in promoting services of questionable benefit under conditions of mortal danger must acknowledge and respond respectfully to these concerns (Beech, 2006).

In order for psychosocial programs to be implemented successfully, effective collaboration among culturally diverse groups of people must take place (Peddle, Hudnall Stamm, Hudnall, & Stamm, 2006). Perhaps the most distinct intercultural partnership is that which forms between the populations indigenous to the disaster-affected areas and the relief agencies that are foreign to those regions. International humanitarian agencies employ expatriate (ex-pat) staff from around the world, so there is also a great deal of cultural diversity among their personnel. However, it is an undeniable reality of the hierarchical structure of these agencies that most of the managerial staff are of European or North American origin, while middle- and lower-level personnel comprise a more diverse assembly representing the less wealthy nations. Providing culturally appropriate psychosocial support under these conditions requires considerable skill and flexibility at every level, since the people with the most useful cultural knowledge and insight are often not those who decide policies and practices. Development of approaches that could be applied in any event and context is perhaps a desirable goal, but an unlikely one given the diversity of situations, values, cultures, and customs. Nevertheless, there are similarities across events that allow for construction of flexibly structured templates based on tested principles of good psychosocial practices (Ager, 2006).

A basic necessity for any relief operation is to assess the needs and resources of the affected populations, and in this regard psychosocial programs are not substantively different. Supplies and services based entirely on typical assumptions are unlikely to accurately match the types, levels, and characteristics of what is truly required in a specific context. Moreover, this profile of needs and resources is a moving target and must be persistently assessed and modified to remain pertinent (Dodge, 2006a). Among the many options for efficiently matching needs and services and making them available and useful to those who are most likely to benefit, the preference has shifted strongly toward community-based models, both for assessments and for intervention designs. Consequently, psychosocial planners and implementing personnel are less concerned with "clinical" training and skills because of the growing importance of methods associated with community psychology (Dodge, 2006b). The roles of ex-pat personnel are also increasingly educational in nature, with direct human services often being reserved for local staff, who are more likely to have the requisite language skills and cultural knowledge to work effectively within the communities where needs are greatest.

Communities constantly gather information to inform their decisions and guide the actions of their members. Thus, the importance of public information in disaster management should never be ignored. The mass news and entertainment media, especially television and increasingly the Internet, provide a critical resource in disasters, and the effective use of these media may spell the difference between success and failure in some instances (Kuriansky, 2006). Inaccurate rumors can have destructive consequences, and urgent transmission of vital information can save lives. And given the education components of psychological support, the print and electronic media are crucial to the mission of disseminating information that can help to reduce distress and direct survivors toward resources that are most likely to meet their needs. Therefore, it is important to make effective use of these techniques and technologies, in the interest of public education and according to well-proven public health models (Cohen, 2006).

Volume 2: Practices and Programs

The second volume of the *Handbook of International Disaster Psychology* addresses various psychosocial programs and the practices they employ to provide services to a variety of populations under difficult circumstances. The contributors describe not only what they do and with whom, but also the underlying reasons for certain decisions and activities. The approaches employed in designing effective intervention programs vary according to the types of problems being targeted and the types of people being helped. Some interventions are designed to work with people one at a time, though most are conducted with small groups or across entire communities. For instance, faculty at Massey University in New Zealand have developed and refined a model for providing optimal psychosocial care to youth and families (Ronan, Finnis, & Johnston, 2006). Their approach identifies the family as the basic unit of intervention, but it also makes optimal use of community resources such as schools and the news media. Under very different conditions, however, adaptations to cultural and sociopolitical conditions such as those encountered in Southeast Asia may require very different and innovative approaches (Armstrong, Boyden, Galappatti, & Hart, 2006). As is clear in these two examples, the approaches to such interventions are also profoundly influenced by the operational assumptions made by the designers and practitioners involved.

Ongoing violent conflicts produce perhaps the most difficult situations in which to implement such services, but the psychosocial needs that became evident during the collapse of the former Yugoslavia were urgent and could not wait until more peaceful times (Kapor-Stanulovic, 2006). The fact that hostilities have not ceased creates a perpetual sense of danger and dread, making it almost impossible to promote hope and healing with any sincerity. Similar horrors have been experienced across the African continent, whether stretched out over decades in such places as Uganda (Agger, 2006), or compressed into genocidal rampages as in Rwanda (Neugebauer, 2006). Although there are many important differences between conditions of persistent violence and singular events such as the terrorist bombing of the U. S. embassy in Nairobi (Ndetei, Kasina, & Kathuku, 2006), the psychological impact on survivors and the principles of psychosocial support are mostly similar.

Natural disasters can also wreak tremendous havoc, and they often occur in parts of the world where poverty, disease, and civil strife have already weakened the local capacity for coping with adversity. Latin American countries provide an example of such conditions (Cohen, 2006), with a recent string of major earthquakes and deadly storms having killed tens of thousands and left many times that number homeless and destitute. The prime example can be found in the recent history of Venezuela. That country was overwhelmed in 1999 by flooding and mudslides that killed over 30,000 people (Blanco, Villalobos, & Carrillo, 2006) and has since experienced a military junta, rioting, a disputed election, and extreme economic hardships. Given these worsening conditions, the psychosocial interventions initially mobilized for the flood survivors taught lessons about the need for developing long-range plans to deal with a succession of crises.

Among the organizations best suited for developing such capacities are the International Federation of Red Cross and Red Crescent Societies (IFRC), which has played an important role in teaching its member societies how to develop and sustain a national program of psychological support. An exemplary application of the IFRC model took place recently in Cuba, which had invited the psychosocial training director of the Danish Red Cross to provide a "training-of-trainers" for local Red Cross staff and volunteers. Those receiving the training then became trainers of others until, in just one year's time, they had disseminated the information and skills to every corner of their country (Atherton & Sonniks, 2006). The Cuban Red Cross has sustained and implemented its psychological support activities with great success as Cuba has endured a series of hurricanes and other disasters. More recently, the IFRC has published a manual consisting of six modules that is used to train its national societies in community-based principles of psychological support (Simonsen & Reyes, 2003). Training-of-trainers workshops employing that manual were field tested in Eastern Europe, Southeast Asia, and the Middle East and have since been conducted in several other regions around the world.

Concurrently, a number of other humanitarian NGOs have developed their own training procedures and begun to proliferate them wherever such a need is identified. Additional sources of training exist across various academic and clinical institutions scattered around the globe. Some of these institutions take a general approach to disaster mental health, while others specialize in assisting with a particular problem or population. What works best in any given instance is still an open question requiring further examination and resolution. What is clear, however, is that people and institutions interested in learning about the psychosocial programs and practices employed with disaster survivors now have access to more information and training options than ever before.

Volume 3: Refugee Mental Health

The third volume of the *Handbook of International Disaster Psychology* addresses several key issues confronted by those who have been involved in mental health work with refugees. Among the most persistently troubling aspects of international affairs in the twentieth century was the sharp increase in forced international migrations, which created refugee crises on a massive scale. This was one of the earliest and most pressing issues facing the fledgling United Nations, and it led to the creation of the United Nations High Commissioner for Refugees (UNHCR) in 1951. Worldwide estimates from international relief organizations indicate that there are more than 10 million refugees and twice that number of internally displaced persons (IDPs) at this time. The psychosocial impact of the countless horrific events that characterize the refugee experience are sometimes temporary and manageable, but can also be enduring and disabling. Among survivors of war, the prevalence of psychological distress and mental disorders is often strikingly elevated, as studies of Vietnamese and Cambodian refugees demonstrated over two decades ago (Kinzie, 2006).

To accurately assess the mental health needs of displaced and transient populations is a difficult task under the best of circumstances, and to do so during the emergency phase is in some ways the most difficult option (Jacobs, Revel, Reyes, & Quevillon, 2006). However, if we are to respond with immediacy and accuracy to refugee mental health needs, such an option must be explored and developed. Furthermore, it is important to conduct research that clarifies not only the most prevalent psychopathologies seen among refugees following migration, but also the risk and protective factors that differentiate the most resilient outcomes from those requiring clinical intervention. Culturally diverse perspectives and assumptions compound the difficulty of such research, which is most often conducted in Western industrialized nations to which large populations of refugees have migrated. However, since most people displaced by forced migrations return to their regions of origin, it is important to conduct culturally sensitive research that is congruent with local customs, rather than erroneously imposing a Western psychiatric perspective (Bolton, 2006). Moreover, if we are to fully comprehend how psychosocial healing can best be supported across varying conditions and cultures, we must find ways to study the most important factors with simultaneous sensitivity and responsiveness to the needs of the survivors.

Programs serving the mental health needs of refugees are often located in the Western nations where they have settled. Europe, Australia, and North America are the most popular destinations for refugees, and nearly all of the published studies evaluating intervention programs originate from these regions. Sweden and other Scandinavian countries are among the most welcoming of refugees, and many excellent programs have been developed to help relieve postmigratory distress and improve the adjustment of forced migrants to cultural conditions that are entirely foreign to their experience (Ekblad, 2006). Australia has also experienced an influx of refugees fleeing persecution and violence, many of whom arrived from neighboring Asian nations. Innovative and culturally sensitive programs have been implemented in response to trauma and torture that can serve as models of blending individual and community intervention strategies into a more integral whole (Silove, 2006). The United States also receives large numbers of refugees and has become home to many who fled the wars and persecution across the Balkan republics following the disintegration of the former Yugoslavia. An abundance of intervention programs have been implemented in major American cities to assist refugees with psychosocial concerns, some of which have become particularly influential examples of innovation. Among those is a program in Chicago that employs family therapy and other techniques to apply a framework of intervening with groups composed of multiple families (Raina et al., 2006).

The work with refugees taking place in postmigration countries is often enhanced by experiences working with corresponding populations that remained in their country of origin. Several researchers and clinicians who work with postmigratory refugees in the West also invest great effort in working with former IDPs in the countries from which refugees have recently fled. The mental health infrastructures of such countries were often poorly developed and are typically overwhelmed and underfunded for meeting the needs of their postconflict population. International collaborations between mental health professionals from poorly resourced and highly resourced settings offer countless opportunities for improvement on both ends of such partnerships (Weine, Pavkovic, Agani, Ceric, & Jukic, 2006). Of particular merit is the movement to assign the same level of human rights, commitment to healing, and compassionate regard for mental illness as that which is felt toward those with physical ailments and injuries.

As wars and other levels of massive violence continue to erupt in repetitious cycles in many parts of the world, some patterns and principle are clear. Among those is that hatred and revenge have long memories and can reemerge after extended periods of apparent peace. One approach to breaking the cycle of violence has been to seek social justice through human rights instruments and international criminal tribunals. Another approach emphasizes rapprochement through community processes of communicative expression, such as the Truth and Reconciliation Commissions in South Africa, Peru, East Timor, Sierra Leone, and elsewhere. Unfortunately, the idealistic goals of such an undertaking often run headlong into the sheer force and brutality of the hatred they are created to alleviate. Moreover, for many who continue to endure an ever-present pain borne of atrocities that can never blend into an innocuous past, forgiveness seems like a form of betrayal that joins victims with perpetrators in a profane alliance belying all truth. Nevertheless, without forgiveness, complete psychosocial health cannot be achieved and the transmission of violence is more likely continue across generations as children enact themes of revenge in a perverse pursuit of honor and retribution (Borris, 2006).

Volume 4: Interventions with Special Needs Populations

The fourth volume of the *Handbook of International Disaster Psychology* addresses populations whose needs differ in some critical way from more general expectations. There are many reasons why this might occur, including that the "special" population is at elevated risk of harm or that key aspects of what they have endured differ from the experiences of most disaster survivors. Another reason may be that the group's needs are not well matched to the practices that are typically effective with people. Groups with "special needs" have been identified in regard to several variables, including developmental characteristics (e.g., children, the elderly), gender, types of traumatic experiences (e.g., torture, sexual assault), and occupational roles (e.g., relief workers, military personnel, journalists). Although several elements of good psychosocial practice reliably combine to form a strong core that can be applied across most populations and conditions, it is important to take special needs into account and not to expect any approach to be universally effective.

The manner in which different groups of people are treated in disasters and humanitarian crises usually reflects how they are treated under more normal circumstances. That is, if categories of people are less privileged in general, they are unlikely to receive better treatment in the worst of times. If anything, the social destabilization characteristic of most crises tends to amplify disparities in power and encourage opportunistic exploitation of the weak and vulnerable. Among the populations most often targeted for exploitation are women and children. Gender inequities are prevalent in most societies and, from a global perspective, the gains resulting from social justice movements such as feminism have been meager and fragile. Thus, while women have made remarkable progress on some issues in some nations, the worldwide economic and human rights advances for women have been shamefully slow and sporadic in their progress. Therefore, to understand the special needs of women in disasters, wars, and other crises, one must grasp the conditions and obstacles with which women are faced even in the best of times (Hudnall & Lindner, 2006).

Among the many ways in which women and girls are demeaned and exploited, one of the most humiliating and pernicious is widespread sexual violence (Reis & Vann, 2006). Sexual coercion and assault are all too commonplace in women's lives, and the protection of women and girls against such violations is pathetically inadequate. When war and social upheaval are entered into this equation, the levels of sexual depravity against women achieve sickening proportions. Tenuous social restrictions designed to at least postpone the exploitation of female children until they have reached sexual maturity are easily swept aside in times of lawlessness and war. Civilian women have historically suffered under the domination of conquering armies, who have subjected them to systematic rapes and sexual slavery. The history of these atrocities has been disputed and denied by governments unwilling to take responsibility for the heinous acts that transpire under cover of war.

Given that, there is perhaps some comfort to be taken behind international human rights protections when governments war against one another. No such restrictions exist for outlaw bands of militia and other paramilitary fighters that dominate many regions of conflict in today's world. Therefore, while the member states of the UN enact resolutions and other instruments, such as the Convention on the Rights of the Child, to protect children from harmful practices such as child labor, sexual exploitation, early marriage, and premature military service, these problems persist and worsen in the darkest corners of civilization. Wherever societies crumble into chaos and bitter conflict, children are exposed to countless hazards and may also be drawn into battle, either as fighters or as captive workers to support the troops (Boyden, de Berry, Feeny, & Hart, 2006).

While the prototypical child soldier is a young boy armed with a light machinegun, girls too are forcibly ensnared into service (McKay. 2006). In such instances, girls are used as porters, domestic servants, sexual slaves, and "wives." Whether they are boys or girls, once these children escape captivity or are otherwise returned to civilian lives, the process of reunion and reintegration is often one of stigma, rejection, and shame. Girls in particular may be viewed as damaged goods and never regain the status and opportunities that were once within reach.

The type and intensity of traumatic events can also create differential impact characteristics that translate into unique needs for certain kinds of survivors. For instance, the impact of torture on the mind can be uniquely complex and intractable, thus requiring exquisitely precise skills unlike those which suffice for other types of disaster and trauma interventions (Holtz, 1998). In response to this need, dozens of excellent facilities, such as the Rehabilitation and Research Centre for Torture Survivors in Copenhagen, have developed noteworthy expertise in helping people who have suffered terribly at the hands of others (Berliner & Mikkelsen, 2006).

A paradoxical aspect of disasters and humanitarian emergencies is that, while most people flee from these zones of mayhem and destruction, others rush into the breach to assist survivors and pursue altruistic ends. The impact of facing death and other gruesome consequences of disasters fall particularly hard upon humanitarian aid workers, emergency services personnel, members of the military, and other occupations who perform heroic services. International humanitarian organizations (Ehrenreich, 2006), civilian fire and police departments (De Soir, 2006), and other agencies have recently come to recognize the importance of responding to the psychosocial needs of their employees and volunteers. Managing occupational stress among their personnel challenges these organizations not only to add a psychosocial component to their existing employee health services, but also to modify their systems so that they are less likely to create the stress that must then be managed. It is at least ironic, if not hypocritical, that humanitarian organizations charged with the mission of relieving the suffering of any and every unfortunate soul whom they encounter often fail to treat their own staff and volunteers with comparable compassion and regard for their dignity and well-being.

As noted earlier, the role of the news media in providing reliable information about crises and relief operations has become a critically important component of marshaling resources and public opinion in helpful directions. In viewing the "media" as a mammoth multinational corporate operation involving cameras, satellites, and high technology, it is easy to overlook the fragile human elements. International correspondents and their coworkers, many of whom are poorly paid local citizens, sometimes cover these stories at great risk to their own lives. In recent events it has become clear that journalists reporting from war zones and humanitarian crises are being killed and injured at historically high rates, sometimes due to their own risky decisions, though often at the hands of military forces they had trusted to protect them. Perhaps in part because the status of war correspondents in the journalistic community is so high, they are expected to shake off the ill effects of their occupation without complaint and bask in the glory they have earned through daring deeds. But recent collaborative projects have been initiated between journalists and psychologists that examine the psychological effects of covering traumatic stories, assess the mental health needs of journalists exposed to trauma, and design proactive interventions to reduce the negative psychosocial impact on those who inform the public about these critically important events (Newman & Shapiro, 2006).

Appendix of NGO Profiles (Volume 4)

The international humanitarian relief community that developed over the past century was pioneered by a small number of organizations dedicated to serving victims of war, disease, famine, and other natural calamities. Paramount among these was the Red Cross movement, which began in Switzerland in 1863 and slowly spread throughout most of the world over the next several decades. The red cross on a white background came to be recognized as a symbol of neutrality and compassion in the face of conflict and brutality. Hospitals, ambulances, and personnel marked with the Red Cross emblem earned a status as noncombatants that allowed them to function in war zones and other dangerous places with few direct attacks upon their operations. This philosophy of mercy within a context of violence eventually led to the Geneva Conventions and other international accords designed to provide limited protection for civilians and military prisoners as an ever widening swath of war engulfed the world. As the Red Cross movement proliferated, national societies were founded in dozens of countries and a new emblem, the Red Crescent, was approved to accommodate societies in regions where Islam was the predominate faith.

The founding of the United Nations at the end of World War II fostered a period of growing humanitarian aid through both governmental agencies and nongovernmental organizations (NGOs). Several agencies within the UN system, such as the United Nations Children's Fund (UNICEF), the United Nations High Commissioner for Refugees (UNHCR), and the World Health Organization (WHO), developed programs and policies that saved millions of lives and improved the quality of life for untold numbers of the world's most vulnerable citizens. The scourges of war, disease, and disaster were never abolished, but a countervailing force of hope and compassion was established, and hundreds of NGOs have been founded to serve the needs of people who might otherwise perish or wither.

Perhaps the most recent of humanitarian relief activities is the formal provision of psychosocial support, though this is certainly an element of any compassionate care to the afflicted. The story of international disaster psychology cannot be fully told without repeated reference to the humanitarian NGOs that have developed and disseminated psychosocial support training and services with great dedication and determination. Moreover, volunteers who aspire to work in this field of endeavor will almost certainly work closely with several of these NGOs and will benefit from obtaining at least a cursory knowledge of their missions, philosophies, histories, and activities.

Therefore, the editors of the *Handbook of International Disaster Psychology* have included an appendix consisting of brief profiles that describe some of the prominent humanitarian organizations operating in the world today. The information contained in these profiles was gathered from public sources and may contain accidental inaccuracies. Given the rapidly evolving nature of the NGOs profiled, it is also quite likely that some of the information will soon become outdated. However, these profiles are substantially accurate, and the contact information given for each agency makes it possible for interested readers to obtain more current and detailed information.

References

Ager, A. (2006). Toward a consensus protocol for psychosocial response in complex emergencies. In G. Reyes & G. A. Jacobs (Eds.), *Handbook of international disaster psychology, Vol. 1. Fundamentals and overview*. Westport, CT: Praeger Publishers.

Agger, I. (2006). Approaches to psychosocial healing: Case examples from Lusophone Africa. In G. Reyes & G. A. Jacobs (Eds.), *Handbook of international disaster psychology, Vol. 2. Practices and programs*. Westport, CT: Praeger Publishers.

Armstrong, M., Boyden, J., Galappatti, A., & Hart, J. (2006). Participatory tools for monitoring and evaluating psychosocial work with children: Reflections on a pilot study in Eastern Sri Lanka. In G. Reyes & G. A. Jacobs (Eds.), *Handbook of international disaster psychology, Vol. 2. Practices and programs*. Westport, CT: Praeger Publishers.

Atherton, J., & Sonniks, M. (2006). Implementation of a training of trainers model for disseminating psychological support in the Cuban Red Cross. In G. Reyes & G. A. Jacobs (Eds.), *Handbook of international disaster psychology, Vol. 2. Practices and programs*. Westport, CT: Praeger Publishers.

Beech, D. R. (2006). Peace-building, culturally responsive means, and ethical practices in humanitarian psychosocial interventions. In G. Reyes & G. A. Jacobs (Eds.), *Handbook of international disaster psychology, Vol. 1. Fundamentals and overview*. Westport, CT: Praeger Publishers.

Berliner, P., & Mikkelsen, E. (2006). Serving the psychosocial needs of survivors of torture and organized violence. In G. Reyes & G. A. Jacobs (Eds.), *Handbook of international disaster psychology, Vol. 4. Interventions with special needs populations*. Westport, CT: Praeger Publishers.

Blanco, T., Villalobos, M., & Carrillo, C. (2006). The psychological support network of the Central University of Venezuela and the Venezuelan floods of 1999. In G. Reyes & G. A. Jacobs (Eds.), *Handbook of international disaster psychology, Vol. 2. Practices and programs*. Westport, CT: Praeger Publishers.

Bolton, P. (2006). Challenges in international disaster mental health research. In G. Reyes & G. A. Jacobs (Eds.), *Handbook of international disaster psychology, Vol. 3. Refugee mental health*. Westport, CT: Praeger Publishers.

Borris, E. (2006). The healing power of forgiveness and the resolution of protracted conflicts. In G. Reyes & G. A. Jacobs (Eds.), *Handbook of international disaster psychology, Vol. 3. Refugee mental health*. Westport, CT: Praeger Publishers.

Boyden, J., de Berry, J., Feeny, T., & Hart, J. (2006). Children affected by armed conflict in South Asia: A regional summary. In G. Reyes & G. A. Jacobs (Eds.), *Handbook of international disaster psychology, Vol. 4. Interventions with special needs populations*. Westport, CT: Praeger Publishers.

Burnett, J. S. (2004, August 4). In the line of fire. *The New York Times*, Late Edition–Final, p. A17, col. 1.

Cohen, R. (2006). Implementation of mental health programs for survivors of natural disasters in Latin America. In G. Reyes & G. A. Jacobs (Eds.), *Handbook of international disaster psychology, Vol. 2. Practices and programs*. Westport, CT: Praeger Publishers.

De Soir, E. (2006). Psychosocial crisis intervention with military and emergency services personnel. In G. Reyes & G. A. Jacobs (Eds.), *Handbook of international disaster psychology, Vol. 4. Interventions with special needs populations*. Westport, CT: Praeger Publishers.

Dodge, G. R. (2006a). Assessing the psychosocial needs of communities affected by disaster. In G. Reyes & G. A. Jacobs (Eds.), *Handbook of international disaster psychology, Vol. 1. Fundamentals and overview*. Westport, CT: Praeger Publishers.

———. (2006b). In defense of a community psychology model for international psychosocial intervention. In G. Reyes & G. A. Jacobs (Eds.), *Handbook of international disaster psychology, Vol. 1. Fundamentals and overview*. Westport, CT: Praeger Publishers.

Ehrenreich, J. (2006). Managing stress in humanitarian aid workers: The role of the humanitarian aid organization. In G. Reyes & G. A. Jacobs (Eds.), *Handbook of international disaster psychology, Vol. 4. Interventions with special needs populations*. Westport, CT: Praeger Publishers.

Ekblad, S. (2006). Serving the mental health needs of postmigratory adult refugees in Sweden: A transitional augmentation approach. In G. Reyes & G. A. Jacobs (Eds.), *Handbook of international disaster psychology, Vol. 3. Refugee mental health*. Westport, CT: Praeger Publishers.

Gall, C. (2004, June 3). Aid agency halts operations in Afghanistan. *The New York Times*, Late Edition–Final, p. A5, col. 3.

Holtz, T. H. (1998). Refugee trauma versus torture trauma: A retrospective controlled cohort study of Tibetan refugees. *Journal of Nervous & Mental Disease, 186*, 24–34.

Hudnall, A., & Lindner, E. (2006). Crisis and gender: Addressing the psychosocial needs of women in international disasters. In G. Reyes & G. A. Jacobs (Eds.), *Handbook of international disaster psychology, Vol. 4. Interventions with special needs populations*. Westport, CT: Praeger Publishers.

Jacobs, G. A., Revel, J. P., Reyes, G., & Quevillon, R. P. (2006). Development of the Rapid Assessment of Mental Health: An international collaboration. In G. Reyes & G. A. Jacobs (Eds.), *Handbook of international disaster psychology, Vol. 3. Refugee mental health*. Westport, CT: Praeger Publishers.

Kapor-Stanulovic, N. (2006). Implementing psychosocial programs in the Federal Republic of Yugoslavia: Was it really mission impossible? In G. Reyes & G. A. Jacobs (Eds.), *Handbook of international disaster psychology, Vol. 2. Practices and programs*. Westport, CT: Praeger Publishers.

Kelly, A. (2004, December 15). Caught in the crossfire. *The Guardian Weekly*. Retrieved March 4, 2005, from http://society.guardian.co.uk/societyguardian/story/0,,1373410,00.html

Kinzie, J. D. (2006). Personal reflections on treating traumatized refugees. In G. Reyes & G. A. Jacobs (Eds.), *Handbook of international disaster psychology, Vol. 3. Refugee mental health*. Westport, CT: Praeger Publishers.

Kuriansky, J. (2006). Working effectively with the mass media in disaster mental health. In G. Reyes & G. A. Jacobs (Eds.), *Handbook of international disaster psychology, Vol. 1. Fundamentals and overview.* Westport, CT: Praeger Publishers.

MacDonald, C. M. (2003). Evaluation of stress debriefing interventions with military populations. *Military Medicine, 168,* 961–968.

McKay, S. (2006). How do you mend broken hearts? Gender, war, and impacts on girls in fighting forces. In G. Reyes & G. A. Jacobs (Eds.), *Handbook of international disaster psychology, Vol. 4. Interventions with special needs populations.* Westport, CT: Praeger Publishers.

Ndetei, D., Kasina, R., & Kathuku, D. (2006). Psychosocial responses to the bombing of the American Embassy in Nairobi: Challenges, lessons, and opportunities. In G. Reyes & G. A. Jacobs (Eds.), *Handbook of international disaster psychology, Vol. 2. Practices and programs.* Westport, CT: Praeger Publishers.

Neugebauer, R. (2006). Psychosocial research and interventions after the Rwanda genocide. In G. Reyes & G. A. Jacobs (Eds.), *Handbook of international disaster psychology, Vol. 2. Practices and programs.* Westport, CT: Praeger Publishers.

Newman, E., & Shapiro, B. (2006). Helping journalists who cover humanitarian crises. In G. Reyes & G. A. Jacobs (Eds.), *Handbook of international disaster psychology, Vol. 4. Interventions with special needs populations.* Westport, CT: Praeger Publishers.

Peddle, N., Hudnall Stamm, B., Hudnall, A. C., & Stamm, H. E. (2006). Effective intercultural collaboration on psychosocial support programs. In G. Reyes & G. A. Jacobs (Eds.), *Handbook of international disaster psychology, Vol. 1. Fundamentals and overview.* Westport, CT: Praeger Publishers.

Pupavac, V. (2006). Humanitarian politics and the rise of international disaster psychology. In G. Reyes & G. A. Jacobs (Eds.), *Handbook of international disaster psychology, Vol. 1. Fundamentals and overview.* Westport, CT: Praeger Publishers.

Raina, D., Weine, S., Kulauzovic, Y., Feetham, S., Zhubi, M., Huseni, D., & Pavkovic, I. (2006). A framework for developing and implementing multiple-family groups for refugee families. In G. Reyes & G. A. Jacobs (Eds.), *Handbook of international disaster psychology, Vol. 3. Refugee mental health.* Westport, CT: Praeger Publishers.

Reis, C., & Vann. B. (2006). Sexual violence against women and children in the context of armed conflict. In G. Reyes & G. A. Jacobs (Eds.), *Handbook of international disaster psychology, Vol. 4. Interventions with special needs populations.* Westport, CT: Praeger Publishers.

Reyes, G. (2006). International disaster psychology: Purposes, principles, and practices. In G. Reyes & G. A. Jacobs (Eds.), *Handbook of international disaster psychology, Vol. 1. Fundamentals and overview.* Westport, CT: Praeger Publishers.

Rieff, D. (2002). *A bed for the night: Humanitarianism in crisis.* New York: Simon & Schuster.

Ronan, K. R., Finnis, K., & Johnston, D. M. (2006). Interventions with youth and families: A prevention and stepped care model. In G. Reyes & G. A. Jacobs (Eds.), *Handbook of international disaster psychology, Vol. 2. Practices and programs.* Westport, CT: Praeger Publishers.

Silove, D. (2006). The impact of mass psychological trauma on psychosocial adaptation among refugees. In G. Reyes & G. A. Jacobs (Eds.), *Handbook of international disaster psychology, Vol. 3. Refugee mental health.* Westport, CT: Praeger Publishers.

Weine, S., Pavkovic, I., Agani, F., Ceric, I., & Jukic, V. (2006). Mental health reform and assisting psychiatric leaders in postwar countries. In G. Reyes & G. A. Jacobs (Eds.), *Handbook of international disaster psychology, Vol. 3. Refugee mental health*. Westport, CT: Praeger Publishers.

Wessells, M. G. (2006). Negotiating the shrunken humanitarian space: Challenges and options. In G. Reyes & G. A. Jacobs (Eds.), *Handbook of international disaster psychology, Vol. 1. Fundamentals and overview*. Westport, CT: Praeger Publishers.

CHAPTER 1

CRISIS AND GENDER: ADDRESSING THE PSYCHOSOCIAL NEEDS OF WOMEN IN INTERNATIONAL DISASTERS

Amy C. Hudnall and Evelin Gerda Lindner

"we lose husbands, children [all of our] lives are made fragile" by war.
—e-mail from an African woman (Hudnall, 2003, p. 101)

Introduction

Why is it necessary to include in these volumes a chapter devoted to the special problems that women may encounter during and after disasters? Everyone suffers: men, children, and women. Are women more vulnerable? Have their interests been largely ignored? "Psychological trauma is an affliction of the powerless. At the moment of trauma, the victim is rendered helpless by overwhelming force" (Herman, 1997, p. 33). How often are these words, which here describe the effect of traumatic incidents, used when women describe events in their lives? Women often are more vulnerable; since they occupy a central role in community life, however, they can also be empowered to protect communities from disasters. In a speech titled "The Role of Women in Protecting Communities for Disasters," Natalie Domeisen (1997) states:

> Women do have specific issues that make them more vulnerable. This needs to be more widely understood or accepted. Until recently, researchers felt that natural disasters didn't discriminate among their victims. But research shows that at least for famines and earthquakes, there is a convincing case that mortality rates are higher for women than for men. A recent Canadian

study on post-disaster stress shows that women and children are the first to be marginalized or abused. Stressful situations are harder for women because they lack control over resources and have more family responsibilities.

Indeed, recent studies seem to indicate that in many instances women are more vulnerable to the effects of trauma than men, although it is not yet clear what other factors, such as culture, may play a role in these outcomes (Holbrook & Hoyt, 2004; Murray & Lopez, 1996; Norris, Perilla, Ilbañez, & Murphy, 2001).

Cultural influences on psychosocial needs of women are significant in a multitude of ways. It has, just to name one area, been widely acknowledged that rape (of men and women) has acquired an infamous frequency in armed conflicts around the world, including resulting pregnancies for women. Particularly women are often too ashamed and humiliated to seek adequate help for their plight. Hartling has found that these dynamics particularly affect women who reported greater "cumulative humiliation" and greater "fear of humiliation" than men (Hartling & Luchetta, 1999). Moreover, the consequences of women being perceived to have humiliated men are grave indeed. In cultural contexts that endorse so-called honor killings, they face the prospect of death by the hands of their male relatives. Domeisen (1997) provides the following example:

> One woman from a development NGO in Bangladesh noted that "A woman is under great pressure because of the practice of purdah, a traditional custom not to leave the house when the husband is away. Without her husband to escort her, she cannot go alone to the cyclone shelter. And many husbands work away from home. . . . After a cyclone, women have often been left alone in their damaged homes, unreached by aid workers, unable to contribute to community rehabilitation decisions!"

In other words, Domeisen concludes, failing to address cultural issues makes it more difficult to access women's concerns or contributions. This can keep valuable female perspectives from being incorporated into the planning of suitable crisis interventions; furthermore, when taken to an extreme, it can put women's lives in danger.

Wiest, Mocellin, and Motsisi (1994) warn that:

> Widespread subordination of women . . . means women typically must bear more stress than men. . . . Sexual abuse of girls is common. . . . In some countries, many displaced women may end up as prostitutes, hoping to gain income to sustain their families. The longer the situation of unemployment remains unresolved, the greater the likely incidence of prostitution. . . . Physical and mental abuse arising out of the sexual exploitation of displaced women and girls has not been adequately documented. (Executive Summary)

We may conclude that if it is the case that women are more vulnerable, it is important, as aid workers, to understand what different kinds of situations women may face and to which they must respond. Not least among these, female aid workers might face stress and subsequent burnout, compassion fatigue, or vicarious traumatization that is related to female victims of disaster. By the end of this chapter, we hope that you can more clearly relate to how gender differences and cultural roles create unique and demanding expectations on women, making their suffering sometimes even worse. Because of this, those working in the field have to approach their work with women in different ways.

We begin this chapter by discussing a brief, modern history of the international women's human rights movement. We then move to a discussion of human rights violations unique to women. This includes a section on women in wartime and the multiple roles women are expected to take on during conflict: psychologically and physically. To elucidate, we will provide historical examples of these unique and often unanticipated burdens. By gaining an understanding of women's history, one can naturally move into the next section of the chapter, a discussion of how aid workers can best support the women enmeshed in disasters or violent conflicts.

Modern History of Feminism and the International Women's Human Rights Movement

It is difficult to disentangle the feminist movements from the earlier peace and emancipation movements. Beginning in the 1800s, female activists (e.g., antislavery, civil rights, or antiwar) naturally began to make demands for women's rights. In other words, these activists were ultimately always fighting for human rights. Geographically, the demand for women's rights as an organized movement began in the United States and Western Europe, spreading to Eastern Europe, and then parts of Asia, Latin America, Africa, and the Middle East—although there were pockets of progress that do not fit this chronology. Often, the success of these changes was attributable to the economic stability of the country.

Organized activism for women's rights is young. Living around the time of the French Revolution, British Mary Wollstonecraft and French native Olympe de Gouges are often considered the "mothers" of the movement, forming what came to be known as the "first wave of feminism." Throughout the eighteenth and nineteenth centuries, European and American women fought for their rights to an education and to vote, believing that these two rights were necessary to gain a voice in the political process. Not until the twentieth century, however, did women begin to make any gain. The United States gave women the vote by a narrow margin in 1920, Great Britain in 1928, Switzerland in 1971, while much of Africa, Asia, and Latin America granted women suffrage after 1980.

In the twentieth century, the World Wars necessitated women's entrance into industry. To sustain each nation's economy, women had to fill industrial labor needs. This seemed to create a watershed; women's debut into the public sphere changed everything from dress to education to politics. Had emancipation been achieved?

Forty years later, American author Betty Friedan suggested it had not, in her landmark book, *The Feminine Mystique* (1963). Friedan set out to examine what she coined the "problem with no name." According to Friedan, women were still chained—heart, soul, and intellect—to the private world and patriarchal dominance; they were still—only—the "keepers of hearth and home." Friedan's articulation of the problem—what she called "is this all there is"—was revolutionary. Were women in some way defective, as they had been told, or did the problem lie in society's expectations of them? Thus was born the "second wave," which moved beyond the West and began to engulf women worldwide; advocates began to theorize about human rights as women's rights.

Women's rights in everyday life and women as a unique party in war were not recognized until 1979 (see International Committee of the Red Cross, 2004, 2001). From the creation of the United Nations' (UN General Assembly, 1979) document, the Convention on the Elimination of All Forms of Discrimination against Women (CEDAW),[1] to the UN-sponsored Beijing Conference on Women's Rights in 1995, the majority of the world's nations today agree that women have not achieved equality and in fact, face singular and unusual violations of their person strictly because of their gender. CEDAW, often described as an international bill of rights for women, is composed of a preamble and 30 articles. It defines discrimination against women as:

> Any distinction, exclusion or restriction made on the basis of sex which has the effect or purpose of impairing or nullifying the recognition, enjoyment or exercise by women, irrespective of their marital status, on a basis of equality of men and women, of human rights and fundamental freedoms in the political, economic, social, cultural, civil or any other field. (UN General Assembly, 1979, Introduction)

Further, CEDAW set up an agenda for national action to end discrimination against women. Signatory states committed themselves to:

- Incorporate the principle of equality of men and women in their government, abolish discriminatory laws, and prohibit discrimination against women
- Establish public institutions that ensure protection of women
- Ensure the elimination of discrimination against women by persons, organizations, or enterprises (UN Development Programme, 2000).

Thus, CEDAW is intended to provide the basis for "ensuring women's equal access to, and equal opportunities in, political and public life, as well as education, health, and employment" (UN General Assembly, 1979, Introduction). Interestingly, CEDAW is the only human rights treaty acknowledging that gender-specific demands are shaped by culture, and the only treaty that demands reproductive rights for women. Countries that have ratified or acceded to the Convention are legally bound to put its provisions into practice. They must also submit to providing national reports, at least every four years, on measures they have taken to comply with the treaty.[2]

Women's Roles during Natural Disasters and Violent Conflict

Women play, willingly and unwillingly, a variety of roles during disasters. Many of these are not new, although some tasks seem to have been honed to a fine edge in the twentieth century. Most frequently, women offer the following support:

- Serving as nurses or some form of healer
- Serving as tools to dilute or destroy a culture or ethnic group
- Sex slaves and rape victims
- Keeping the "home fires" burning
- Supporting the war effort
- Instigating wars
- Holding together communal systems while signifying group identity
- Providing emotional support for returning "frontline" workers
- Serving as combatants

Women as Nurses

Women have nursed wounded soldiers on and off the battlefield since the first wars. However, Florence Nightingale (1820–1910) is often considered the pioneer of modern and wartime nursing. Nightingale and women like her fought public and private opposition to revolutionize the nursing field and formalize the recognition of women as trained professional nurses in wartime. By 1914, for example, the British opened uniformed services to women. Gaining this recognition afforded female nurses some measure of protection. Unfortunately, in the last 20 years, ignoring the sanctity of medical workers, male or female, is becoming more and more common.

Women as Tools to Dilute or Destroy a Culture or Ethnic Group

Rape has always been considered an inevitable byproduct of war, and thus when it occurred in war it was largely ignored; the Bosnian conflict (1992) brought the act of rape to a new level, however, by using it as a "weapon" of war. To create a "Greater Serbia," leaders enacted a policy of "ethnic cleansing" through the Serbian and Bosnian Serb armies and paramilitary groups. Their intent was to create a "religiously, culturally, and linguistically homogenous Serbian nation" (Salzman, 1998, p. 349).

In Serbian culture, a woman is often valued merely for her reproductive abilities. This is supported and perpetuated by all aspects of the culture, from religion to the government, as a way to strengthen Serbian population numbers and nationalism. UN investigators uncovered the existence of a Serbian military policy that designated rape as a specific means for ethnic cleansing. A plan written by Yugoslav National Army Psychological Operations Department officers around the end of August 1991 was intended "to drive Muslims out of Bosnia based on an analysis of Muslim behavior which 'showed that their morale, desire for battle, and will could be crushed more easily by raping women, especially minors and even children'" (Salzman, 1998, p. 356). The "rape camps" became a systematic policy of the Serbian military to create an ethnically pure state (UN Commission of Experts, 1994). The UN General Assembly (1996) was "convinced that this heinous practice [rape and abuse of women] constitutes a deliberate weapon of war in fulfilling the policy of ethnic cleansing carried out by Serbian forces in Bosnia and Herzegovina, and . . . that the abhorrent policy of ethnic cleansing was a form of genocide." The sexual assault of women during war had been taken to unknown depths by completely ignoring women's humanity.

Women as Sex Slaves and Rape Victims

Today, women and children are the product of a thriving commercial business: the global sex trade (Seager, 2003). In 2001–2002 a conservative estimate of 700,000 women were trafficked worldwide. Practices such as these are neither new nor modern, but instead reach back across centuries of history. The establishment of brothels attached to an army during war occurred in the Roman army, the Greek army, and in the American army in Vietnam to name only a few.

The term Comfort Women is a translation of the Japanese *jugun ianfu* (military comfort women). During World War II, *jugun ianfu* referred to women of various ethnic, social, and national backgrounds who were forced into sexual labor for Japanese troops. Comfort Women were handpicked to fill the brothels that were organized by the government for Japanese military officers. There is no way to determine precisely how many women served as comfort women, although the estimates range from 80,000 to 200,000, about 80 percent of whom were Korean. Other nationalities included Japanese, Taiwanese, Filipina, Indonesian, and Burmese. Japanese authorities believed that providing the soldiers with recreational sex enhanced morale and allowed the government to control the spread of sexually transmitted diseases; they also hoped it would help prevent soldiers from random sexual violence against women in occupied territories. At the war's end, the only military tribunal concerning the comfort women took place in 1948 in Batavia (Jakarta today). Several officers were convicted of forcing 35 white Dutch women into the institutionalized brothels. The fate of other comfort women was completely ignored.

In many strongly patriarchal cultures women are little more then property; thus, rape and sexual violence are acts against the perceived owner, not the woman. Even in supposedly advanced countries, "women quickly learn that rape is a crime only in theory; in practice the standard for what constitutes rape is set not at the level of women's experience of violation but just above the level of coercion acceptable to men" (Herman, 1997, p. 72). This cultural attitude results in gross underreporting of rape, skewing data on the victims,[3] and harkens back to early etymology of the word rape, which dealt solely with the idea of ownership and family honor, not harm to the victim. This prompts the question of whether rape is an act of sexual desire or an act of violence and "power over" another. Perhaps it is a product of one or the other or both depending on the circumstances. However, the fact that "rape in war is at epidemic proportions" (Seager, 2003, p. 58) seems to indicate that it is more often an issue of power, not sex drive.

Women "Keeping the Home Fires Burning"

The most traditional of all expectations that fall to women concern roles and duties within the household. Some say it is the most important job a woman fills, nurturing her children and family, feeding the soul of her traditions. But in war all of this is disrupted. Events that should be joyful, such as childbirth, become driven by fear and danger. Mundane and routine tasks—milking the cow or driving your child to school—are eliminated. Some women will lose their homes, while others will be driven from them. Women lose husbands, sons, and fathers, never knowing if they survived. The tasks that surround "the home fires" are often invisible and difficult to quantify. For the aid worker it is easy to anticipate a woman's physical need in this regard, but it is difficult to anticipate the emotional needs of a woman who has lost her home or is at threat of losing it. The woman is expected to re-create "home" in whatever environment or condition she may find herself; her needs aside, she is expected to maintain a semblance of normalcy for her family and community.

Women as Supporters of the War Effort

Across time and space women have taken up the cause of their society's wars. They have done the work left uncompleted by their now-fighting men while continuing to mother, nurse, and take care of the home. In many cultures the division between the public and private spheres, the spheres of men and women respectively, were and are clearly defined. But with the onset of war, these lines become blurred and women must move between their traditional roles and new public roles if the culture is to continue (Lorentzen & Turpin, 1998). This blurring is apt to create unusual physical and emotional hardships. In post-conflict conditions, the stress of either re-establishing the former roles or renegotiating new ones is a tremendous burden on the whole culture.

Women as Instigators and Perpetuators of Wars

Women throughout history have been described as the instigators of wars (e.g. Mernissi, 1993; Meltzer & Andersen, 1998). In Britain, during World War I, Admiral Fitzgerald founded the Order of the White Feather, which encouraged women to hand a white feather to any young man who had not enlisted (Gullace, 1997). To be given the white feather meant you were a coward—a stigma that you bore for the rest of your life. Women can also act as more direct supporters of a war. On June 25, 2004, a middle-aged Hutu woman stood trial in Tanzania accused of inciting rape and genocide. Multiple witnesses took the stand to testify that Nyiramasuhuko had urged the Hutu militiamen "to slaughter the Tutsi 'cockroaches'" (Landesman, 2002).

Women have generally been afforded little personal empowerment and even less overt power. Often, an outcome of disempowerment does not mean complete acceptance of the other's wills, but the grasp for power in subversive ways, much like that of the British woman with a "white feather" or the Hutu woman egging on her male counterparts.

Holding Together Family Systems While Signifying Their Group Identity

During conflicts, it is expected that a group's women will maintain family and community rituals, provide the emotional and physical wherewithal to stay together, and maintain the group's traditions, even to death. In addition, "discourse on the preservation of cultural values usually centers on women's sexuality, although this may not be explicitly stated" (Espín, 1999, p. 13). If the family or group is displaced, the expectations placed on women in maintaining the group's identity becomes even more inflexible. Female gender-specific behaviors "are used by enemies and friends alike as proof of the morality—or decay—of social groups or nations" (p. 6). Their status or signification is not a reflection of the signified's (i.e., woman's) actions or attributes, but a reflection of the signifier (i.e., patriarchy), their beliefs about themselves, their models, and culture (Hudnall, 2002). These responsibilities can be simple traditions like public veiling to represent their honor, or they can become physically challenging (e.g., creating shelter after one's home is destroyed).

Often, women signify the values of the community through legal dictates. In World War II, the national court of Iceland forbade Icelandic women to associate with American GIs stationed there in the fear that unwanted pregnancies would dilute their Icelandic blood. We are all familiar with stories of "honor killings" perpetrated in the name of familial dignity. Now we see that not only are women expected to fulfill the physical aspects of community building during a crisis, but they are the most important social and psychological representation of that community. The woman is expected to carry the culture; she cradles it, keeping the stories, the laws, and the morality alive. This places an enormous burden on women already pushed to the limits of their resources.

Women as Caregivers for Returning "Frontline" Workers

Many soldiers return as different, "unknown" people, who are less able to talk to their families, disillusioned, more mature, and often bearing physical and emotional wounds. They return home anticipating and expecting stability and sameness: the same wives, the same homes, the same friends, and the same traditions. Rarely is this possible. Wives, daughters, and mothers bear the brunt of the shock facing returning soldiers. They take on the role of counselor and nurse, wife, girlfriend, or daughter. The adjustments are manifested in a number of ways, from increased unemployment to increased reporting of somatic illness among soldiers. For women, the changes often lead to higher divorce rates and increasing domestic violence (Herman, 1997).

Women as Combatants

Women have long fought in wars, but until the twentieth century they were a decided minority and often fought in secret. The now-famous Long March in China, 1934, occurred when Mao Tse-Tung's Communist Red Army was under threat by the imperial Chinese government. To escape the Imperial Army, 100,000 men and women fought side by side as they fled 6,000 miles to safety. Today, one can find Israeli women, Russian women, and women in several African countries serving alongside men. Many countries' military are composed of more than 10 percent women, with New Zealand, the United States, Australia, and South Africa leading the "ranks." In these nations, women combatants are becoming viewed as able partners, challenging the stereotype of women as the protectors of peace and men as the perpetrators of violence. However, this has placed a strain on cultures in which women remain in the private domain. For example, the U.S. military deployment in Afghanistan during 2002 was made up of 6 percent women (Seager, 2003), yet there is no way for these women to address Afghani males without implying an insult. The tensions that these kinds of strictures create among Afghani men tend to be released in violence against Afghani women while increasing the pressure on American female soldiers. At its extreme, this kind of strain finds ease by "dehumanizing the dehumanizer," as in women playing leading roles in humiliating the Iraqi prisoners in Abu Ghraib Prison, Iraq.

Challenges to Women's Roles in Crisis

A great deal of attention has been given to the variety of roles that women might play in periods of violent conflict. Usually they are fulfilling multiple roles. This is not to imply that men are not also important; however it does highlight the fact that women, by their physical and cultural-bound difference, offer unique functions in conflict and disasters and, as mentioned earlier, often are more vulnerable to trauma (Holbrook & Hoyt, 2004; Murray & Lopez, 1996; Norris et al., 2001).

Compounding the difficulty of their tasks are some global biases against women that deprive them of educational opportunities, access to health care, and life-sustaining jobs. Of the nearly one billion illiterate persons in the world, two-thirds are women. If women are allowed an education, it is generally only in the primary grades, in which they are given the cast-off texts and often the weakest teachers. The biggest gap in education today occurs in sub-Saharan Africa, a region fraught with violent conflict.

Many people in the world lack sufficient or even existing health care. Women are at a high risk for illness or death. Approximately 200 million women become pregnant yearly, and only half of these women will survive their pregnancy. Another 50 million will be permanently disabled during the birth. Women are vulnerable to outside risks during pregnancy because of some nations' and cultures' population policies and gender preferences. Unsafe abortions, female genital mutilation (FGM), and some forms of contraception all pose serious threats. Of particular concern is the ongoing practice of FGM, originally rooted in parts of Africa and the Middle East. Approximately two million young girls each year receive the "surgery," which is frequently performed in unsanitary environments without the use of anesthesia or sterile instruments.

The pandemic of HIV/AIDS continues to be a staggering global problem, especially in Africa. Often, women are unwittingly infected with AIDS because of rape and their inability to negotiate safe sex partners. Many African men still believe that sex with a virgin will cure them of HIV/AIDS, placing young women and girls in a particularly vulnerable situation. In sum, because of women's physical differences and reproductive ability, they continue to be unable to protect their physical well-being.

The functions women perform often go unnoticed, even though these jobs may require tremendous personal strength and stamina. The world's poor are disproportionately represented by women, while they form the majority of unpaid workers in family businesses and in housework.[4] Globally, women spend 65 percent of their time in unpaid work. When a woman finally does acquire a paying job, she is paid less than her male counterparts across all jobs. For example, in the United States women earn, on average, 24 percent less than men. In times of conflict, when men are either away fighting or are dead, women are unable to secure a sufficient income to support their families, thus increasing their overall risk. Ignoring the significance of women's roles in wartime only exacerbates their emotional and physical risk. Aid workers around the world face particularly difficult dilemmas when propelled into crisis situations that are fraught with the difficulties that afflict women. These dilemmas are so severe that helpers may be burnt out rapidly. To avoid the risk of secondary trauma when working in high-risk environments, one should consider these points (adapted from Saakvitne & Stamm, n.d., and Stamm, Higson-Smith, & Hudnall, 2003):

1. Educate yourself and those with whom you work about secondary trauma and know the support systems your organization provides.
2. Ensure that you have people you can safely express your distress to.
3. Have a strong foundation within/about the culture you are working in.
4. Develop an environment in which you can relax or rejuvenate and which is as physically and emotionally safe as you can create.
5. Never work alone.
6. Try to maintain healthy eating habits, exercise habits, and sleep habits.

Lindner's work on humiliation is anchored at the juncture between human rights and feelings of humiliation, as well as at the juncture between help and humiliation. These points of intersection are extremely difficult to explore, not only for victims, but also for helpers. To illustrate, consider the following situation: A health worker comes across a wife who is being battered and abused by her husband. The health worker speaks to the wife and explains to her that she should no longer accept such humiliating treatment (invoking the principle that the handling she receives represents a violation of her basic human rights). The wife agrees to seek refuge in a house for battered women. However, the wife returns to her husband after a short while, asserting that she does not feel humiliated by him, but loved. The husband, on his side, accuses the health worker of undue meddling and claims that it is he who feels humiliated and degraded by such treatment. And, since feelings of humiliation, albeit often translated into apathy and depression, may also lead to violence, the husband might actually intimidate the health worker with threats of violence.

Transposed into international situations of crisis, helpers might find themselves being accused that their understanding of "help" is "disrespectful of local culture," and helpers may be accused of disregarding local customs and traditions. In certain cases, helpers are insensitive to local customs and traditions; cross-cultural training is often sorely lacking. However, what about situations when helpers perceive particular aspects of local culture as humiliating to some of their members, for example, their women? What do they do when helpers do not see how they can condone customs and traditions they regard as humiliating? The resulting dilemma is extremely hard.

In the course of her fieldwork in Africa, Lindner met numerous disillusioned aid workers who had left their ideals behind and had become tired, even cynical.[5] Humiliation appeared to be a ubiquitous phenomenon, not only among African victims of disaster, but also among international aid workers. Their "disillusionment" had—simplified—two sources (Lindner, 2001): the first was that many aid workers felt betrayed by their own aid organizations, leaving the lower ranks, with their human rights ideals, looking naïve. The second source of disillusionment was the lack of appreciation for help by the recipients; help was often perceived as humiliating by recipients, and this perception in turn had humiliating effects on the helpers. In other words, even though victims often do feel demeaned by aspects entailed in the ongoing crisis itself, they can also feel humiliated again by incoming helpers. At the same time, helpers see their efforts to help being sabotaged, degraded, and ridiculed, and they as caregivers feel humiliated by the lack of recognition for their help.

Lindner learned, for example, that an average African view of incoming helpers could be described as follows:

> You . . . come here to get a kick out of our problems. You pretend to want to help, but you just want to have some fun. You have everything back home, you live in luxury, and you are blind to that. You arrogantly and stupidly believe that you suffer when you cannot take a shower or have to wait for the bus for more than two hours! Look how you cover our people with dust when bumping childishly and proudly around in your four-wheel drive cars! Look how you enjoy being a king, while you would be a nobody back home in your country! All you want is having fun, getting a good salary, writing empty reports to your organization back home, in order to be able to continue this fraud. You pay lip service to human rights and empowerment, but you are hypocrites! And you know that we need help—how glad would we be if we did not need it! And how good would it be if you were really to listen to us once, not only to the greedy among us who exploit your arrogant stupidity for their own good! (Lindner, 2000, p. 17)

Helpers react with deep distress to such outbursts (see also Maren, 1997; Hancock, 1989).

What can be done? The story of Tostan is illuminating. Tostan, an NGO based in Senegal,[6] has been highly successful in eliminating the practice of FGM (Tostan, 2002, 2003). Since 1997, its efforts have led 1,271 communities representing 600,000 people to abandon this practice. According to Molly Melching, Tostan Executive Director, "It was through learning about women's human rights and responsibilities concerning health that discussions of FGC [FGM] first arose" (Wellesley Centers for Women, 2004, p. 16). Kerthio Diarra, a Senegalese village woman who became a human rights activist for the Tostan program, explained: "Before, we thought that the tradition [FGM] was a religious obligation. But when we began to learn about the dangers and consequences of the tradition, we understood we needed to change. It was learning about human rights that changed everything" (p. 17).

Admittedly, the Tostan example is not easy to emulate. Female helpers, witnessing female victims who are trapped in human rights violations, are often particularly disturbed by the experience. Often, all they manage to do, is "close their eyes," as described to Lindner in a personal message (April 10, 2004):

> When Zainab went to Afghanistan two weeks after the Taliban fell, . . . [s]he saw so many injustices to women and children, but stayed focused on her purpose and key mandate of her organization which was to provide immediate relief to the suffering and retrain the women within the context of their culture, so they could be somewhat self-reliant. She had to close

her eyes to many of the political issues, and worked with what would make results, not in the big picture, but in the immediate moment—eat, find shelter, re-establish dignity.

Julia Taft, Assistant Administrator and Director of the Bureau for Crisis Prevention and Recovery at the United Nations Development Program (UNDP), urges a mainstreaming of gender in all development activities (Taft, 2002). The International Crisis Group (ICG), a private, multinational organization, developed a detailed set of recommendations as to how gender equality may be mainstreamed; even though these recommendations have been developed with Afghanistan in mind, they are referred to here since they represent a detailed example of how this task may be approached (see Appendix to this chapter). And, to conclude, aid workers are the ones caught in the middle, a sensitive position in which to be, particularly when women's faring is at stake.

Rising awareness of human rights transforms the lowliness that formerly went unseen and unquestioned into an injustice. As women around the world redefine their positions, many feel unjustly humiliated, no longer duly humbled. They translate these feelings of humiliation into resistance—sometimes destructive resistance and sometimes constructive resistance leading to benign social change. Formerly privileged elites may also develop feelings of humiliation when accused of arrogant superiority and asked to humbly descend from domination and oppression. In other words, adherents of patriarchal social structures—men and women—who are asked to dismantle the concept of male superiority may cry "foul." Intense feelings of humiliation may lead to other painful consequences, ranging from depression and apathy to spiraling acts of rage and violence.

Conclusion

It is important to remember that white middle-class women from the economic North have dominated the feminist movements. Moreover, many aid workers and the people creating treatment plans and policies for humanitarian operations also represent the goals and ideals of privileged Western societies, so that most of the tactics and strategies employed by humanitarian psychosocial staff are informed from this world view. Remember how women and their families displaced by war and conflict must struggle constantly merely to survive, and that finding food for their families and finding safe places to rest are often their most critical needs.

These women are not concerned about whether they are diagnosed with post-traumatic stress disorder (PTSD), or which NGO should be delivering food shipments. They do not know if they will live beyond the moment. Such debates become insignificant when women are fighting to stay alive, feed their children, avoid torture, or find some warm, dry place to sleep. A consequence of this is that there is no way to fully understand the needs of women outside of your own culture. To be successful, it is imperative to incorporate into your disaster program women from within the culture in which you are working. Allow them to inform and guide you on the needs of the women you are trying to aid and learn the best way to fulfill those needs. You will be surprised at some of the answers.

Also, remember that you cannot remove gender from violent conflict, since most social and political structures are patriarchal. Because the nature of war is defined in part by gender, one must consider the needs of men and women differently. It is in periods of great stress that gendered roles become most clearly defined and rigid. Men dominate in most cultures; thus a crisis serves to reinforce male control. Therefore, taking gender into account—or better yet, mainstreaming gender in public policy planning as well as in crisis management—seems to be central.

Particularly important for the topic of this chapter is the role of UN Development Fund for Women (UNIFEM). We suggest that you consider the core strategies guiding UNIFEM's work (2005):

1. Strengthen the capacity and leadership of women's organizations and networks.
2. Leverage political and financial support for women from a range of stakeholders.
3. Forge new partnerships among women's organizations, governments, the UN system, and the private sector.
4. Undertake pilot projects to test innovative approaches to women's empowerment and gender mainstreaming.
5. Build a knowledge base on strategies for engendering mainstream development.

The key idea is to work for new human rights–based social environments, both in general and in cases of crisis, by using appropriate methods that are infused with the human rights spirit. This is all the more important when crisis is the norm in vast regions of the world; for them "normality," as it is known in the wealthier parts of the world, is a state of affairs that lies years of hard work ahead. To create human rights–based social structures and practices worldwide, both in general and in times of crisis, always remember that the use of strategies that humiliate the women you are trying to help— or are perceived as humiliating—are not conducive, but counterproductive.

Appendix

Recommendations to Afghanistan's Transitional Administration by the International Crisis Group:

1. Request the Ministry of Women's Affairs to study and adopt, a streamlined administrative structure that establishes crosscutting links within its departments.

2. All ministries should name officials with gender focal points at the rank of deputy minister or department head and link those gender focal points to the Gender Advisory Group, so that policy recommendations can be disseminated within the government.
3. Appoint permanent managerial and technical support staff to the Gender Advisory Group and other bodies that are meant to mainstream gender policy in line ministries.
4. Appoint members of the civil service commission, give it a professional secretariat and use its developed employment selection criteria for appointment to government posts and review of existing appointments, including the Ministry of Women's Affairs.
5. Develop methods of ensuring that gender policy concerns are incorporated within budgetary allocations of line ministries.
6. Establish family courts in each provincial centre, with jurisdiction over divorce, compulsory marriage, child custody and inheritance, and ensure that judges presiding over the courts are conversant with civil code and applicable international treaties.
7. Incorporate women with experience in public life and advocacy into the Constitutional Commission to ensure visible and meaningful gender balance.
8. Ensure that input from the public consultation process, particularly with women, is reflected in the final draft of the constitution presented to the Constitutional Loya Jirga.
9. The selection process will facilitate women's Constitutional Loya Jirga participation.

To the Judicial Reform Commission:

10. Incorporate CEDAW into the civil and criminal codes, in particular with family law.
11. Identify progressive statutory systems as sources for revision of the civil and penal codes consistent with Afghan norms.

To the International Community:

12. Include capacity building in the aid given to the Ministry of Women's Affairs.
13. Support micro-credit loan programs and training in loan management for women.
14. Ensure that gender and development assistance is based on field research and consultations with Afghan women, including market research into income-earning opportunities, women's mobility in the target areas, and accessibility of services.
15. Help the Ministry of Education develop curricula that explain women's rights under the civil code and CEDAW in terms accessible to both male and female students.

16. Support financially a consultation process on the constitution that gives women a genuine voice and identify and support a constituency for women's rights within and without the government in up to the Constitutional Loya Jirga.

To the United Nations:

17. Refocus UNIFEM's efforts on effective needs assessments, income-generating projects with training, and projects building women's roles in the political process.

To the States Participating in ISAF:

18. Extend ISAF or an equivalent mission to additional areas of the country, beyond Kabul so that Afghan women activists can operate there effectively.

Notes

1. A *convention* is a legally binding instrument concluded by the UN, signed by UN body members, and established by international law. This is in contrast to the other document that the UN can pass, a declaration, which is not legally binding.
2. Today, most of the world has adopted CEDAW, although the outcome is mixed. Only two nations have signed but not ratified CEDAW, Afghanistan and the United States. Those states who have neither signed nor ratified the convention include Sudan, Somalia, Iran, Oman, Syria Micronesia, Brunei (not an inclusive list) (Seager, 2003).
3. According to Seager (2003), "estimates suggest that the actual incidence of rape may be up to 50 times the numbers reported" (p. 58), depending on how you define rape. In most countries forcible sex within a marriage is not considered rape or a crime. Also, sex outside of the marriage, whether rape or consensual, is often considered a crime for which a woman can be imprisoned or sentenced to death in some instances.
4. In Sweden women average 33 hours a week on housework, men 24. In Japan women spend 29 hours on housework and men only 4 hours.
5. Lindner conducted a four-year doctoral research project (1997–2001) at the University of Oslo, entitled *The Feeling of Being Humiliated: A Central Theme in Armed Conflicts. A Study of the Role of Humiliation in Somalia, and Rwanda/Burundi, between the Warring Parties, and in Relation to Third Intervening Parties.* She carried out 216 qualitative interviews addressing Somalia, Rwanda, and Burundi and their history of genocidal killings. The interviews were carried from 1997 to 2001.
6. For more information about Tostan, see www.tostan.org.

References

Domeisen, N. (1997). *The role of women in protecting communities for disasters.* Speech presented at United Nations panel discussion on women and emergencies. Retrieved August 19, 2005, from http://www.disaster-info.net/crid/eng/info/idndrgen.htm

Espín, O. M. (1999). *Women crossing boundaries: A psychology of immigration and transformations of sexuality.* New York: Routledge.

Friedan, Betty. (1963). *The feminine mystique* (5th ed.). New York: Norton & Co.

Gullace, N. F. (1997). White feathers and wounded men: Female patriotism and the memory of the Great War. *Journal of British Studies, 36,* 178–206.

Hancock, G. (1989). *The lords of poverty. The power, prestige and corruption of the international aid business.* New York: Atlantic Monthly Press.

Hartling, L. M., & Luchetta, T. (1999). Humiliation: Assessing the impact of derision, degradation, and debasement. *Journal of Primary Prevention, 19*(5), 259–278.

Herman, J. (1997). *Trauma and recovery: The aftermath of violence—from domestic abuse to political terror* (2nd ed.). New York: Basic Books.

Holbrook, T. L., & Hoyt, D. B. (2004). The impact of major trauma: Quality of life outcomes are worse in women than in men, independent of mechanism and injury severity. *Journal of Trauma, Injury, Infection, and Critical Care, 56*(2), 284–290.

Hudnall, A. C. (2002, August). *The necessity of cultural relativism and universalism for effective implementation of the United Nation's CEDAW and the establishment of International Women's Equality.* Paper presented at the International Congress of Women's World 2002. Makerere, Uganda.

———. (2003). Feminists around the world protest war with Iraq-photo essay. *NWSA Journal, 15*(2), 101–110.

International Committee of the Red Cross. (2001, October). Women and war, fact sheet. Retrieved April 4, 2004 from http://www.icrc.org/Web/eng/siteeng0.nsf/iwpList138/

———. (2004, February). *Addressing the needs of women affected by armed conflict: An ICRC guidance document* (Ref. 0804, executive summary). Retrieved January 20, 2005 from http://www.icrc.org/WEB/ENG/siteeng0.nsf/htmlall/p0840?OpenDocmment&style=Custo_Final.4&View=defaultBody2

Landesman, P. (September 15, 2002). A Woman's Work. *The New York Times Magazine.*

Lindner, E. G. (2000). *How humiliation creates cultural differences: The psychology of intercultural communication.* Unpublished manuscript, University of Oslo.

———. (2001). *The psychology of humiliation: Somalia, Rwanda/Burundi, and Hitler's Germany.* Unpublished doctoral dissertation, University of Oslo.

Lorentzen, L. A., & Turpin, J. (Eds.). (1998). *The women and war reader.* New York: New York University Press.

Maren, M. (1997). *The road to hell: The ravaging effects of foreign aid and international charity.* New York: Free Press.

Meltzer, M., & Andersen, B. (1998). *Ten queens: Portraits of women of power.* New York: Dutton Books.

Mernissi, F. (1993). *The forgotten queens of Islam.* Cambridge: Polity Press.

Murray, C. J. L., & Lopez, A. D. (Eds.) (1996). *The global burden of disease and injury series: Vol. 1: A comprehensive assessment of mortality and disability from diseases, injuries, and risk factors in 1990 and projected to 2020.* Cambridge, MA: Harvard University Press.

Norris, F. H., Perilla, J. L., Ilbañez, G. E., & Murphy, A. D. (2001). Sex differences in symptoms of posttraumatic stress: Does culture play a role? *Journal of Traumatic Stress, 14*(1), 7–28.

Saakvitne, K. W., & Stamm, B. H. (n.d.). *Fostering resilience in response to terrorism among mental health workers* (Fact sheet). Washington, DC: American Psychological Association. Retrieved January 24, 2005, from http://www.apa.org/psychologists/pdfs/mentalhealthworkers.pdf

Salzman, T. A. (1998). Rape camps as a means of ethnic cleansing: Religious, cultural, and ethical responses to rape victims in the former Yugoslavia. *Human Rights Quarterly, 20*(2), 348–378.

Seager, J. (2003). *The Penguin atlas of women in the world* (3rd ed.). Brighton, UK: Penguin Group.

Stamm, B. H., Higson-Smith, C., & Hudnall, A. C. (2003). The complexities of working with terror. In D. Knafo (Ed.), *Living with Terror, Working with Trauma: A Clinician's Handbook* (pp. 369–399). Northvale, NJ: Jason Aronson.

Taft, J. (2002, March). *Afghan women today: Realities and opportunities.* Speech presented at United Nations panel discussion. Retrieved August 19, 2005, from http://www.un.org/events/women/2002/taft.htm

Tostan. (2002). Tostan annual report. Dakar, Senegal: Author. Retrieved January 24, 2005 from http://www.tostan.org/articles.htm

———. (2003). *Tostan: Putting African communities at the center of development* [Brochure]. Dakar, Senegal: Author.

United Nations [UN] Commission of Experts. (1994, May). *Final Report of the Commission of Experts.* Retrieved June 24, 2004, from http://www.ess.uwe.ac.uk/comexpert/REPORT_TOC.HTM

UN Development Fund for Women [UNIFEM]. *Core strategies guiding UNIFEM's work.* Retrieved January 24, 2005, from http://www.unifem.org/index.php?f_page_pid=2

UN Development Programme. (2000). *Human development report 2000.* New York: Oxford University Press.

UN General Assembly. (1979). *The Convention on the Elimination of All Forms of Discrimination against Women (CEDAW).* Retrieved January 24, 2005 from, http://www.un.org/womenwatch/daw/cedaw/text/econvention.htm

———. (1996, February 23). *Rape and abuse of women in the areas of armed conflict in the former Yugoslavia:* Resolution adopted by the General Assembly [on the Report of the Third Committee (A/50/635/Add.3)] (No. A/RES/50/192). Retrieved June 24, 2004, from http://www.unhchr.ch/Huridocda/Huridoca.nsf/0/954885f1c9492e7b8025666d0058d49b?Opendocument

Wellesley Centers for Women. (2004). Human rights activists from West Africa visit WCW. *Research & Action Report, 25*(2), 16–17.

Wiest, R. E., Mocellin, J. S. P., & Motsisi, D. T. (1994). The needs of women in disasters and emergencies. Retrieved January 24, 2005, from http://online.northumbria.ac.uk/geography_research/gdn/resources/papers.html

Yoshimi, Y. (2001). *Comfort women: Sexual slavery in the japanese military during World War II.* New York: Columbia University Press.

CHAPTER 2

SEXUAL VIOLENCE AGAINST WOMEN AND CHILDREN IN THE CONTEXT OF ARMED CONFLICT

Chen Reis and Beth Vann

Sexual violence in the context of armed conflict and displacement is a serious, life-threatening issue that affects primarily women and children. While men and boys have also been victims of sexual violence, research suggests that the vast majority of those experiencing sexual violence are women and girls and that the majority of perpetrators are male combatants. It is well documented that sexual violence is a widespread international public health issue, and that adequate, appropriate, and comprehensive prevention and response are lacking in most countries worldwide (Heise, Pitanguy, & Germain, 1994). Sexual violence is especially problematic during armed conflict and in displaced settings, where civilian women and children constitute the greatest numbers, are often targeted for abuse, and are the most vulnerable to exploitation, violence, and abuse simply by virtue of their gender, age, and status in society.

Sexual abuses such as rape, exploitation, and sex-for-survival in displaced settings are increasingly recognized as pervasive problems worldwide. Although reports of rape, sexual exploitation, sexual bartering, domestic violence, and other forms of sexual violence are frequently detected in conflict and displaced settings, few reliable numbers are available at this time. Nevertheless, wartime sexual violence perpetrated by combatants is a serious and persisting risk for women across the world and can no longer be ignored or denied.

Since the early 1990s, the humanitarian community has given increased attention to the problem of sexual violence. Efforts are underway to address sexual violence in many conflict and displacement settings. So far, the most promising efforts to prevent sexual violence and provide services to survivors have required integrated and coordinated action by multisectoral actors from the refugee community, international humanitarian organizations (nongovernmental [NGOs] and the UN), national organizations, and host government ministries. A minimum set of services must be provided for health care, psychosocial support, security and protection, and legal justice (both formal and traditional). To achieve integrated and coordinated action, there must be collaboration, skill, knowledge, training, coordination, and high-level support and commitment within all organizations.

Published resource materials, best-practice recommendations, guidelines, and field tools for designing and managing prevention and response to sexual violence are continually emerging as the pool of knowledge and experience grows. Materials specific to displaced populations are sometimes difficult to identify and obtain, especially by field programs in countries with limited access to the Internet. Because the field is so new and wisdom is evolving rapidly, materials specific to displaced populations may be difficult for some organizations to identify and obtain. Nevertheless, materials are available that organizations can use to build the capacity of their staff and develop good programs to address sexual violence.

Overview of Conflict-Related Sexual Violence

The world's awareness that sexual violence can be used as a deliberate strategy to undermine communities was raised during the crises in Rwanda and the former Yugoslavia and their aftermath. The convictions by the ad-hoc tribunals for Rwanda and Yugoslavia on rape as a war crime and crime against humanity and the inclusion of sexual violence as a crime against humanity in the statute of the new International Criminal Court indicate the reduced tolerance for these crimes. The problem, however, is ongoing; recent events in the Democratic Republic of the Congo and the Darfur region of Sudan demonstrate that sexual violence continues and that the majority of perpetrators escape justice. Even when trials occur and those who are responsible for sexual violence are punished, there is little assistance for the survivors. True justice requires that the survivors receive assistance for their psychological, physical, and social needs. In most settings, unfortunately, these services are lacking.

Sexual violence is believed to have been common in armed conflicts throughout history worldwide as a spoil of war or as an unavoidable byproduct of the chaos and violence of war. Until recently, sexual violence in conflicts received little attention from the international community, and we still do not know enough about sexual violence in crises. There is little or no research on the magnitude or prevalence of sexual violence, causal factors, risk factors, prevention sexual violence in a crisis, or addressing its consequences. Moreover, little is known about the short- and long-term effects of conflict-related sexual violence on women and their communities. Reviews and evaluations of interventions are also unavailable. Conducting research in crises is exceedingly difficult because of resource constraints, safety, and other logistical considerations. Furthermore, the specific challenges of conducting research on the sensitive matters of sexual violence, difficult in relatively stable settings, are magnified during crises, when lack of stability, disruption of family or community support mechanisms, and other experiences of the population may prevent full disclosure.

Nature of Recent Armed Conflicts

Over the past century, the impact of war on civilians has increased substantially. Although only about 5 percent of casualties in World War I were civilians, it was estimated that 80 percent of war casualties in the 1990s were civilians. This significant increase in the impact of conflict on civilians is a product of the changing nature of conflicts. Today, most conflicts target civilians and civilian institutions as a deliberate tactic of war. Between 1989 and 1996 there were 101 armed conflicts around the world. Of these, the vast majority were deemed to be internal disputes involving the use of small arms by decentralized groups of combatants. Because of the systematic targeting of civilians and institutions key to their survival, these conflicts have devastating consequences for the populations residing in the affected countries. The majority of those who become displaced or refugees while fleeing the conflict are women and children. Often, families are separated or the men are killed, leaving women as heads of households and many children to fend for themselves. Those who are internally displaced (IDPs) receive fewer protections than those who cross an international border. IDPs generally receive fewer services, are harder to reach, and experience increased insecurity both during flight and while displaced. At the mercy of local officials, women may be targeted when they go looking for firewood, or they may be forced to engage in sexual activities to obtain necessities for survival.

Another relevant aspect of recent armed conflicts is that many are long-term, seemingly intractable disputes that result in high numbers of displaced civilians who remain displaced for many years, sometimes for several generations. Living in "temporary" sites of refuge, with almost total dependence on humanitarian aid, populations suffer from stress, depression, ongoing trauma, and even boredom. In these situations of extreme and long-term dependence, populations are vulnerable to many forms of abuse and exploitation, including sexual violence.

The use of sexual violence to intimidate, humiliate, control, and punish during conflicts has been documented in wars around the world, including Kosovo, Sierra Leone, Democratic Republic of Congo, Darfur, Mozambique, former Yugoslavia, Angola, Rwanda, Kashmir, Liberia, Indonesia, East Timor, and Uganda. The use, nature, and prevalence of sexual violence vary from conflict to conflict. The following section discusses the types and definitions of sexual violence and addresses the range of actors who have perpetrated sexual violence in crises.

Characteristics of Sexual Violence in Armed Conflicts and Displaced Settings

Sexual violence is defined in the World Report on Violence and Health (WHO, 2002) as "any sexual act, attempt to obtain a sexual act, unwanted sexual comments or advances, or acts to traffic a person's sexuality, using coercion, threats of harm or physical force, by any person regardless of relationship to the victim, in any setting, including but not limited to home and work (p. 149). Sexual violence takes many forms, including rape, sexual slavery, forced pregnancy, sexual harassment, virginity testing, forced marriage, forced pregnancy, and forced abortion.

Rape is defined by the *World Report on Violence and Health* as "physically forced or otherwise coerced penetration—even if slight—of the vulva or anus using a penis other body parts or an object." Sexual violence may also "include other forms of assault involving a sexual organ, including coerced contact between the mouth and penis, vulva or anus" (p. 149). For the purposes of this chapter, the existence of an intimate or marital relationship between the perpetrator and victim/survivor does not mean that rape could not have occurred, although national laws vary. In fact, studies in relatively stable settings have shown that intimate partners are the most common perpetrators of sexual and other violence.

In the context of armed conflict, sexual violence can occur during the fighting, in flight, in settings of refuge such as refugee and IDP camps, or within host communities. Rape is often used as a weapon of war to terrorize the population and undermine the enemy's morale. Gang rape, a particularly horrific form of rape, has been documented in numerous conflicts. In a study conducted among internally displaced populations in Sierra Leone, one out of every three reported rapes was of the gang variety. Rape may also include forcing an individual to have sex with someone else. Human rights groups have reported instances of young men being forced to have sex with others, including family members, as a way of severing their ties to their communities. In some settings, such as Rwanda and the former Yugoslavia, rape is used as a tool of ethnic cleansing. Rape and impregnation of the women of the targeted community, so that they give birth to "mixed" children, was considered a way of eliminating the targeted community as well as insulting the honor of the men.

Although a woman or girl may be left by the perpetrator after the rape, in some instances, as in Sierra Leone and Uganda, women and girls are abducted for long periods of time and made to provide sexual and other services to combatants. Women and girls subjected to sexual slavery may be forced to have sex with many men or may be selected by one man and forced to have sex only with him and to bear his children. While many attempt to flee in such situations, others eventually consider that they are married to a man from the group who abducted them. The reasons for this are complex and may include fear, inability to return home, the need for stability, and social acceptance, as well as economic dependence. Many of these women and girls have multiple children born as a result of rape and have no alternatives for care and support of themselves and their children.

During flight, women and girls are also subject to abuse by members of communities that they pass through, as well as by officials, such as border guards, who have a significant influence over who is allowed to cross the border and who is not. This abuse may include rape or other sexual assault, including being forced to undress. The lack of shelter for displaced persons—particularly women and girls—means little protection if attacked by combatants or others.

Even in a refugee or IDP camp women and girls may be subject to rape and sexual abuse by others in the community. Physical security in these settings is often lacking—especially at night. Women may be attacked while in the camp, for instance when going to use the latrines, or outside the camp, when going to fetch firewood or returning from the market. Women also experience sexual violence at the hands of intimate partners, including husbands. Domestic violence has been documented in camp settings; it includes sexual as well as physical and psychological abuse. One of the most disturbing manifestations of sexual violence in the camp setting is exploitation and abuse by humanitarian workers and peacekeepers. According to the Interagency Standing Committee (IASC, 2002):[1]

> Exploitation and abuse occurs when this disparity of power is misused to the detriment of those persons who cannot negotiate or make decisions on an equal basis. Exploitation and abuse can take the form of physical and psychological force or other means of coercion (threats, inducements, deception or extortion) with the aim of gaining sexual or other favors in exchange for services. In institutional terms, sexual exploitation and abuse by humanitarian staff represents a failure on the part of humanitarian agencies, whose stated role is to provide protection and care. (p. 13)

Perpetrators

What is known about these crimes suggests that most perpetrators are male and most victims female. The issue of sexual abuse of boys and men is receiving increased attention, and most of these acts are also committed by men. Sexual violence can happen within the family and the community, and it can be committed by anyone in a position of power. Perpetrators may include individuals close to the survivor as well as combatants, members of host communities, and those charged with roles of protection and assistance to refugees and IDPs.

In the context of disasters, conflict, and forced population movements, sexual violence may also be perpetrated by husbands or boyfriends. Such violence by intimate partners likely reflects the status of women in the society and may increase with the societal and personal stress associated with conflict. Women often rely on their partners for protection or food and fear increased reprisals should they fight back or resist. In communities where abusive behavior by intimate partners is an accepted norm, these women will likely not get the support they need to leave the abusive relationship. Sexual violence by intimate partners, including marital rape, is an important aspect of the problem of sexual violence in emergencies and one that is not always addressed. Similarly, other members of the family or community may also perpetrate sexual violence against women and girls. The forms of sexual violence will range from rape to incest to harmful traditional practices such as female genital cutting, wife inheritance, and forced marriage. People in positions of authority within the community such as teachers and other community leaders may also use their power and authority to commit acts of sexual violence through coercion—and with impunity.

As discussed above, sexual violence as a tactic of war is increasingly recognized as a significant problem in recent and ongoing conflicts. Armed personnel, even those with a specific mandate to protect civilians, such as police and peacekeepers, may abuse their power by committing crimes of sexual violence. Women who are separated from family, young children, and those forced to flee and who come into contact with combatants may be at increased risk of sexual violence. Those who rely upon armed forces for permission to cross borders or pass checkpoints may face increased risk of experiencing sexual violence. Sexual violence has also been committed by those charged with protecting and assisting people in times of crisis, including staff of humanitarian aid organizations, UN agencies, and host government officials in the case of refugees. Perpetrators may include international staff (i.e., expatriates) and staff recruited locally (i.e., indigenous) including some from within the affected communities.

The nature of conflicts and their consequences contribute to the vulnerability of women and girls. Conflict leads to separation of families as people flee, are killed, or are taken away. The targeting of civilian institutions and civilians leads to flight. As people flee, they become separated from family members. Others, often men, may be taken away to fight or to be killed. The loss of property, family, and community protections during flight and displacement contributes to the vulnerability of women to all forms of sexual violence. The lack of security during flight and in refuge, the poverty that arises from loss of property and livelihood, and the dependence on host communities, governments, and aid workers also increase the vulnerability of women to sexual violence, abuse, and exploitation.

Consequences of Sexual Violence

Those who experience sexual violence are at risk for many serious, debilitating, life-threatening long- and short-term physical and mental health consequences. Sexual violence can be linked with injury and death by homicide or suicide. More frequently, it is associated with a range of sexual and reproductive health problems, including unwanted pregnancy and, related to this, unsafe abortion. Even in countries in which abortion is legal in cases of rape, these services are often not available or may be associated with stigma. Women may therefore be forced to undergo unsafe abortions or have unwanted children. Other sexual and reproductive problems that are associated with sexual violence include sexually transmitted infections (STIs), including HIV/AIDS, and gynecological problems such as pelvic inflammatory disease, chronic pelvic pain, urinary tract infections, pelvic fistulae, and genital injuries such as tears, bruising, and abrasions.

Sexual violence is also associated with psychological and emotional problems; including depression, post-traumatic stress disorder, anxiety, and eating disorders, and suicidal behavior, including suicide attempts. Survivors may also experience problems in the long term, including chronic headaches, sexual difficulties, and sleep disturbances. Those who experience sexual violence may also adopt high-risk behaviors such as having multiple sexual partners or substance abuse.

The social consequences of sexual violence can also have a significant impact on the life of the survivor. The violence and the inequalities that women face in emergencies do not exist in a vacuum; rather they are direct results and reflections of the violence, discrimination, and marginalization that women face in times of relative peace. Similarly, societal attitudes and norms relating to how crimes of sexual violence are addressed, if at all, are often reflected in the response to sexual violence in emergencies.

As in times of relative peace, there are often a variety of factors in conflict settings that will discourage the woman from disclosing that she has experienced sexual violence. The stigma and shame associated with sexual violence in most settings worldwide may prevent the victim from reporting what happened to her, as may fear of ridicule and concerns about personal safety or retribution. Furthermore, disclosure may result in abandonment by a partner or rejection by family or community, and the social opportunities and status of a woman may be affected by disclosure. For instance, a woman may be considered unsuitable for marriage because she is no longer a virgin; in societies where marriage provides women with status, this is likely a significant deterrent to reporting. In some instances, the woman may be forced to marry the perpetrator. Even when women do not disclose, the fear and trauma from the event may lead them to isolate themselves from their family and community. A tendency to blame the victim for the assault or for not stopping it exists in many societies during both conflict and relative peace and serves as a further disincentive to disclosure.

When the sexual violence happens within an intimate partnership, there is often a tendency to consider the act as not inappropriate or to consider the matter a personal affair that does not require interference. Disclosure, furthermore, may not result in justice for the victim, as laws may be discriminatory and the infrastructure not present to enable the victim to bring a successful case. In cases of government complicity in the acts of sexual violence, or where it is not in the political interest of the government to record and prosecute these crimes, a woman seeking redress from governmental authorities is unlikely to find it. Traditional or customary law is frequently the preferred form of legal justice among displaced populations. Such traditional tribunals, usually composed of male elders in the community, adjudicate cases based on traditional and cultural beliefs and norms, which are usually not supportive of women's equal rights and need for justice. Even when a case is brought, whether using formal or traditional law, the survivor often is subjected to unnecessary invasive exams, does not receive social or psychological support or protection when engaging with the legal system, and, because of attitudes that blame the victim, may feel that she herself is on trial rather than the perpetrator. Disclosure may therefore result in further adverse consequences to the survivor beyond those that are a direct result of the sexual violence.

Humanitarian Efforts to Address Sexual Violence

Wisdom from 15 years of experience with sexual violence demonstrates the importance of addressing three interrelated sets of activities: prevention, response (survivor assistance), and coordination. All of these activities involve women and men, adults and children from the displaced community, staff in NGOs, UN agencies, and host government authorities. Addressing sexual violence among displaced populations has become an increasingly high priority over the past 15 years, coinciding with the growing worldwide attention to human rights and women's rights. The United Nations High Commissioner for Refugees (UNHCR), mandated to protect and assist refugees worldwide, is the designated leader for efforts to address sexual violence among refugee populations. Since the early 1990s, UNHCR and its NGO partners have been implementing comprehensive programs to address sexual violence against women and children.

To date, experience indicates that the most promising prevention and response strategies require integrated and coordinated action by multiple actors from the displaced community, international humanitarian aid organizations (international NGOs and UN agencies), national NGOs, and host governments. The key sectors, or functional areas, that must be involved are the health, psychosocial, security, and legal justice systems (both formal and traditional). To achieve integrated action, there must be collaboration, coordination, communication, technical training, and high-level support and commitment among and between all of these actors.

The first set of guidelines, *Sexual Violence against Refugees: Guidelines on Prevention and Response,* was published by UNHCR in 1995. It was UNHCR's first attempt to establish comprehensive and specific standards for prevention and response to sexual violence in refugee populations. In October 1998, the United Nations Foundation awarded $1.65 million to UNHCR to strengthen efforts to prevent sexual violence in five countries in sub-Saharan Africa—Kenya, Tanzania, Guinea, Sierra Leone, and Liberia—and to put into place services that respond compassionately to survivors. It marked the first time that funds were targeted for coordinated interagency development of comprehensive multisectoral services that were to be implemented by well-trained and well-equipped staff from an array of UN, NGO, government- and community-based entities. Along with this injection of funds, UNHCR expanded its programming to include other forms of violence against women and children beyond specifically sexual violence. Thus, in the late 1990s, the humanitarian community broadened its view to incorporate issues of gender and gender discrimination into a more comprehensive understanding of gender-based violence, which includes sexual violence.

The knowledge base of sexual violence programming in displaced population settings grew significantly with the UNHCR/UN Foundation programs. Multisectoral, interdisciplinary, and interagency programming became the recommended approach for all settings. By 2001, UNHCR and NGOs were developing more comprehensive programs tied into multiple sectors or disciplines in an increasing number of settings. Initiatives in many countries included health care, emotional support, social reintegration, and, often, police and legal action. Interventions were targeting many different forms of gender-based violence, including war-related sexual violence, domestic violence, incest, and harmful traditional practices. Prevention strategies were developing; they included engaging interested and committed members of the displaced community in influencing changes to their own society's beliefs and practices about gender issues and women's rights.

In 2001, UNHCR hosted an international conference to bring together multisectoral actors from displaced settings worldwide. Conference participants developed a set of minimum standards and recommendations for continued development of these important programs. Participants identified that there are many forms of violence against women and children, including but not limited to sexual violence, that are serious problems in displaced settings and stated that more guidance is needed in the field. They called for revision and expansion of UNHCR's 1995 *Guidelines*. Participants also urged all organizations to establish codes of conduct for staff. During the conference, participants identified that some national and international aid staff, including peacekeepers—sometimes including high-level managers— are known to engage in sexual exploitation and abuse of their beneficiaries.

Interestingly, in 2002, a story appeared in the international media about sexual exploitation of women and children in refugee camps in West Africa, reportedly perpetrated by humanitarian and peacekeeping staff. Organizations identified included NGOs, UN agencies, the government, and international peacekeepers. The scandal and attention that resulted from this public news story pushed UN agencies and NGOs into developing codes of conduct for staff. The IASC established a set of minimum standards for all aid staff; these standards are now required in codes of conduct for all UN staff, and for staff of NGOs receiving certain donor funds.

In 2003, UNHCR issued a revised and updated version of its 1995 *Guidelines, Sexual and Gender-Based Violence against Refugees, Returnees, and Internally Displaced Persons: Guidelines for Prevention and Response*. The new version includes minimum standards for prevention and response action, roles, and responsibilities of specific staff and organizations in displaced settings, as well as new recommended forms, checklists, and monitoring and evaluation tools.

In 2001, WHO and UNHCR jointly produced concrete and user-friendly guidelines for clinical management of post-rape care, including specific treatments, dosages, and recommendations for actions to be taken by all health providers in displaced settings. These guidelines have now been revised based on input from field sites and were republished in 2004.

Recommended Standards and Strategies

There are now recommended standards and practices for addressing sexual violence with displaced populations. These are based on field experiences and lessons learned over a 15-year period. Although the standards and recommendations exist, implementation remains challenging. This section describes the current guidelines and recommendations for action. The next section looks at successes and challenges in implementation.

Situation Analysis

In order to design effective interventions, organizations must understand the situation vis-à-vis sexual violence in any specific setting. In most societies, however, sexual violence is a very sensitive topic that, when broached, often elicits denial from communities, as well as embarrassment, shame, and even anger and defensiveness. Situational analyses about sexual violence must be carried out with good planning, care, sensitivity, and awareness of potential security issues for community members.

Understanding sexual violence begins with a situation analysis that gathers, at a minimum, information about the following factors in the setting. Information can be gathered through individual interviews, focus group discussions, and record reviews.

- Demographic composition (age and sex) of the population
- Information about flight, movements, and the population's direct contact with combatants during fighting and in flight
- Social and cultural norms for gender roles and expectations, use of power, and decision making in the community
- Family and community systems for protection that were in place before flight and those that are in place now
- Groups and individuals at greater risk of sexual violence

- Types and extent of sexual violence that occurred during flight and may be occurring in the site of refuge
- Societal attitudes and beliefs about sexual violence and how the community views survivors (blaming the victim, preferring she marry the perpetrator, etc.)
- Knowledge, attitudes, and behavior of people in positions of power in the community—and in aid organizations working at the site
- Physical environment, site layout, and access to services and facilities, including the population's level of awareness of their rights and entitlements
- Formal (national) and traditional systems for law and administration of justice

Interagency Coordination and Collaboration

No single organization, sector, or discipline has sole responsibility for preventing and responding to sexual violence. Everyone must work together to understand the problem and design strategies to address it. "Everyone" includes the displaced communities; without active community involvement, interventions cannot be fully successful. Given the multisectoral and interagency nature of prevention and response, there is a need for coordination and leadership: a lead agency. In some settings, UNHCR leads the efforts; in other settings, an NGO with interest, commitment, and (sometimes) funds provides the capacity for the high levels of activity needed for this coordination and leadership.

The design, monitoring, and evaluation of interagency and multisectoral action must be a coordinated effort. Some key components for coordination must be established and agreed upon by all actors, including the following:

- Community participation in all stages of program design and implementation
- Guiding principles for how everyone will maximize confidentiality, survivor respect, and safety
- Systems for receiving and documenting incident reports
- Referral mechanisms between and among organizations
- Systems for information sharing, problem solving, and coordination
- Continuous monitoring and evaluation to guide action in both prevention and response

Recommended Standards for Assisting Survivors (Response)

Response to sexual and other forms of gender-based violence comprises a group of comprehensive services for survivors that reduce the harmful after-effects and prevent further trauma and harm. Consequences and after-effects, as described above, can include health problems, psychological trauma, physical safety and security concerns, and criminal justice needs. Help can be provided, however, only if an incident is reported and the survivor requests assistance. Response, therefore, begins with establishing assistance services and building trust in the community that appropriate, confidential, and useful help is available.

Building and maintaining community trust in the response services requires adherence to three fundamental guiding principles for all who assist survivors:

1. At all times, ensure the safety of the survivor.
2. Maintain confidentiality.
3. Respect the dignity, choices, and rights of the survivor.

All actors in all organizations engaged in response must also have sufficient capacity to provide the services needed by any individual survivor. For this reason, a large part of the work in addressing sexual violence is building the capacity of the responders. There are usually needs for training; for developing clear and consistent protocols, procedures, and policies for actions to be taken; and for materials and equipment. Minimum response requires action from at least four primary sectors or functional areas. In most displaced settings, there is at least one organization providing minimum services in each of these four areas. The recommended standards are as follows.

Health care (outpatient clinic, hospital)

- Outreach and identification of survivors
- Examination and treatment by trained staff using appropriate protocols and with adequate equipment, supplies, medicines to
  - Treat injury
  - Prevent unwanted pregnancy
  - Treat/prevent sexually transmitted infections, including HIV/AIDS
  - Assess mental trauma
- Medical evidence documentation for legal proceedings, as requested and required
- Follow-up care and treatment
- Referral (and transport) to appropriate levels of care
- Collaboration and coordination with traditional healing practitioners

Psychosocial support (community services, social services programs)

- Outreach and identification of survivors: designated place(s) where survivors can go to receive assistance and assurance of safety and confidentiality, without stigma
- Counseling (e.g., short-term listening and emotional support) for survivors and families
- Referral, advocacy, and assistance (case management) for survivors with health care, security, and legal justice systems, and other needed services

- Group activities—including income generation and micro credit projects—for survivors and other vulnerable women that focus on building support networks, reintegration into communities, confidence building, skill building, and promotion of economic empowerment
- Community education—targeting the community, UN and NGO staff, and local government authorities—for protection awareness, rights awareness, and knowledge of available assistance

Security (police, security workers, UNHCR staff)

- Appropriately trained, competent, and adequately equipped police force
- Private interview space in police posts to receive complaints
- Presence of police/security workers, especially after dark and in high-risk areas
- Analysis of incident data and communication with all actors and community of security risks and issues
- Concrete security solutions to address identified risks and problems (e.g., fencing, lighting, use of radios)
- Strategies and options for immediate protection of survivors (e.g., separation of ration cards, relocation, "protection area," safe houses in the community)

Legal justice (national courts, traditional/customary law)

- Nondiscriminatory laws and practices that protect human rights
- Court system with adequate training and capacity to adjudicate cases with minimal delays and with respect for the dignity and rights of the victim

Recommended Strategies for Prevention in Displaced Settings

Prevention involves first understanding the root causes of sexual violence as well as the situation-specific factors that contribute to, perpetuate, or increase the risk of sexual violence. Once these are understood, prevention activities seek to address the causes by influencing changes in knowledge, attitudes, and behaviors; and to reduce the contributing factors by launching targeted prevention strategies. Prevention activities target potential survivors and potential perpetrators in both their behavior and their environment.

Sexual violence involves the abuse of power and is rooted in gender expectations, limitations, privileges, opportunities, and inequalities. Preventing sexual violence therefore involves influencing changes in knowledge, attitudes, and behavior among women and men, young and old, displaced and helper, concerning issues of gender, power, and human rights.

There are also any number of situation-specific factors that may contribute to the risk of sexual violence. Populations fleeing conflict experience a breakdown in traditional family and community support systems. Families separate. Women, separated from their husbands and extended families, raise children alone, often without job skills or means for generating income. Children separated from parents or other family have no trusted adult to protect them. This environment of poverty and dependence contributes to many forms of abuse and discrimination, including sexual exploitation.

With a solid understanding of the community-in-need and its environment, the interagency team can target prevention activities to potential perpetrators, potential survivors, and the people who assist both groups. Historically, efforts have focused on empowering women because they are the majority of potential survivors. This focus is important, but, on its own, it ignores the other half of the abuse equation, namely, the perpetrator. Another component receiving increased attention now is working with children and with men and encouraging men to work with men. Prevention, then, includes activities that address both the root causes and the contributing factors; it includes activities such as the following.

- Problem solving with humanitarian aid staff about security risks in the setting, and the types, places, and circumstances under which sexual violence and other forms of gender-based violence occur.
- Educating potential survivors about where to go for help if they are victimized, and what help would be available.
- Establishing and enforcing standards of behavior for humanitarian aid staff, such as codes of conduct, accountability systems, and consequences for violations.
- Promoting changes in national and traditional laws and practices to bring about stronger protection of the human rights of women and children. This may include education and advocacy with displaced leaders and advocating with government lawmakers through partnership with national women's rights and legal aid organizations.
- Implementing behavior change communication (BCC) strategies about gender, power, human rights, and violence, using a variety of participatory methods that promote discussion and reflection about attitudes and beliefs, and ultimately lead to changes in behavior. This effort, often called *awareness raising*, includes many different types of activities targeting all the demographic groups within the refugee and aid communities. Education can empower potential victims and change the attitudes and behavior of potential perpetrators and the community at large that may be perpetuating violence and abuse through silent acceptance of abusive behavior and blaming the victim.

Successes and Challenges

Implementing comprehensive, interagency, and interdisciplinary services for survivors and effective strategies for prevention of sexual violence is a major challenge in stable, well-resourced settings such as the United States and countries in Europe. In humanitarian settings, implementing these programs involves an additional set of obstacles and challenges. This section highlights some of the major successes and weaknesses of humanitarian efforts to date.

Humanitarian Emergency versus Long-Term Development Project

Addressing sexual violence—the after-effects and consequences for individual survivors and their families as well as the causes and contributing factors—is a long-term process. There are immediate services that can and should be provided in all emergency settings. Nevertheless, the majority of issues around sexual violence require a long-term resource commitment and access to the population in order to follow through on long-term emotional, social, and legal justice needs and to effectively influence changes in behavior to prevent sexual violence.

Populations receiving humanitarian aid are, by definition, are unstable. There may be frequent influxes of new arrivals and outflows as people try to return home or find a better place of refuge. In many recent armed conflicts, populations flee fighting to find refuge and then return home when the fighting ceases, only to be displaced again when the conflict re-erupts.

Another significant challenge is that funding for humanitarian aid programs is usually short-term. Most humanitarian aid projects fall into emergency funding streams, regardless of how many years the "emergency" may continue, and projects are implemented in 3-, 6-, or 12-month funding cycles. It is difficult, if not impossible, for organizations to develop effective and sustainable long-term programs to adequately address sexual violence given such short funding cycles and the constant insecurity of continued funding.

Development programs in nonconflict settings have historically accessed a wider range of funding opportunities, and multiyear projects to address many forms of gender-based violence are underway in sites with more "stable" populations around the world. These development programs have the luxury of time, continuous access to a stable population, and resource commitment, and many are demonstrating success. In fact, the recommended standards for addressing sexual violence in conflict and displaced settings are based on lessons from development programs and strategies used in North/Central/South America and Europe.

Internally Displaced Persons versus Refugees

According to international definitions, a *refugee* is a person who crosses a country border seeking safety. People who flee from their homes but remain in the country where the conflict is occurring are deemed *internally displaced persons* (IDPs). IDPs are often unable to escape their country because of fighting. It can be argued that providing humanitarian aid to refugees is easier. In most situations, the host government works with the UN refugee agency, UNHCR, to provide many protection services. These include designated refugee camps or settlements with security, food, shelter, and health care. In many refugee settings there are also schools, social services programs, churches, mosques, and an array of other community services.

IDPs, however, are considered to be under the care and protection of their own government. In most conflicts, the government is unable to provide sufficient care and protection. The UN World Food Program (WFP) tries to distribute food to IDPs, and other organizations try to provide care and protection. In most conflicts, the International Committee for the Red Cross (ICRC) has some presence and provides emergency medical care. ICRC's services in emergencies have included post-rape medical management. Frequently, humanitarian efforts are delayed or prevented entirely because of insecurity, looting, and other factors directly related to the conflict. If a victim of sexual violence is an IDP, it is unlikely that she will receive basic medical care, and she will probably not have access to emotional/social support or legal justice.

Integration and Interagency Coordination and Collaboration

To its credit, UNHCR has been a leader in efforts to bring sexual violence and other forms of gender-based violence into the forefront of protection concerns in humanitarian settings. Most of the large international humanitarian organizations that are present in emergencies are working with UNHCR in this leadership role. Yet there are many humanitarian organizations that view sexual violence interventions as "luxury" or "fashionable," rather than essential humanitarian aid. This attitude continues, despite the fact that sexual violence is a well-documented public health problem worldwide and that sexual violence is a common weapon of war.

Earlier in this chapter, it was established that an array of services is needed to assist survivors in recovering from sexual violence. Those services must be well coordinated among and between the various organizations and actors. Coordination is essential in order to minimize trauma to the survivor and prevent delays in receiving needed help. In many displaced settings, humanitarian actors who should be providing some basic sexual violence services—and participating in coordination efforts—are not doing so because of negative attitudes toward the issue, conflicting priorities, inadequate funding, or lack of knowledge and capacity to provide appropriate services. Although UNHCR's guidelines and other relevant publications lay out guidelines, standards, and recommendations for prevention and response to sexual violence, many humanitarian actors are not aware of their specific responsibilities, and many have not been trained to carry them out.

In many settings, particularly in African countries, there are specially funded "gender-based violence" programs in place. These programs generally offer leadership for coordination and training with all actors, counseling and case management for survivors, and community-based prevention activities. For the most part, these programs are implemented parallel to existing services such as social service programs, children's programs, and sometimes reproductive health care programs. There are distinct advantages in these programs, proven in refugee settings in Kenya, Tanzania, and Sierra Leone, among others. An infusion of specific and targeted funds enables humanitarian actors to develop some minimum services and allows for adequate training and capacity building. The disadvantage is that many of the services, especially counseling, case management, and coordination leadership are difficult to integrate into existing and continuing services in the setting. Thus, if the special funds are reduced or eliminated, attention to the problem is likely to be similarly reduced or eliminated. Effective prevention and response require good interagency planning, coordination, collaboration, and communication. In humanitarian settings, interagency coordination is one of the greatest challenges because of infrastructure limitations, staffing constraints, and competing priorities.

Health Care

Publication of the UNHCR/WHO clinical guidelines for post-rape care and other concrete tools and guides for health organizations has enabled many health NGOs to develop appropriate sexual violence treatment protocols and implement training for health care staff. Medicines to prevent unwanted pregnancy and treat sexually transmitted infections are more available in humanitarian settings than in the past. Post-exposure prophylaxis (PEP) for HIV infection is gaining popularity. For example, an NGO health program in refugee camps in Tanzania recently began to offer PEP as part of its post-rape medical care. In those camps, the reporting rate of sexual violence increased dramatically. It is suspected, though as yet unproven, that the increase in rape reports is due to survivors' perception that good help is now available for them. Surprisingly, however, the availability of a set of minimum health services for post-rape care is the exception rather than the norm in humanitarian settings. The reasons for this are complex, but the scarcity is largely due to negative attitudes and limitations in knowledge, capacity, and funding.

Psychosocial Support for Survivors

Counseling and emotional support for survivors of sexual violence is available in specifically funded "gender-based violence programs" in many refugee and postconflict settings. Sites include Kosovo, Bosnia, Tanzania, Kenya, Eritrea, Sierra Leone, Liberia, Thailand, and Zambia, among others. In these settings, an NGO has obtained funding to hire and train staff from among the displaced community to serve as counselors—and sometimes also as case managers. Adequate funding at these sites has enabled organizational capacity to properly train and supervise these refugee counselors and case managers. Training and supervision are important aspects of the work.

Another key issue is to clearly define the roles, responsibilities, and limitations of staff who live and work in the community. Addressing sexual violence and other forms of gender-based violence is emotionally demanding and often frustrating work. Domestic violence or sexual abuse survivors who do not want to report the case to the police (and therefore have limited options for security and safety) present special challenges for the staff. Refugee counselors have been known to place themselves in unsafe situations in order to "solve" cases. Without careful supervision and guidance, these kinds of situations can be disastrous. Refugee counselors have been attacked by angry husbands and other perpetrators living in the community.

In other sites without special gender-based violence funding, there are usually women in the displaced community serving as "focal points" for sexual violence. Their roles are often undefined, and they receive little if any training, but they are interested and committed to helping women in their community. These focal points are often frustrated by not being able to "solve" cases, and they are in desperate need of training, support, and supervision.

The term *counseling* itself has proven to be ambiguous. In many displaced populations, the word *counseling* means giving advice and telling a troubled person what to do in order to solve a problem. Counseling for survivors of sexual violence, however, should not be advice-giving. The perception that some of these difficult cases can be "solved" is an indication that staff do not understand the complex dynamics involved in sexual violence. Counseling in these situations should involve reassurance, normalizing feelings, giving clear and honest information, then supporting and empowering the survivor to make her own choices about what action, if any, to take.

Given the dependence and poverty in displaced settings, as well as the fact that most of these populations are unaccustomed to psychological therapy, most survivors do not have time or interest in continuing counseling sessions over the long term. Counseling should, therefore, be aimed at short-term emotional support, empowerment for problem solving, case management and referrals for other requested and needed services, such as social reintegration projects.

In a survey of sexual violence among displaced women in Sierra Leone, over 85 percent of respondents indicated that humanitarian assistance and income-generation projects would be most useful for helping their state of mind and ability to cope with the sexual violence experience. Indeed, one important component of psychosocial support for survivors is social reintegration. This involves building, or rebuilding, a survivor's sense of her own independence and empowerment. Skills-training, income-generation, and small-loan projects have proven effective in supporting survivors to live in the community without shame, with the ability to care for themselves and their children, and to avoid sex-for-survival and other risky behaviors. In refugee camps in Guinea and Kenya, for example, such projects have been implemented with survivors of sexual violence. Outcomes of these projects are consistently positive, showing improved economic, social, and emotional status among the target group.

Safety and Security of Survivors

Security response for survivors of sexual violence is almost entirely lacking in IDP settings. The humanitarian aid community has little experience in this area, and there are no published reports for information about strategies, successes, or failures in ensuring safety and security for survivors of sexual violence in these settings. In refugee and returnee sites, however, strategies have been employed and lessons learned. One important consideration is that in most refugee settings, the host government does not have sufficient resources to adequately staff, equip, and train its police force to deal with high numbers of refugees in addition to the local population. For example, in 2002, there were only 40 police officers covering 45,000 town residents and 78,000 refugees in Kakuma, Kenya. In addition, national police lack basic capacity to do their jobs in most refugee sites; for example, they may not have a vehicle, may frequently run out of fuel if they do have one, may not have pen and paper to take complaints, and may not have access to written national laws, policies, and procedures. In this environment, it will be difficult, if not impossible, to engage the national police force in putting forth effort to address crimes of sexual violence, which is often a low priority concern unless children or severe injuries are involved.

One police success story has occurred in the Dadaab camps in Kenya. With adequate funding from the UN Foundation and the U.S. government, UNHCR and its partners provided financial and material support to the Kenyan police. Training, fencing, radios, police posts in the camp, and other inputs were provided in the late 1990s. Funding for several years was provided, and during this time, the police worked closely with UNHCR, NGOs, and the refugee community to develop a coordinated security system. During that time, trust was built, and now, with fewer funds, the police remain engaged with the community to address sexual violence.

The three guiding principles for response to sexual violence—security, confidentiality, and respect—require that all actors respect the wishes and choices of an adult survivor. In practice, this means that if an adult rape survivor does not want to pursue legal justice and involve the police, she cannot be forced to do so. When police have been notified without a survivor's consent, the survivor frequently does not cooperate because of her fears of stigma and retribution, among other concerns.

Earlier in this chapter, under-reporting and nonreporting of sexual violence crimes were discussed. In fact, only a small percentage of adult sexual violence survivors worldwide seek police intervention and legal justice. In displaced settings, this usually results in the perpetrator continuing to live, with impunity, in the same small community with the survivor. The humanitarian aid community has not been able to successfully resolve these kinds of situations, which are extremely frustrating for all involved, and the survivors are neither safe nor secure. The solution probably lies in improving psychosocial support, case management, and social acceptance and support for survivors. With good emotional and social support, survivors are more likely to officially report these crimes and follow through with lengthy court trials.

In some settings, humanitarian organizations and displaced women's groups have begun establishing safe houses or shelters for temporary refuge. These shelters can serve important functions for security as well as provide the opportunity for the survivor to consider her choices in a safe environment. In a number of settings, however, these shelters have resulted in new security concerns. For example, in Thailand, one such shelter has been used by the refugee leaders as a detention center for women accused of adultery. In small, tightly knit refugee camp settings, the shelters cannot be in concealed locations: everyone knows where the shelter is, and perpetrators usually have easy access to survivors.

Efforts have been made, with mixed success, to support refugee leaders in establishing safe shelters within the community, maintained and managed by trusted leaders, not run by NGOs. In theory, these community-led efforts should be successful in that the community knows best how to establish such services to meet its unique situation.

Legal Justice

A recurrent issue in addressing sexual violence is the under-reporting of these crimes. Even if they are reported, the crime may have occurred days, months, or even years earlier. Collecting evidence and preparing for a successful prosecution can be nearly impossible even in well-resourced settings. National courts are often located considerable distance from displaced settings such as refugee or IDP camps, and they may have the same kinds of capacity limitations as described above in the discussion of police response. In addition, national laws may not include sufficient provisions for prosecution of some forms of sexual violence. Negative and judgmental attitudes of prosecutors and judges may also contravene rigorous attention to and prosecution of these crimes.

Many displaced communities are actually governed by customary and traditional systems of law and justice. For most displaced populations, these customary systems are known from the home setting. The host government system may be frightening and intimidating, and the customary and traditional systems are therefore the preferred method for resolving disputes in the community. Usually composed of male elders from the community, these traditional courts mete out justice in accordance with social and cultural norms that are, in most cases, not supportive of women's equal rights.

In cases of sexual violence, court decisions are usually viewed by sexual violence survivors as unjust and unhelpful. For example, a rapist may be ordered to marry his victim as a way of making her an "honest woman," thus removing the social shame and stigma assigned to her as a result of the rape. Or a father may be awarded a small financial compensation for the rape of his daughter.

Humanitarian aid organizations are considerably challenged by these traditional courts. In refugee settings, the traditional system cannot be officially recognized because the host government is officially responsible for law and order. Yet humanitarian aid organizations are charged with protecting the population they serve, and it is generally believed that traditional courts do not adequately protect and serve survivors of sexual violence. Until recently, the standard practice in many settings has been to educate traditional courts about human rights and appropriate legal standards. Education alone has not, however, resulted in significant changes. In Tanzania and Kenya, national lawyers employed by UNHCR are trying to understand these traditional systems in order to establish strategies to influence changes in practices. Influencing changes in traditional justice systems will not be easy or quick, though, given the long-standing cultural beliefs and practices about women and gender roles, and those systems' limitations, expectations, and privileges.

For war-related sexual violence, legal justice may be available to survivors through international criminal courts. This, too, is a lengthy process, and it is often difficult to find survivors who are willing to testify. There are many protection issues that must be considered and addressed. In Arusha, Tanzania, the International Criminal Tribunal for Rwanda (ICTR) has established a thorough protocol for protecting witnesses (survivors) of sexual violence. The protocol includes using a pseudonym throughout the proceedings, security escorts, and psychological support, as well as a curtain around the witness in the courtroom to conceal her identity from all but the accused person and the judges.

Reporting and Referral Systems

Establishing services that are accessible, confidential, and helpful will increase the probability that survivors will report incidents of sexual violence. One characteristic of "helpful" services is the presence of clear and effective referral mechanisms among and between the various responding organizations, especially health and psychosocial services. Every effort must be made to minimize the number of times a survivor has to repeat her story and talk with another stranger about what happened to her. In many sites, key responding organizations use a common form, the Incident Report Form, as a documentation and information-sharing tool. The 2003 UNHCR *Guidelines* recommends using this form, and there are instructions and training information for staff. Of course, survivor consent must be obtained before this form or any information is shared with others.

In an increasing number of refugee sites, there are interagency procedures in place for sexual violence reporting and referral mechanisms. In these sites, the interagency team parties have discussed and clarified their roles and responsibilities, and agreed on guiding principles, documentation, and specific methods for referrals and follow-up. When these procedures are written and agreed upon by the key organizations involved, they have proven a useful tool for orienting incoming staff, for resolving problems and disagreements among organizations, and for establishing accessible and helpful support for survivors. Written procedures like this were first developed in Tanzania and are now in place in many refugee settings.

In Thailand, where there are many unrecognized Burmese refugees (called "migrants"), the refugee/migrant women's organizations developed their own procedure manual, independent of humanitarian aid organizations. These women's groups were aware that sexual violence was occurring at an alarming rate and little help was available from humanitarian organizations operating along the Thai-Burma border. The Automatic Response Mechanism (ARM) details a 10-step process for assisting survivors of sexual violence. Beginning with the initial report, ARM describes actions to be taken by refugee women helping the survivor, lists potential referrals to be made, and goes further to discuss possible obstacles and problems in each step and suggestions for how to resolve them, including asking humanitarian organizations for assistance.

Definitions, Terminology, and Selecting Focus of Interventions

The 2003 UNHCR *Guidelines* uses the phrase "sexual and gender-based violence" (SGBV) to refer to an array of abuses that primarily affect females. SGBV includes sexual violence, domestic violence (intimate partner abuse), sexual exploitation, sexual harassment, and harmful traditional practices such as female genital mutilation (FGM), forced early marriage, female infanticide, and widow inheritance. In other organizations and UN agencies, these same types of violence and abuse may be called "violence against women" (VAW) or "gender-based violence" (GBV). From time to time, there is debate about which phrase should be used to most accurately reflect the complex issues surrounding these problems.

Some organizations believe that framing the problem in terms of gender clarifies the issues and clearly articulates the ultimate goal, which is to empower women and equalize power relations between males and females. Others perceive that using the term *gender* may cloud the issue, reduce the focus on women's rights, and imply that more needs to be done to help male survivors rather than females. The disagreement about terminology is a reflection of the wide range of issues and priorities inherent in sexual violence and other forms of gender-based violence. If humanitarian actors cannot agree on definitions, terms, and priorities, this will affect the type and focus of programs to address sexual violence and organizations' abilities to coordinate with each other.

Sexual Violence against Children

Available data from displaced settings with sexual violence services in place indicate that the majority of incidents reported are those affecting children under age 18. Qualitative information suggests that higher reporting rates of child sexual abuse are related to the community's perception that sexual violence against a child is a crime and not the child's fault (as opposed to adult sexual violence, where the victim is usually blamed for the assault). Parents of these children frequently want to pursue legal justice, either through traditional or national courts. In most settings, there are few, if any, staff who are trained and prepared to provide the psychological and social support needed by child survivors and their families. This can be especially damaging to a child in the case of incest.

Participatory Community-Based Approaches to Prevention

Prevention of sexual violence involves identifying and addressing the causes and specific factors in the environment that contribute the problem. With the goal of changing knowledge, attitudes, and behavior, humanitarian organizations in many displaced settings are working with displaced communities to raise awareness about sexual violence. To date, methods for awareness raising include street dramas, workshops, posters, radio programs, and other mass communication methods. Topics typically include human rights, gender, power, and various examples of sexual violence that are occurring in the community. These strategies have proven effective in raising awareness and knowledge about the issues but are not useful for taking the next steps to actually change attitudes, beliefs, and behaviors.

Historically, humanitarian aid programs have focused on emergency and short-term projects. By its nature, humanitarian aid has involved "giving" or "doing" for a group of "beneficiaries." Influencing long-standing cultural norms and practices, however, requires a different type of approach: engaging the community in long-term participatory development for change. For most humanitarian organizations—and staff—this approach requires a new set of skills.

Emerging wisdom from HIV/AIDS prevention programs can inform humanitarian efforts to address sexual violence. Behavior change communication (BCC) strategies are proving effective in changing behavior to reduce the risk of HIV infection. BCC is a well-planned process that seeks to change behavior through a changing set of strategies that are based on the population's level of awareness and willingness to change.

According to BCC theories, the sexual violence awareness-raising activities that currently exist in many field sites are effective in raising awareness and promoting interest in the issue. Strategies that are more refined, better targeted and well timed are needed so that individuals can both improve and sustain those changed behaviors over time. Humanitarian aid organizations have not yet consistently used BCC methods as a process to change behavior effectively enough to prevent sexual violence.

Working with men in the community is an important element in effective BCC for sexual violence. Humanitarian organizations in Guinea and Thailand have implemented some projects to involve men in preventing sexual violence. These projects started by including men in community-based committees to explore and address sexual violence. Quickly, the men took over these formerly all-women groups. The Guinea program resolved this by creating separate men's and women's groups. In a different site in Thailand, a new men's involvement project is starting at the time of this writing; this project will establish a group of men engaged in working with other men to prevent sexual violence.

Prevention during Conflict

Prevention of sexual violence during armed conflict presents a host of seemingly insurmountable obstacles and challenges. Written information is not available, and anecdotal reports indicate no success to date. Logic suggests that rigorous prosecution and sentencing of war crimes, including sexual violence, can be a deterrent in future armed struggles. The international criminal tribunals for the former Yugoslavia, Rwanda, and Sierra Leone are prosecuting these crimes. It is too soon to know if there will be any deterrent effect.

In the Democratic Republic of Congo, negotiators implied during peace negotiations with the various fighting factions in 2003 that they (fighting factions) would be more likely to be taken seriously if they were not engaging in atrocities against civilians, such as sexual violence. Some organizations involved in the negotiations were hoping that combatants would view committing acts of sexual violence as hurting their cause. There is no evidence to suggest that this strategy has been successful.

Sexual Exploitation and Codes of Conduct

In 2002, after the public scandal concerning sexual exploitation allegedly perpetrated by humanitarian workers and peacekeepers, the United Nations, NGOs, and donors publicly denounced these practices and declared "zero tolerance." Codes of conduct have been established and staff in humanitarian organizations, including peacekeepers, must agree to abide by the code. The Secretary General of the United Nations mandated specific mechanisms be put in place in all humanitarian settings for identifying cases of sexual abuse/exploitation, receiving reports, conducting investigations, and assisting victims of these acts. Implementation of these mechanisms has been slow, and, to date, most displaced persons are not aware of where, how, and to whom to report incidents of sexual abuse or exploitation perpetrated by a humanitarian worker or peacekeeper.

The problem is widespread, according to anecdotal reports and discussions from the 2001 UNHCR Lessons Learned Conference. Allegations of sexual abuse and exploitation get attention, as humanitarian aid organizations and donors are sensitive and somewhat nervous about the issue. Unfortunately, in most sites, clear systems for response action are not in place, and survivors who report these incidents face multiple and invasive interviews and investigations. There are not yet adequate protection measures in place, and many survivors of these acts also face public shame and sometimes retribution from perpetrators.

Monitoring and Evaluation

Quantitative and qualitative data about sexual violence incidents and interventions in humanitarian settings are maintained to some extent in nearly all field sites. Compiling, analyzing, and evaluating data, however, either is not being done or is spotty and inconsistent.

Data are not consistently used for monitoring program outcomes and guiding strategies for action in either prevention or response to sexual violence. There are written recommended indicators for outputs and outcomes of various actions being taken in humanitarian settings. These indicators are not used consistently, and there are no available reports evaluating progress or outcomes in relation to established indicators. There are also written program evaluations from some projects that specifically address female genital mutilation. In addition, there are data reports from health providers that give information about medical care provided, such as use of emergency contraception medicines and preventing sexually transmitted infections. UNHCR has begun monitoring the numbers of successful legal prosecutions of refugee sexual violence cases. Although efforts to monitor and evaluate sexual violence programming are increasing and improving, no available data or report provides information about the outcomes of humanitarian interventions.

Note

1. The Inter-Agency Standing Committee (IASC) was established in June 1992 in response to a United Nations General Assembly Resolution that called for strengthened coordination of humanitarian assistance. Within the humanitarian community IASC provides a forum that brings together a broad range of UN and non-UN humanitarian partners, including UN humanitarian agencies, IOM, three consortia of major international NGOs and the Red Cross movement (ICRC and IFRC). The primary role of the IASC is to formulate humanitarian policy to ensure coordinated and effective humanitarian response to both complex emergencies and to natural disasters.

References

Heise, L., Pitanguy, L., & Germain, A. (1994). Violence against women: The hidden health burden. *World Report on Violence and Health* [Discussion Paper 255]. World Health Organization. Washington, DC: World Bank.

Interagency Standing Committee. (2002, April 9). *Policy paper on the protection from sexual abuse and exploitation in humanitarian crises.* Rome: Author.

United Nations High Commissioner for Refugees. (2001). *Prevention and response to SGBV in refugee situation.* Interagency Conference Proceedings held March 27–29, 2001. Geneva, Switzerland: UNHCR.

———. (2003). *Sexual and gender-based violence against refugees, returnees, and internally displaced persons: Guidelines for prevention and response.* Retrieved August 15, 2005, from www.rhrc.org/pdf/gl_sgbv03_00.pdf

World Health Organization. (2002). *Clinical management of survivors of rape.* (Publication no.: WHO/RHR/02.08). Retrieved August 15, 2005, from www.who.int/reproductive-health/publications/rhr_02_8_clinical_management_survivors_of _rape/

———. (2002). *World report on violence and health.* Retrieved March 7, 2005, from www.who.int/violence_injury_prevention/violence/world_report/en/

How Do You Mend Broken Hearts? Gender, War, and Impacts on Girls in Fighting Forces

Susan McKay

The compound is spacious, with sun dappling through the trees and women walking by, often carrying goods balanced on their heads. Here live the paramount chief and his extended family. Little children linger, watching the day's events while men lounge in the shadows of the trees. In the center of the compound is a large thatched-roof meeting hut. Nearby are several concrete housing structures, seemingly luxurious against a backdrop of partially destroyed homes and buildings in this small village of Mambolo, Sierra Leone.[1] The cooking room, a stone's throw behind the main house, is a center of women's conversation and activity. An old woman dries grain in the sun, fending off periodic attacks from an insistent chicken. All about us is quiet, and the pace is languid. Are we really in the middle of what has, so recently, been a war zone?

Twice a day, the chief's wife prepares us rice, embellished with vegetables such as cassava or freshly discovered eggs that are scrambled and laced with a bit of chili. As we eat, I look up to the rafters and see pieces of paper tied above one of the hut entries, evidence of activity from the Bondo women's secret society. "Don't touch them," we are told, and their very mystery invades us, invoking small tremors of uncertainty. Our translator explains that the Bondo society is presently conducting initiation rites for girls. Days later when the girls are brought back to their families, we dance down the main road of Mambolo with members of the community.

When heavy rainfall comes, we take advantage of it to shower under the cascades of torrential water. At night, we sleep in the central hut on mattresses, with mosquito nets tucked under the edges, listening to night sounds such as soft drumming that create a rhythm of comfort. Together with my research colleague Mary Burman and assistants Maria Gonsalves and Miranda Worthen, we are staying in this village to learn more about the situations of some of the most invisible actors in the Sierra Leonean war—girls who were impregnated when they were part of the rebel Revolutionary United Front (RUF) fighting force. In the wake of the war's ending in Sierra Leone in January 2001, these girl mothers are struggling to survive. Their children mark these girls as having violated norms such as maintaining virginity and community-sanctioned notions of marriage, despite the knowledge that maternity was forced upon them. The girl mothers are known by the community, but they are seldom spoken about in public nor are they or their children usually given specific help by humanitarian organizations. Compounding their seeming "invisibility," these girls are reluctant to self-identify as former members of the RUF because they fear being stigmatized and provoked. Also, elders are reluctant to bring up the issue of these girls and their children because they aren't comfortable with their presence (McKay, Burman, Gonsalves, & Worthen, 2004). These girl mothers face special challenges because they have experienced extreme hardship, sexual violence, and were forced to witness and participate in atrocities—sometimes against their own families and friends. In essence, their hearts have been broken.

Our research interest in these girl mothers in Mambolo derives from a completed study that was funded by the Canadian International Development Agency (CIDA) on girls in fighting forces in Mozambique, Northern Uganda, and Sierra Leone (McKay & Mazurana, 2004). During this research, which was conducted from 2000 to 2003, I talked with girls and young women in Mozambique, where the 16-year war ended in 1992, in Northern Uganda, which continues to be war-torn more than 18 years after the war began in 1986, and Sierra Leone. Some of the girls with whom I've talked have been as young as nine or 10 when I met them and were abducted when they were six or seven years old. Others are now young women but were girls when they were taken into the force. Some have disabilities—either physical, emotional, or both—and for many this was the first time they had talked to outsiders about their experiences. Most showed evidence of their trauma through their gestures, tears, postures, and muted facial expressions. Each had unique experiences of being in a fighting force.

Anthropologist Carolyn Nordstrom (1999) observed that war's violence is not a monolithic event, and "girls" cannot be constructed as a homogeneous category. Their experiences are shaped by such factors as class, religion, ethnicity, oppression, and whether they hold power in a force or it is used against them. Thus each girl's story will be distinct. As an example, a girl in a fighting force who is educated may have expanded opportunities such as being a spy or intelligence operative as compared with a less educated girl who might spend her time in a force as a domestic servant and wife. Thus some girls may have experienced protective effects from gaining some power, whereas a girl who is primarily a domestic and used for sex has little power except, perhaps, for resistance.

But girls also have commonalities of experiences as I discovered when I pooled data from CIDA study interviews and analyzed them thematically. For example, all the girls suffered severe violations of human rights and witnessed or participated in acts of extreme violence and, except for some of the youngest girls, experienced forced sex. Those who return from a force are deeply traumatized and must negotiate changed relationships and communities. Despite their being victims of rebel forces with almost all abducted and raped, many showed agency through acts of resistance and by positioning themselves so they experienced less harm—such as aligning with a commander who provided a modicum of protection. Some girls gained power within a force because of their roles within the force.

One of the CIDA study's most insistent findings is the dire situation of girls abducted into rebel fighting forces who have returned with children. Many spent years in a force, becoming "wives" of commanders as well as performing roles such as being fighters, spies, and domestic servants. Those who survived the war and have returned to their communities face challenges that most of us can only imagine. For example, prior to coming to Mambolo, we talked with girls in Kambia Town in western Sierra Leone who survive because they have become commercial sex workers by night and do domestic chores and farm small plots by day. None of the girls we talked with have close family members who can help them. They tell us that they want opportunities to be educated and trained in skills to give them an economic livelihood, but training or schooling opportunities are not forthcoming. Each day is a challenge to these girl mothers as they try to feed and clothe their children, protect themselves from sexually transmitted diseases, obtain health care, and locate safe housing.

Now in Mambolo, we witness the day-to-day lives of girl mothers, made more real to us because we are living among them. We see their malnourished bodies and those of their children. Some of the young mothers leave an afternoon meeting with us because they are weak and must seek food for the day's meal. We hear their songs when Maria leads girls and adult women in singing about what happened to them in the bush. Through their poignant words, we glean insight into the nuances of their feelings as they sing about experiences from the bush, searching for their people, escaping the rebels and the men who violated them. We marvel at their courage then and now.

Other girls tell us their stories as we sit on the porches of their houses or in their yards. One of the girls, Kate, was captured into the RUF. She was given loads to carry on her head and forced to eat food that was "not good," implying that she participated in cannibalism. Soon, Kate was impregnated by George, the rebel who had abducted her. She gave birth in the bush to a boy who is now four years old. Knowing that breastfeeding can confer protection from pregnancy, she didn't want to stop when George insisted that she do so.

By the time disarmament took place, she was again pregnant. George, like many "husbands" disappeared at war's end. So, with her child, Kate returned to her parents' village. She found nobody there to care for her so she made her way with friends to Mambolo, where she presently lives. Typical of most girls who leave fighting forces, she did not go through formal demobilization programs and consequently received no benefits that might help her, such as skills in a trade or schooling. Kate's experiences point to some of the gendered effects of war upon girls and women, whereby girls experience discrimination both when they are in a fighting force and when they leave.

In describing scenarios from the village of Mambolo, I have attempted to give a sense of the reality of the present lives and past experiences of some girl mothers who were taken into the RUF fighting forces and their situations within the context of the community where they now live. In the remainder of this chapter, I broaden my discussion to explain how armed conflicts disproportionately impact girls and women and produce gender-specific effects. I then focus upon girls' roles and experiences in fighting forces in Northern Uganda and Sierra Leone. I highlight challenges that await them when they return (reintegrate) to their communities. Lastly, I discuss girls' humanitarian needs and give recommendations of programmatic assistance that is crucial if these girls are to survive and thrive.

War's Impact upon Girls and Women

In the past decade, the effects of war upon women and girls have become a source of increasing international concern, whereas previously their plight has been minimized or dismissed altogether. For example, until recently, rape was thought of as being "normal" during wars rather than being viewed as an intentional strategy, sometimes with genocidal intent (see for example, Fisher, 1996; Physicians for Human Rights, 2002; Sajor, 1998; UN, 1996). Although precise estimates are not available, as many as 85 to 95 percent of civilian casualties are estimated to be women and children. Also, the majority of internally displaced people and refugees are women and children.

Girls and women are especially affected by armed conflict because of their gender and unequal status in society. Women are important tactical targets if one's intent is to destroy a culture, since women as mothers are mainly responsible for transmitting the values of a culture to their children. Because they hold families together as they seek to preserve the social order, women risk their lives when they cross minefields or brave shelling and bombing to seek firewood, food, and water. They therefore disproportionately experience displacement of home and property, loss or involuntary disappearance of close relatives, poverty, family separation and disintegration, sexual violence, sexual slavery, and sexual torture (McKay, 1998).

The public health effects of war worsen their situations. As the public health infrastructure is intentionally destroyed (food and water supplies, access to health care, roads, and electricity), women and girls suffer severe health effects. Among these are pregnancy and birth complications and lack of primary and reproductive health care, with increased risk of illness and death. Sexually transmitted diseases and HIV/AIDS transmission, rampant in war-torn countries, pose an extreme threat to the survival of girls and women. Also, resource shortages such as lack of food, water, and shelter lead to shortened life expectancy.

During wartime, unless they flee as internally displaced people or become refugees, women typically remain in their communities to care for their children as they attempt to protect them from war's brutality. And yet, these very communities are often the locus of fighting, especially during internal wars such as recently occurred in Sierra Leone and Mozambique. Today in Northern Uganda and southern Sudan, on an almost daily basis, homes and schools are torched, girls and women are raped, atrocities and murders are committed, and children are abducted into the rebel Lord's Resistance Army (LRA) that has been fighting the Ugandan Army. Children who escape the LRA and return home risk re-abduction; consequently, thousands and thousands leave their homes each evening to towns—the so-called "night commuters." They sleep in public places and seek food before they return to their communities in the mornings. Margaret, age 17, fears re-abduction by the LRA. She was abducted from her school by the LRA and eventually escaped from the force. Her daughter was born while she was with the LRA and is being cared for by her mother while Margaret completes secondary school. She fears visiting her home village because she might be re-abducted. Consequently, she only occasionally sees her daughter and, when she does, she sleeps in the bush.

Girls in Fighting Forces

How Girls Enter and Their Roles
in Fighting Forces

Throughout the world, girls participate in fighting forces. Little is yet known about their presence in these forces, but some data are becoming available as researchers increasingly focus attention upon them. For example, between 1990 and 2003, girls were present in fighting forces in 55 countries (McKay & Mazurana, 2004). Girls served in 11 countries in the Americas, four in the Middle East, 14 in Africa, 12 in Europe, and 14 in Asia. In 38 countries, girls were involved in armed conflicts, which were primarily internal wars fought within national boundaries.

Girls enter forces in a variety of ways including by joining, volunteering, being recruited, or gang pressed. Some are taken from orphanages or are born into the force where they are trained at young ages to be fighters. Some girls join a force to escape abuse at home or to better their circumstances. They also are abducted in large numbers, usually into rebel forces, as occurred between 1990 and 2003 in 27 countries (McKay & Mazurana,

2004). In the countries where I conducted the fieldwork for the CIDA study, girls also volunteered and were recruited or pressed into governmental forces, but the majority were abducted into rebel forces. Typically they are taken from their homes, schools, and communities, or as they are walking along the road.

Why Take Girls?

The sexual violence that girls and women experience during armed conflicts and as members of fighting forces is widely known. Sexual violence is epidemic, as was the case in Sierra Leone and occurs presently in Northern Uganda and Sierra Leone. Most are forced to provide sexual services to males in the force. Within rebel forces, when girls reach puberty, they are taken as "wives" to perform sexual services and give birth to children who may grow up in the force. However, in some forces sexual relations are forbidden or are consensual.

A less-appreciated reason for taking girls is that they and women are essential to the day-to-day operations of a force—just as they are indispensable to the functioning of broader society because of the productive and reproductive labor they do. In Northern Uganda and Sierra Leone, they typically have overlapping roles such as being both a "wife" of a commander and a fighter and carrying out traditional gender roles such as farming, obtaining water, cooking, cleaning, and serving men—although boys, too, participate in domestic chores. Yet girls also participate in lootings and killings; are porters, spies, and intelligence agents; train other fighters; and sometimes become commanders within a force.

Girls' Experiences within a Force

Girls have described the harsh conditions they experience as members of a fighting force—including long marches, being trained to use weapons, strenuous work, limited sleep, fighting, looting, and burning villages, and killing people. Elizabeth's story is an example. She was abducted at a young age in the town of Kono early in the Sierra Leonean war and stayed with the RUF for almost a decade. She was taught how to fight and use guns and took part in the fighting, killing others and participating in cannibalism. Elizabeth said that in the jungle they ate humans, reptiles, and "every kind of thing" that one can eat in the jungle. If she didn't eat what was given to her, Elizabeth would have been killed. She saw most of her companions die because they refused to eat. She ate because she wanted to survive. Forced to have sex at puberty, she became the "wife" of a commander. She miscarried[2] one child when she was with the commander.

The brutal life in a force and the violence to which they are subjected means that many girls are badly injured or die. They die from wounds, complications of pregnancy and childbirth, sexual violence, and are killed outright by the rebels. Others die from self-induced abortions, bad water, malnutrition, malaria, tuberculosis, injuries, or because they are killed during fighting. Many have chronic health conditions such as pelvic inflammatory disease and sexually transmitted diseases. Emotionally, they are all traumatized. Girls have shared heartrending stories about crying for their mothers, missing their families, being lonely, and their broken hearts.

Returning Home

When girls return to their communities, assuming their families are alive and their communities still intact, entire communities are challenged to respond to them, to come to terms with what has happened, and to heal as a collective. Girls need caring adults, especially their mothers, to support them as they readjust to community life and to assist them with healing. When these adults are not a part of the lives of returning girls, they experience even greater difficulties—such as the girls I described from Kambia Town who were commercial sex workers so that they and their children could stay alive. We also talked with girl mothers in Mambolo in similar situations. With no parents to help them, they survived through sex work and begging for food.

Although international and national nongovernmental organizations (NGOs), supported by United Nations (UN) agencies such as the UN Children's Fund (UNICEF) and the U.S. Agency for International Development (USAID), have worked with communities to develop psychosocial programs for children, girls usually have not been recognized in terms of their wide prevalence in fighting forces and the traumatic experiences they have had. Sexual violence, a taboo topic in most communities where I did fieldwork, is seldom discussed unless NGOs facilitate a dialogue using community-based methods such as forming child protection or sexual violence committees.

How Girls Return

When they leave a force, for the most part, girls make their own ways back to their communities or flee to urban areas. They usually experience "second-rate reintegration," meaning that they don't receive the assistance boys typically do and are seldom demobilized and helped with reintegration through official programs. Instead, they slip back into their homes and communities or sometimes go with friends when they have no family to care for them or their communities are destroyed. Because girls are seldom helped with reintegration, they are at higher risk than boys because communities and their families may not be prepared to accept them. This is particularly true when long separations have occurred, they have committed violations against community members, or girls return with children who, like the girls themselves, may be ostracized and called "rebels." In Mambolo, girl mothers said that community members provoked them and their children until the paramount chief delivered an edict that the provocation must stop. Girls may also encounter stigma, threats, physical abuse, and sexual violence committed by boys and men in the community. Further, they lack economic and marital opportunities, and some have changed so much that they no longer fit into the community.

Girls' Behavioral and Emotional Responses

When girls return to their communities, they may show culturally and gender-inappropriate and violent behaviors that they learned in a force. For example, community elders in Sierra Leone explained how girls returning from the RUF withdrew and wouldn't talk with anyone. Some girls provoked others and were aggressive in their behavior. Girls have been reported as using offensive language, abusing drugs, and smoking, and killing and eating animals that belonged to others. For girls, these behaviors violate gender norms in ways they do not for boys, and impair the ability of communities to respond positively to them.

Shame is a prominent emotional response of returning girls, and so is guilt, because girls have violated cultural taboos within the gendered cultural dictates of sanctioned marriage—such as being shamed for underage and unmarried sex, which boys are not although boys experience shame for other reasons. In Northern Uganda and Sierra Leone, girls' shame is amplified when the baby was born of multiple rapes and without an identifiable father. Also, girls experience shame from having tattoos, scars, and carvings that identify them as participants in combat. Community members, in turn, experience shame for not having protected girls from harm.

Devastated Communities

Because community infrastructures are extensively damaged because of armed conflict, communities may be radically changed from what they were when the girls were taken. Thus communities, beset by their own survival challenges, require focused assistance to develop their capacities to protect returning girls and assist them in reclaiming their lives. However, this seldom happens unless NGOs or grassroots groups work with communities since governments are typically engaged in priorities with national, not local, focus.

For some girls, no community exists for them to return to either because they are destroyed or their parents are dead. Rosie's story is a common one. Rosie, a deaf girl who was about six years old when she was abducted by the RUF, escaped from the force when she went across the Sierra Leonean border to Guinea to buy goods at a marketplace. Being resourceful, she hid from the others. She then made her way down a road by herself, crying as she walked. A sympathetic woman stopped to help her and took her home with her to Makeni where she now lives. Rosie's disability and not knowing where her parents were, or even if they were alive, made it impossible for her to return to her community. Like many war-affected children, she is now being fostered by a caring adult.

Other girls, willingly or unwillingly, accompany a commander "husband" when he is officially demobilized. For some, despite having been abducted into a force, staying with him is the best option she can see for her future. This may be because her family is dead, she has children whom she fears will be ostracized if she returns to her community, or her rebel "husband" has some benefits that will give her some support, whereas she has none if she returns to her home. Although these "wives" also deserve to be demobilized, they typically are treated as "camp followers" (women and children who follow male combatants), rather than participants in the force who deserve benefits, including assistance with reintegration.

Rituals to Assist Reintegration

In Northern Uganda and Sierra Leone, community rituals can be instrumental in alleviating shame, both for the girls and community members, and to begin mending their broken hearts. Rituals can support reintegration and healing for the girls and the community and help them reconcile with their parents and know they are forgiven. Different from Western modes of addressing trauma on an individualistic basis, which emphasize psychotherapeutic recounting of experiences, community rituals act to create a rupture with the past and begin a new life. In recognition of the importance of rituals, some NGOs in Northern Uganda and Sierra Leone have supported new forms of rituals or provided materials so rituals can be conducted—since items such as goats and eggs can be too costly.

In both Northern Uganda and Sierra Leone, community-based rituals have been used when girls and boys return as a way to reconnect the child to the community of both living and dead, facilitate social reintegration, protect the community from evil influences, and call upon ancestors for assistance. These rituals may consist of traditional practices such as slaughtering a goat or stepping on an egg before entering the community, and ritual herb baths to cleanse girls, religious practices such as prayer, song, and dance, or both. Some are gender-specific rituals such as rituals dealing specifically with sexual abuse. Those conducting these rituals may be religious leaders, traditional healers, traditional leaders, or a combination. Also, community elders often talk with the returned girl, giving her advice, and encouraging her to have hope for her future. When Ann returned to her community in Northern Uganda, she stepped on an egg. A goat was then slaughtered for her, and the community gathered to rejoice. Ann also was taken to church, where there was fasting and thanks given to God for returning her home safely. She then returned to school.

Health Care

An immediate priority for returning girls is that they receive primary health care. In addition to injuries and chronic illnesses, many have severe disabilities, including loss of sight, hearing, amputated limbs, scars or burns from torture, or injuries during battle. Those with disabilities have particular difficulty accessing health care and are usually left out of broader reintegration initiatives.

Unfortunately, few girls are diagnosed and treated except for some who go through disarmament, demobilization, and reintegration (DDR), rehabilitation centers, or are assisted by NGOs.

A key concern for returning girls is reproductive health care. Girls often have genital injuries and infections, such as swelling, fistulas, vaginal discharge, genital itch, and pain from their vaginas being cut. Profound trauma to genital, urinary, and anal regions caused by sexual violence increases vulnerability to sexually transmitted diseases (STDs) and other infections (McKay & Mazurana, 2004). The majority of girls returning from the LRA or the RUF are infected with STDs including syphilis, gonorrhea, chlamydia, and HIV/AIDS. Also, many have genital injuries. These infections may subsequently develop into pelvic inflammatory disease, chronic pain, and infertility. Also, mother-to-child transmission of HIV/AIDS during pregnancy and childbirth and from breast milk means that the children of girl mothers may also be infected and require treatment, although at present, treatment with antiretroviral drugs is seldom available to either the girls or their children. If community health centers are still intact and can provide some services, as in Mambolo, girls may still not be able to access health care because some services, including prescriptions, may be available only if a fee is paid. Also, supplies in health centers may be inadequate for treatment and testing not available. Even when they receive care, it is not designed for girls nor is it sensitive to the physical and psychological health issues they face as ex-combatants.

Only a limited number of programs developed by local and international NGOs are helping the large number of girls who have experienced sexual violence. Few programs are designed for rape survivors, and girls are understandably reluctant to discuss rape experience or are in denial about what happened to them. Remedying this lack of primary and reproductive health care should become a priority goal of humanitarian organizations, consistent with UNICEF's call for universal access to basic services for children affected by conflict in Uganda (UN Wire, 2004).

Skills Training and Schooling

One of the most powerful ways to help girls move on with their lives, to heal, and build upon their strengths and resilience to learn a skill or continue their education. Otherwise girls may believe they have no choices, no skills, and that help does not exist for them. Girls who are mothers face even greater difficulties because they fear that they are not marriageable, and they are discriminated against in obtaining education. For example, in Northern Uganda and Sierra Leone, pregnant girls and mothers traditionally have been ineligible to go to school. Repeatedly girls stressed how important it was for them to gain training, even if only to learn fundamental literacy and math skills, learn a trade, or receive help in setting up a small business.

Because they have not received DDR benefits, girls are usually prevented from enrolling, their parents are unable to pay for their school fees and uniforms or skills training, they are kept at home to do domestic labor or are heads of households, they are ashamed to go to school because they are older than other children, or they have children of their own and are therefore not eligible to attend school. Another detriment to attending school is that these can be dangerous places to be as in Northern Uganda where LRA rebels abduct children from primary and secondary schools. Also, skills training for girls, even when available, may provide limited economic opportunities because girls tend to be taught gender-specific skills such as tailoring, tie-dying or candle making with oversaturated and limited markets when they would benefit much more by learning how to do welding or be electricians or skills demanded by the local economy.

Like health care, schools and training programs should be girl-friendly. Also, they should have relevant curricula and options such as accelerated programs to teach them basic literacy and numerical skills. Importantly, within these various programs, psychosocial programs should be developed to help build girls' sense of agency, self-esteem, and confidence. For example, in Sierra Leone the Forum for African Women Educationalists (FAWE) has developed countrywide schooling for girls that includes pregnant girls and girl mothers who can attend school with their children. Psychosocial assistance is recognized as an important aspect of the girls' schooling.

Increasingly the importance of girls' schooling is being recognized. A U.S. Department of Labor $3,000,000 educational grant is now being implemented by the International Rescue Committee to reach war-affected children, both girls and boys, in Northern Uganda and improve their educational and training opportunities. During the CIDA study, I visited skills programs in Sierra Leone; most of the girls found in these programs were among the few who had received DDR benefits. In Mambolo, we visited a skills program called "Youth Pack," a one-year program for former combatants that was sponsored by the Norwegian Refugee Council. The program enrolled equal numbers of girls and boys, including girl mothers. An innovative program with children who were obviously thriving in the school setting, the girls mothers who attended required parental or community help with child care because the program lacked such services. Thus the mothers could not bring their children with them. Without such accommodations, most girl mothers are prevented from participating in training programs or school because they are unable to obtain care for their children. We talked with girl mothers in Mambolo who wanted to attend this program but could not because they lack child care.

Humanitarian Assistance for Girls in Fighting Forces

Although girls' roles within fighting forces vary by country and cultural contexts, in Northern Uganda and Sierra Leone, girls reported that being a fighter was one of their top two to three primary roles (McKay & Mazurana, 2004). Among these were many who were either pregnant at the time or had young children to care for. Therefore, humanitarian groups err when they assume that returning girls were used only as "wives," domestics, and "camp followers" who were not on the front lines of fighting. Instead, girls *must be seen* for the central productive and reproductive roles they hold within a force. Also, recognizing that girls and young women may be the last to be released from a force—if at all—should increase advocacy on the behalf of these girls rather than explaining their low numbers by assuming they were not present in a force. For example, toward the end of the fighting in Sierra Leone, between May 20 and May 29, 2001, the RUF released 1088 boys, but only 15 girls. Yet, in the CIDA study, a conclusion reached was that girls constituted approximately one-quarter of the RUF child soldiers. These numbers, therefore, may not accurately reflect the reality of girls' presence but clearly points to qualities of invisibility and expendability because their gender makes them less valuable to recover and rehabilitate into postwar societies (McKay & Mazurana, 2004).

Because formal DDR processes discriminate against girls and few receive its benefits, most girls who do return from a fighting force will be found within a community setting, whether rural or urban, and girls do not receive the assistance they deserve. Since we know that girls are "known but invisible," humanitarian organizations should assume that these returning girls are present even if they are not spoken about by community members. A key aspect of humanitarian work, therefore, is to involve community members in developing problem solving strategies to identify and work with these returning girls; such strategies include community members learning conflict resolution, dialogue, and mediation processes, and being educated about girls' and children's rights. This is best accomplished when humanitarian organizations work with communities over time to increase their capacity to accept returning girls (and boys) and better understand their experiences. By empowering community leaders, parents, relatives, and neighbors, returning girls and young women who were once controlled in captivity by violent men may see these adults as positive influences in rebuilding their lives.

Although too often a neglected aspect of community-based work, utilizing the expertise of the community's women is central to girls being able to reintegrate and move forward with their lives and in developing their self-confidence, self-esteem, and capabilities. Women leaders can support and advise girls over time in helping them develop a more positive future. Important to remember, is that women leaders are also war traumatized and require support for their work by humanitarian groups, including enhancing the work of local women's organizations. In Mambolo, women leaders, midwives, and healers said that if they were given assistance, they would be able to help girl mothers. Some had already made small efforts to help these girls, but they wanted training to know how to help them better. Several said they could teach skills to the girls if they were re-supplied with the tools of their trade, such as midwifery equipment, that were taken from them during the war. The teacher who served as our translator said she would be willing to train these women, if she was supported to do so. In our assessment, supporting local women's capacity in this community could be instrumental in improving the situation of girl mothers.

Principles for Humanitarian Groups Working with Reintegrating Girls

Programmatic approaches should be developed to ensure attention to girls who were unjustly left out of DDR. Importantly, girls should be involved in meaningful ways in the planning, implementing, and evaluating of these programs, and their own perceptions of their situations should serve as a basis for needs assessment. Also, girls should be educated about their rights.

Specific and practical assistance should be prioritized for disabled, separated (from their families), orphaned girls, and girl mothers and their children. These girls are at high risk, and have greater difficulty in fulfilling gender roles and in securing resources for survival (McKay & Mazurana, 2004). As highly vulnerable populations, they require long-term support and follow-up. Also, girls who survive through commercial sex work need targeted assistance that includes family tracing, reconciliation and reintegration counseling, health care and education, skills training, and income-generating activities to provide an alternative to sex work.

In working with reintegrating girls, care must be taken to understand the context into which they reintegrate since their experiences are diverse. A girl who returns, was young when taken, did not remain in a force for an extended period, and returned with other children who were taken with her, will have a very different reintegration experience than one who was abducted at a young age, remained in a force for many years, became a "wife," and returned with three children of a father unknown to the community and, perhaps, to the girl herself. The reintegration experience of the latter is likely to be far more difficult.

Rather than assuming individualistic Western approaches to addressing trauma, community-based programs must be based upon the premise that communities have the capacity to care and protect children. Although support and counsel by indigenous leaders can be crucial to the process of girls' healing, one-to-one professional therapeutic intervention is seldom appropriate in cultures because community responsibility to care for and protect children is a social concern. Communities may, however, require assistance in developing communication skills so members can understand and better respond to the psychological and social implications of girls' experiences. For example, programs developed in the community to support girls' expression of sadness and grief may benefit girls. Opportunities to tell their stories through drama, music, and the arts can facilitate healing within cultures where these art forms are key modes of expression.

In Sierra Leone, appropriate humanitarian assistance and collaboration with male and female community elders and influential community leaders occurred when a group of communities that were concerned about sexual violence was supported in its work with war-affected, sexually abused girls. Knowing that singling out girls who were in fighting forces could "brand them," the approach the communities used was to identify a cohort of sexually abused girls who needed assistance. From this cohort, community members selected a subset, which then met with community leaders to participate in programming developed by locals. Partnerships such as this, between humanitarian organization and grassroots groups and individuals who know the girls and are best equipped to work with them over time, should emphasize capacity building, partnership, and empowerment. Also, bringing into the open information about the extent of sexual violence both toward girls in fighting forces and within the community itself, holds the potential to further address a subject that has long been taboo in Northern Uganda and Sierra Leone—as it is in much of the world.

In addition to working with communities to help girls heal from trauma, girls need practical assistance. Their health, both physical and psychological, has received little attention by humanitarian organizations. Further, girls are at risk because of gender discrimination, lack of health care access—especially for girls in rural areas—and because of reproductive injuries from their sexual abuse within a fighting force. Humanitarian groups should offer medical screening and care and health care support to *all* returning girls with follow-up, and develop links with referral services. A major challenge is to identify these girls without stigmatizing them and to be innovative when designing treatment and follow-up care.

In addition to treatment of chronic and acute illnesses and wounds, reproductive health care and psychosocial assistance should be key components of care. Because primary health structures are often destroyed, innovative ways to reach girls should be developed—such as converting existing structures or using mobile health clinics. All girls should be tested for STDs and HIV/AIDS and given counseling and health education about results of the testing. The babies of girl mothers also should be tested.

Another key area of practical assistance is for humanitarian groups to work with returning girls to find opportunities for them to gain economic skills and/or to attend school. As a priority, girls' schooling and training should be funded. Schools and training programs should be girl-friendly, have relevant curricula, and offer accelerated programs to help girls catch up with basic literacy and numerical skills. Importantly, girls should be active in shaping, monitoring, and evaluating their programs for relevancy to their lives (McKay & Mazurana, 2004).

Girls should also be given life skills training within programs in which they are enrolled. Also, economic schemes such as micro-credit programs for girls should be developed so that they have income potential. However, girls should not be segregated into "gender-appropriate" training that cannot be firmly linked to viable economic markets within the community.

Mending Girls' Broken Hearts

Whether Western or community-based approaches are used, healing is not a process that comes easily. For girls returning from fighting forces who have been invisible within the gaze of humanitarian organizations working in war-torn countries, healing from acute and chronic trauma may be particularly difficult. Invisible and neglected, typically they forge their own ways to survival. Some return to loving families and supportive communities that provide the vital bridge to healing. Others, because of injuries, mental and physical illnesses, and sexually transmitted diseases, do not survive. Their children also die or become orphans in the wake of their mothers' deaths. For many, commercial sex work may be their only option.

Yet, as I have learned in talking with these girls and with grassroots, NGO, and UNICEF, and other organizational leaders, girls have the capacity to develop positive futures and productive lives if they are recognized, supported, helped to build upon the strengths they bring back with them, and empowered. The challenge for humanitarian organizations is to work in partnership with communities to find ways that girls' hearts can mend— even if they remain frayed around the edges and occasionally miss a beat.

Notes

1. Save the Children, Sierra Leone, was our partner organization and generously facilitated our work in Mambolo, which was funded by a University of Wyoming Faculty Grant-in-Aid. We requested that Save the Children place us in a community where there had not yet been much NGO activity but where a positive relationship had already been forged with the community. Our intent was to gain clearer insights about the state of the community and its girl mothers prior to NGO involvement in programming. After we completed our site study, we met with the NGO team to share our findings and make recommendations for their work with girl mothers in Mambolo.
2. Miscarriage is the usual word that girls used to describe a pregnancy that ended in the bush although, in addition to natural causes, the reasons the pregnancy ended may include abortion initiated by the mother, or she may be forced to abort.

References

Fisher, S. (1996). Occupation of the womb: Forced impregnation as genocide. *Duke Law Journal, 46,* 91–133.

McKay, S. (1998). The effects of armed conflict on girls and women. *Peace and Conflict: Journal of Peace Psychology, 4,* 381–392.

————, Burman, M., Gonsalves, M., & Worthen, M. (2004). Known but invisible: Girl mothers returning from fighting forces. *Child Soldiers Newsletter, 11,* 10–11.

————, & Mazurana, D. (2004). *Where are the girls? Girls in fighting forces in Northern Uganda, Sierra Leone and Mozambique: Their lives during and after war.* Montreal, Canada: Rights and Democracy.

Nordstrom, C. (1999). Visible wars and invisible girls, shadow industries, and the politics of not-knowing. *International Journal of Feminist Politics, 1,* 14–33.

Physicians for Human Rights. (2002). *War-related sexual violence in Sierra Leone.* Boston: Physicians for Human Rights.

Sajor, I. L. (Ed.). (1998). *Common grounds: Violence against women in war and conflict situations.* Quezon City, Philippines: Asian Center for Women's Human Rights.

United Nations [UN]. (1996). *The impact of armed conflict on children: Report of the expert of the Secretary-General, Ms. Graça Machel.* New York: Author.

UN Wire. (2004, July 16). *U.N. urges better services for Uganda's war-affected children.* New York: UN Foundation.

CHAPTER 4

CHILDREN AFFECTED BY ARMED CONFLICT IN SOUTH ASIA: A REGIONAL SUMMARY

Jo Boyden, Joanna de Berry,
Thomas Feeny, and Jason Hart

Introduction

This chapter summarizes key findings of a research project studying children affected by armed conflict and forced migration in South Asia conducted in 2001. It is based on interviews with academics and humanitarian workers living in, or at least knowledgeable about, Afghanistan, Bangladesh, Bhutan, India, Nepal, Pakistan and Sri Lanka. It also draws upon a review of "gray" and published literature about conflict and its impact upon children in these countries. A key aim of this study was to think as broadly as possible about the ways in which children's lives may be affected, both directly and indirectly. Although concerns about underage recruitment and the psychosocial effects of conflict are considered, we also explore issues less commonly heard in discussions about children and armed conflict, such as the additional responsibilities borne by the young, access to educational and health services, disruption to family life, and so on. Discussion of such issues is framed in relation to the complex causes and nature of armed conflict in the region.

The Nature of Armed Conflict in South Asia

Many of the countries in the region have experienced multiple forms and levels of conflict concurrently. Sometimes armed violence has begun at the local level with a minor dispute that spiraled out of control, and sometimes it has involved the opposing forces of nation states. In most affected areas, armed conflict has not been continuous but sporadic, and it has shifted from one area and one community to another. In Sri Lanka, the conflict has been characterized by ongoing violence during the entire two decades of the conflict. Full-scale battles between the parties, however, have been few and periods of calm frequent, if short-lived. For the most part, conflicts in South Asia have followed this trend and may be described as low-intensity, involving the use of unsophisticated weaponry. Conflict of this kind may continue for many years producing comparatively few casualties.

Even when exposure to actual armed violence is limited, the effects are considerable in terms of repression; loss of security, income, and service access; displacement; military harassment; and other phenomena. The imposition of security checks, patrols, curfews, restrictions, discriminatory employment practices, closure of schools and other facilities, and so on have all been critical parts of military strategies across South Asia. Therefore, low-intensity conflict may have an immense impact on the lives of children and their families.

Physical Destruction

Forced migration, both internal and international, is a common feature of armed conflict in South Asia, affecting countless individuals, families, and communities. Displacement in Afghanistan alone has produced the greatest number of forced migrants in the history of modern warfare. The social and economic consequences of displacement for families have been severe. The vast majority of displaced peoples live from their own devices, often in extreme poverty and economic insecurity and in constant fear of discovery and banishment. They also generally lack effective voices to advocate for their protection and assistance, nationally and internationally. Only a small proportion of those displaced were officially registered and in receipt of humanitarian assistance. This is the case, for example, with the Rohingya, 25,000 of whom remain in official camps in Cox's Bazaar, Bangladesh, with a further 150,000 estimated to be living illegally in the same region.

Factors Contributing to Conflict in South Asia

Attempts to ensure the safety and well-being of children and their communities must include addressing the factors that gave rise to conflict in the first place. To do otherwise is to deal only with symptoms. In this section, we consider some of the most significant causes of conflict in the South Asian context.

Governance

Governments of conflict-affected countries have frequently held non-state players, such as political activists from ethnic or religious minorities, to be the prime agents of violence. Certainly it is true that insurgency is more prevalent in minority communities, which generally lack the resources and power to use democratic means to bring about social justice and change in a peaceful manner. However, in many cases poor governance at the national and subnational levels has also played a major part. This has been manifested in a range of ways: exclusion of certain sections of the population from decision-making processes; the development of a culture of impunity and nonaccountability; nationalist politics that marginalize certain groups; direct discrimination as demonstrated by the Sinhalese-dominated government toward the Tamil minority; and the widespread discrimination shown toward low-caste, Dalit communities in India. Finally, it is important to consider the impact of budgetary decisions: over recent decades governments in South Asia have spent a high proportion of gross domestic product (GDP) on the military while giving relatively little to health and education provision (Stockholm International Peace Research Institute, 1999). Such budgetary decisions inevitably lead to shortfalls and inconsistencies, and exacerbate the frustrations and sense of disenfranchisement of ordinary people.

Economy

Economic hardship commonly contributes to the development of conflict. This is inevitably the case in South Asia, where half a billion people, including some 250 million children, live in poverty. Such a level of poverty has contributed significantly to other social problems, including poor health and nutrition, exploitative child labor, HIV/AIDS transmission, trafficking of women and children, and violations of basic human rights. Although commitments have been made by the region's governments to address these problems, some countries/states and provinces have remained stagnant in many key indicators, and various multilevel conflicts across the region have substantially hindered the achievement of targeted goals (UNICEF, 2001).

Societal and Cultural Factors

Most of the factors discussed above concern the role of government, directly or indirectly. However, it is also the case that conflict emerges from and is exacerbated by various factors at the societal level. The tremendous upheavals witnessed at the level of family and community throughout the region have inevitably played a role in fueling tensions that may lead to armed conflict. Throughout most of South Asia the size of population and the rate of population growth are issues with profound implications for the creation of conflict. Most significantly, with the exception of Sri Lanka, all of these countries still have fertility rates and annual population growth rates that are well above the world average.

The potential implications of such large, fast-growing, and young populations for the emergence and spread of conflict are numerous. These include the additional strain placed upon existing resources and social problems associated with overcrowding and rapid urbanization. The high percentage of children within the total population places strain upon structures of care, social control, and discipline already threatened by processes of family and community dispersal. Moreover, the economic burden that families and the state must bear by providing for so many young people—their education, health, and general welfare—only adds to the competition, fears, and resentments that may fuel violent conflict.

The ready availability of arms in many parts of South Asia is a major contributory factor to conflict, facilitating resort to weaponry in the resolution of grievances and the escalation of local disputes to a larger scale. The prevalence of small arms increases the likelihood that children will become involved in conflict because they can handle, carry, and load such weapons with comparative ease. This abundance of arms is compounded by the growing problem of the drug trade, which helps enormously in funding arms purchases. As an indication of the fast-growing prevalence of small arms, one commentator claims that from 1980 to 2000, the numbers of AK-47s in the possession of state and non-state actors in South Asia went from virtually none to nearly 8 million (Kartha, 2000).

Children's Experiences of Conflict

Experiencing physical violence, displacement, death, and disappearance of loved ones along with the general militarization of the environment poses major challenges to the psychosocial well-being of children in many areas of South Asia. Scholarship on children in these kinds of situations tends to highlight the apparently self-evident effects of stressors such as violence, bereavement, or family separation. For example, it is a common assumption that long-term exposure to conflict and the challenges to structures of family and community cause children to develop distorted values, in which violence is accepted as an appropriate means to resolve social and political problems. However, it is our contention that the experiences and impacts of conflict are diverse, complex, and often unpredictable. For example, a national survey of the attitudes of nearly 3,000 Sri Lankans in the age range 15–29 (Centre for Anthropological and Sociological Studies, 1999), suggests very little difference between Sinhalese and Tamil youth nationwide in response to questions about the legitimacy of violence (e.g., roughly 30% thought violence to be a "proper" behavior). Furthermore, in the specific areas most affected by the conflict, the young people who participated in the survey were below the national average in terms of the number who viewed violence as legitimate. A causal relationship between the experience of conflict and dysfunctional behavior is also rendered questionable by examples of young people engaged in activities of a highly constructive and socially responsible nature. It is also worth highlighting that engaging in constructive and meaningful activities may well have beneficial psychological effects in children who have been exposed to conflict.

In seeking to understand the impact of long-term violence on the attitudes and behavior of the young and on their survival, development, and emotional and psychological well-being, we need to consider numerous mediating factors that play an exacerbating or mitigating role. Conflict entails transformations and hazards at the multiple levels of society, with diverse implications for children. Sometimes the effects of adverse circumstances induced by conflict—such as grinding poverty or security constraints—can have far more detrimental effects on children's well-being than exposure to violence. How children are affected also varies markedly according to their gender, age, social, religious, or ethnic status and position within the family, but due to the dearth of child-focused studies in war-affected communities in South Asia, it is virtually impossible at this point to discern the specific risks experienced by different groups and categories of children. However, even in the absence of systematic research, it is very apparent that children in all social categories are likely to experience one or more of the following: social disruption, loss of service access, impoverishment, civil and political violations, threats to physical integrity, and transformations in roles and responsibilities.

Social Disruption

As discussed earlier, displacement is a key characteristic of conflict in South Asia, and it invariably has very direct impacts upon the schooling, nutrition, and health of children. It is sometimes assumed that a shared communal identity, shared experiences of persecution, and a shared sense of injustice bring displaced peoples together in mutual understanding and support. But this is a simplistic view, since displacement frequently occurs in an atmosphere of profound fear and mistrust. As such, it is likely to disturb the coherence of familiar networks of community, friends, and family, which provide a basis of consistency and security for the young. The economic effects of displacement are also likely to be severe, with particular pressures for children to engage in some form of labor in support of themselves and their families.

Many displaced people opt for self-settlement on the grounds that it enables them to have freedom to move around and work. However, self-settled refugees are generally defined as illegal immigrants and hence live in constant fear of discovery and deportation, forcing them often to conceal or re-fashion their identity in order to avoid discovery. Due to the risk of discovery, many self-settled refugee families fall prey to extortion or exploitation by unscrupulous property owners, law enforcement officials, or employers. As illegal immigrants, refugees living outside camps seldom receive assistance from aid agencies, which are often working under constraints imposed by host governments.

In contrast to the chronic and ongoing insecurity of those unofficially displaced, a camp or welfare center may offer great improvements in protection, shelter, nutrition, and health. However, as the experience of camp-dwelling communities in countries across the region demonstrates, life in such an environment entails its own risks and difficulties. Simply by being crowded together in a clearly identified place, camp residents are vulnerable to a range of malevolent forces. Traffickers seeking out girls for their trade and militant groups looking for disaffected youth to enlist are often attracted by the large concentration of desperate people. One report described a case of local villagers dropping snakes into wells used by displaced Tamils in order to prevent them from drawing water.

In situations of protracted conflict in particular, young camp dwellers may become trapped for years—decades even—in a confined space, without meaningful employment or leisure opportunities, and cut off from the social and political life of their host community. This is apparent in the case of both Bhutanese children in Nepal and the Rohingya in Bangladesh, many of whom have known no other life. Clearly the right of free movement does not exist for many forced migrants.

The family is the core social unit for the care, nurture, socialization, and emotional support of children. However, in addition to the death and injury of members, conflict creates challenges to the family unit through forced migration and dispersal, as well as intense economic, psycho-emotional, and social pressures. Rates of suicide and attempted suicide are particularly high among women in the north and east of Sri Lanka, leaving many children orphaned or partly orphaned. In Kashmir, the highest proportion of reported suicide is in women between the ages of 15 and 25. Apparently this is not attributable to direct experience of armed violence so much as to the heavy toll taken on family life and social relations by conditions of insurgency.

The solidarity of many families in situations of conflict is seriously threatened, while the incidence of domestic abuse and neglect is commonly believed to rise. In the north and east of Sri Lanka, women and children complained bitterly of the extraordinarily high levels of domestic violence perpetrated by men. They attributed this largely to high levels of alcohol consumption among men, many of whom are able to find only part-time or intermittent work and are idle much of the time. Domestic strife has apparently led a number of adolescents to join the Liberation Tigers of Tamil Elam (LTTE), which is regarded by many young people as offering a less oppressive and more exciting and rewarding existence than civilian home life and civilian employment.

Families and households commonly scatter during conflict and displacement, and are sometimes never reunited. New configurations of family also emerge as orphans, stepparents, and isolated extended relatives are absorbed. It may prove difficult for children to adjust to these truncated and revised family relations. The situation of female-headed households and their children in war-affected populations of South Asia is of great concern, partly because of the sheer numbers involved, and partly because such families appear to face particular hardships. This is especially true in Muslim societies and communities where the public domain is exclusively in the hands of men and in areas where there is a significant social stigma attached to widows. In 1992, two-thirds of those who died among the Rohingya refugees in Bangladesh were female, with those in women-headed households being especially at risk (Newman, 2003). This trend was attributed to a variety of factors, particularly women's profound reluctance to queue for rations alongside men and the lack of other household members in female-headed units to assume this task for them.

Factors that lead to the separation of children from their families, such as poverty, death of key family members, and discord, all become more commonplace during conflict. Frequently, the loss of a family member starts a chain reaction that drastically affects children in very practical ways. Children alone are particularly susceptible to abduction and forced recruitment, labor exploitation, and school deprivation. They are also subject to many physical, psychological, and emotional risks. Children who are associated with the "enemy"—possibly because of the military or political involvement of parents or other relatives—may be especially vulnerable. Fear of discovery by government authorities can act as a strong deterrent for these children to access basic services. Concern about such situations has been raised with respect to children displaced by the conflict between the Maoist insurgents and the government forces in Nepal.

The death, disappearance, or desertion of male breadwinners creates the need for women to find viable employment. Where women obtain work locally, girls are often required to abandon schooling in order to take on extra domestic responsibilities. The involvement of boys in income-generating activities to support the family also becomes likely. When widowed mothers are obliged to travel further afield, as many Sri Lankan Tamil women have done in search of work as domestic servants in the Middle East, the children left behind are often taken in by aunts, uncles, or grandparents. However, the extended family may be severely stretched in order to provide proper care for existing offspring, let alone additional members. Often unnoticed and unsupported by governmental and nongovernmental agencies, children are left to run households of younger siblings, or simply to fend for themselves on the streets of larger towns. Some mothers, especially women without male partners, work abroad in a desperate bid to support their children. As a consequence of this outflow, there are households consisting solely of child-headed sibling groups, with no grandparents or other relatives to assume guardianship. Some of these households receive remittances from their mothers, while others are assisted intermittently by neighbors.

Fosterage is often favored by aid agencies as a solution for children without families, but foster children are also vulnerable to physical, verbal, and sexual abuse and neglect. Children fostered by families in refugee camps may be taken in solely because they bring an additional ration into the home, leading to abandonment at repatriation (when rations normally cease). In the case of host-population fosterage, there may also be cultural differences between the child and the foster family, threatening children's sense of identity and self-efficacy. Thus, not only are the physical needs of these children not adequately met, but their particular psychological and emotional requirements may be ignored.

Orphanages seeking to accommodate children who have lost the care of their families due to conflict have become commonplace in some countries. In the best of circumstances these children enjoy a safe, loving environment, good nutrition, and health care, and they are enabled in their education. However, in some cases residence in such institutions can expose children to new risks. For example, rumors abound that certain orphanages in the Vanni area of Sri Lanka are acting effectively as training establishments for the LTTE. In the Chittagong area orphanages are often run by Buddhist monks, who have at times found themselves unable to protect the children from incursion and torture by the security forces. Outraged by the violence they have witnessed, a significant number of children from these orphanages went on to join the insurgent Shanti Bahini movement. The establishment and maintenance of effective systems for monitoring orphanages are likely to be a low priority in conflict-affected areas. Thus, the way may be left open for unscrupulous business people to make profits from the desperate circumstances of a growing number of vulnerable children.

Service Access

It is commonly accepted that the maintenance of educational services is crucial for children's psychosocial well-being during periods of conflict and upheaval. Many of the areas of South Asia that are affected by conflict have established systems of formal schooling comparatively recently and, in most cases, conflict has had a seriously adverse effect on access. In Kashmir a total of 891 schools have been deliberately attacked or destroyed in the course of military confrontation, and under half of these have been reconstructed (Bose, 2000). Security forces have used other school buildings as barracks, thus putting them out of bounds. Thousands of adult and nonformal education centers have closed in the region because of financial constraints and staff shortages (Madhosh, 1996). Many teachers have left since the troubles began, and those who remain, wary of traveling long distances to work, are too often absent. Strikes, security threats, bomb blasts, arrests of teachers, and absenteeism have taken their toll on educational performance.

Problems of safety while traveling to and from school and during class are also common in conflict-affected areas. In Sri Lanka, children face immense challenges in order to attend school on a regular basis, including a lack of local facilities and very poor infrastructure. The absence of a public transportation service obliges many children to walk for hours each day in order to study. In addition, many parents claim that the numerous "hidden" costs of educating a child are prohibitive. This is particularly a problem for families living in camps where the opportunities for employment are scarce and poverty endemic. In some areas children risk abduction and forced military recruitment while walking to and from school.

During conflict, the education system can become a vehicle for the militarization of children, especially in the context of refugee camps, since children's containment in camps makes them highly accessible to political activists and combatants. Thus, many of the Taliban fighters in Afghanistan were children in Pakistani refugee camps and were recruited through a highly militarized education system provided in the Madrassa schools. The presentation to children of rigid communal identities and of negative stereotypes in many refugee settings has implications for the extension of conflict over generations. School curricula, cultural and religious activities, everyday social practices, and the media can all become means by which the young are encouraged to see themselves as members of distinct and exclusive groups threatened by, or unable to coexist with, others. In this way, opposition and antagonism toward the members of other communities can come to appear as natural, even necessary.

Embargoes, curfews, the damage and destruction of facilities, and the departure of many health professionals all impact on the health services available to the young. The maintenance of properly functioning health facilities in conflict-affected zones is often immensely difficult. As with educational establishments, health centers may be deliberately attacked, with staffing a severe problem in the clinics that survive, and health care professionals are often reluctant to remain in conflict-affected areas. Hospitals are often left without vaccines for months on end and no proper refrigeration facilities for preserving them when and if they do arrive. Pregnancy and childbirth are particularly hazardous because of a severe shortage of trained midwives. Overall, health workers report a high incidence of death due to maladies such as malaria, tuberculosis, anemia, and snakebite, for which preventative measures and routine treatments are often unavailable.

Impoverishment

While poverty is a major contributory factor in armed conflict in South Asia, conflict also tends to marginalize further those who are already vulnerable economically. The impoverishment of families impacts upon children in a number of important ways. It increases pressures on the young to work, frequently at the expense of their schooling and safety. Children's work tends to be more flexible than adults, and in war-affected areas, the young can sometimes obtain work when adults remain unemployed due to a decline in labor demand. In Afghanistan it is considered shameful for adults to beg and scavenge, but not for children, so with the war, many boys in particular were drawn into this activity. Boys' work has always been valued in Afghanistan, but their work roles and conditions have changed radically with the war. Collecting firewood and water has become more arduous and time-consuming with the decline in infrastructure, and a large number of boys have been maimed or killed while collecting scrap metal among unexploded ordnance and in minefields. Research revealed that the boys were fully aware of the risks associated with entering minefields, but they argued that they had no other option given how lucrative the sale of metal is and its importance for family survival.

Poverty also contributes to malnutrition, to the inability of parents to pay for basic educational necessities (e.g., uniforms and materials), and to children's withdrawal from social events (e.g., religious or cultural) in which some offering is necessary. Negative impacts on family structures are also apparent. In Kashmir, the Hanji community has been particularly affected by the loss of revenue from tourism due to the conflict. Increasing numbers of boys from this community are migrating long distances for work. Social life is also affected. Young Bhutanese refugees in Nepal note that they are not able to celebrate weddings in the proper manner. This loss of socioeconomic status compounds a sense of alienation from their homeland.

Civil and Political Violations

Children in communities affected by conflict are at constant risk of being subjected to violations by both state and nonstate military and law enforcement bodies. The Armed Forces (Special Powers) Act in India entrenches the impunity of security forces. It grants the right to shoot to kill, to search and arrest without warrant, and to detain people on suspicion as a "preventative measure" without a strong case against them. The looseness of this act and the degree of power accorded by it means that an extremely broad range of events and situations can be construed and acted upon as a threat to national security. For example, Dalit activists in Bihar have faced charges of terrorism and of being "habitual offenders." In Kashmir, 20 percent of those detained in prison were found to be boys under the age of 18 who had been arrested under "preventative detention measures," to curb potential political threat.

The presence of large numbers of security personnel often entails the militarization of society, leading to constant vigilance, restriction of movement, and intimidation. Checkpoints, surveillance operations, interrogations, searches of homes and places of work, curfews, and restrictions on journalists and activists all undermine normal interaction and community life in many conflict regions. Human rights abuses include harassment, sexual violence, extortion, torture, extra-judicial detention, and killing. Eyewitness accounts pinpoint the arbitrary arrest, detention, burning, and stabbing to death of tribal children in the Chittagong Hill Tracts in Bangladesh by security forces. Tribal girls have been systematically raped by both security forces and illegal Bengali settlers. These conditions create a climate of fear and mistrust that pervades all aspects of community and family life.

Because of high levels of harassment and extortion, children in the east of Sri Lanka would often avoid going to school if it meant going through an army checkpoint. They also expressed concerns about passing nearby LTTE checkpoints, since these are used to identify and monitor children of recruitment age. Emergency legislation often leads to children being detained, frequently without charge, and to interrogations, commonly without the presence of a legal representative or parent. Both during arrest and in detention there is an extremely high risk of sexual abuse, torture, and other forms of ill treatment. Significant numbers of children disappear and remain missing and unaccounted for after conflict has ceased.

The militarization of society has other negative ramifications as well. Many young people are forced to forgo their education due to mobility restrictions. As refugees they are often unable to secure jobs, and they turn to unlawful means of earning income. In the Chittagong Hill Tracts and the Nagalands of northeastern India, militant ethnic minority groups have become embroiled in the smuggling of drugs and small arms as a means of funding weapons purchases. Access to these commodities has become increasingly easy in both areas. In the Chittagong Hill Tracts this has led to notable increases in interpersonal violence, much of which is perpetrated by dissatisfied tribal youth.

Children's rights to citizenship and nationality are also infringed in many conflict-affected communities within South Asia. Although states party to the UN Convention on the Rights of the Child are obliged to uphold the rights of all children resident on their sovereign territory, in practice the denial of citizenship and nationality renders them vulnerable with respect to all other rights. In Bhutan many members of the Nepali-speaking population, who did not leave the country in the early 1990s under alleged threat from government forces, have been effectively denied citizenship status. As a consequence their children have lost their entitlement to free school provision. The Bhutanese government maintains that most of the refugees living in camps in Nepal were illegal immigrants with no rights to Bhutanese citizenship or return. In the meantime, their status in Nepal is highly tenuous and ambiguous.

Threats to the Physical Integrity of Children

Combat activities lead to the injury and death of child civilians in a wide range of situations. Among the most common of these are bystander injury, bombing and shelling, direct military combat, communal massacres, and landmines. Children are particularly vulnerable to the use of landmines and unexploded ordinances (UXOs), which are usually scattered indiscriminately and increase the risk of harm to noncombatants. Because of children's generally smaller stature and the proximity of their vital organs to the body surface, devices that are intended to injure and maim adults cause death to the young. In addition, the domestic activities in which the young may typically engage—such as collecting firewood and water—often expose them to particular danger. Among younger children especially, casualties sometimes occur when playing with explosive objects that appear shiny and interesting.

In South Asia gender differences appear to affect the likelihood of casualty, with boys' greater freedom of movement outside the home putting them at a greater risk of injury than girls. This appears to be the case in Afghanistan and in Jaffna, where there have been three times more boys injured and killed than girls.

In situations of armed conflict, levels of rape, sexual exploitation, and other forms of sexual violence generally rise. Women and girls are the most frequent targets, although men and boys can also be very vulnerable and their victimization may be exacerbated by societal stigma, which forces them to keep their experiences secret. In 1990 information from one of the refugee camps for tribal peoples in the Chittagong Hill Tracts indicated that 10 percent of the total female population had been raped, security forces being the overwhelming majority of perpetrators and over 40 percent of victims being girls under age 18. Often sexual violence is associated with the general level of lawlessness and climate of impunity that prevails in conflict-affected communities. It also reflects the desperation of impoverished and vulnerable families that find themselves forced to sell daughters to traffickers, or offer them to military personnel as protection against attack, extortion, and other abuses. In refugee camps, women and girls may be forced to have sexual intercourse with officials who distribute rations as the only means of gaining access to food.

It is clear, however, that sexual violence during conflict is far more than an arbitrary side effect of the breakdown of law, order, and social custom. Rather, it has become an instrument of terror with the rights of girls and women systematically violated as a deliberate policy. Frequently it takes the form of multiple rapes and may be accompanied by torture, forced marriage, and maternity. Such violations are particularly common in the context of ethnic cleansing, tribal conflict, and boundary disputes, where they are used explicitly both to humiliate individuals and to demoralize the community as a whole.

In order to understand the full impact of conflict upon children's physical well-being, we must also consider their everyday health and the nutrition they receive. Indeed, it is likely that children's health is damaged to a broader and more enduring extent in this indirect way than directly through violence. For example, illnesses such as malaria, diarrhea, and respiratory infection—all of which may be easily cured with the appropriate medication—often become more prevalent and lethal in situations of conflict for a range of reasons. However, these are generally not recorded as conflict-related casualties. In areas of eastern Sri Lanka under direct LTTE control, a high incidence of snakebite among children has been noted, especially during the rainy season, when snakes move close to human settlements in search of dry land. Measures to reduce the threat (e.g., management of the forest around villages and use of building materials that make it harder for snakes to enter homes) have not been taken. Because of delays in getting patients to distant hospitals caused by curfews, checkpoints, and transport shortages, many children have died. When children were asked about their major concerns, worries, and fears, snakes and snakebites featured prominently, alongside abduction and forced recruitment. This is a poignant example of the diverse ways in which conflict affects children's health, which might easily be overlooked by agencies focused only on the most obvious and direct impacts. Yet, in some settings, commonplace concerns, such as snakebite, may seriously endanger large numbers of young people.

The Graça Machel report (United Nations, 1996) emphasizes the strong links between armed conflict, the prevalence of sexual violence and exploitation, and high levels of transmission and incidence of HIV/AIDS. Some countries and areas in South Asia are known to have among the highest rates of HIV transmission in the world, and further research is needed to detect how and in what way this phenomenon is connected to conflict. The most obvious sources of risk include intravenous drug use and a high level of promiscuity and unprotected sex among combatants and other groups affected by conflict. Similarly, it has been noted that militant political groups tend to consist mainly of highly mobile young men, presumed to be sexually active and relatively free of prevailing sexual prohibitions.

Transformations in Children's Roles and Responsibilities

Armed conflict and forced migration propel many children and adolescents into adultlike roles and responsibilities. As noted, when families become dispersed or adults are killed or disappear, children may become heads of household. In effect, this means that young people who are already suffering extreme personal loss must assume the added burden of responsibility for younger siblings, many of whom may confront serious emotional and psychological problems. In addition, children heading households may have to engage in paid work in order to support their dependents.

Significant numbers of adolescents and, in some cases younger children as well, are directly embroiled in armed struggle in both government and opposition forces. Young recruits tend to perform ancillary tasks, as porters (carrying arms, ammunition and loot), messengers, intelligence gatherers, cooks, and weapon-cleaners, to support the military enterprise. Some occupy combat functions, as soldiers, guards or political agitators, and are responsible for patrolling and manning checkpoints, the laying, detection, and clearing of land mines, and bearing arms in battle.

Adolescents were heavily involved in the Shanti Bahini movement in the Chittagong Hill Tracts. Many became engaged only in intelligence activities, but some Chakma youth (the most educated and politically active of the tribal groups in the region) and many others from the refugee camps in India took up arms. Children are drawn into combat through several routes. Since the young tend to be particularly obedient and loyal and have a special talent for escaping surveillance, their recruitment is an overt strategy of many armed forces. Some children are abducted and forced to fight, and others join up through a range of processes and due to a number of factors. Both forced and voluntary recruitment are noted in Sri Lanka and Nepal. Children sometimes equate armed violence with power. Enlistment may also be linked to political commitment, ethnic loyalties, peer pressure, hunger, and the opportunity to engage in looting.

When families undergo times of deprivation and material loss, it is unsurprising that they may turn to their children as an economic resource. This often occurs in poor communities, but particularly so during conflict when regular breadwinners are absent, killed, or injured. Children may also be sold into hazardous forms of employment as an economic coping strategy of their family. Some families have become so indebted that they have committed their children in bonded labor in factories or resorted to selling their daughters to international trafficking rings. Entering children into militant groups may provide rewards in the form of food for the children themselves and provide families with access to rations controlled by these groups. The likelihood of hazardous work increases during conflict because of the reduction in normal economic opportunities and the prevailing climate of lawlessness and impunity. However, prevalence of hazardous work will also depend on local cultural factors that, for example, may create few obstacles to the employment of boys but ensure that girls are largely prevented from pursuing any public economic activity.

The obstacles to freedom of movement created by conflict prevent children from gaining access to schooling and health facilities and hinder their ability to enjoy leisure and play activities among their peers. Curfews severely restrict the ability of children to play outside with friends, leading to feelings of isolation, loneliness, and boredom. Conflict also affects children's relationships. One study from northeast India showed a distinct change in children's friendship patterns before and after communal violence. After the rioting, parents were much less likely to allow their children to mix with friends from other ethnic groups.

Conclusion

The present survey of expert knowledge and literature has revealed that, in general, the plight and psychosocial well-being of war-affected and displaced children in South Asia continues to be seriously neglected. Claims about the militarization of children in some areas seem to be borne out by the flimsy evidence that does exist. In other cases, assertions about the negative effects of war merit much closer investigation; for example, over 20 years of conflict in the Chittagong Hill Tracts has left a "culture of violence" in which all disputes, whether domestic or public, involving children or adults, entail physical violence of one sort or another. Also, much remains unknown about how children respond to the multitude of adversities associated with conflict in South Asia and what legal and practical means exist to aid and support them. This has serious ramifications for policy and pro-grammatic intervention in this important field, since effective measures require a full understanding of the overall situation with respect to armed political struggles, the specific circumstances of children caught up in these struggles, and the available forms of assistance and protection.

Hence, a key recommendation from our study concerns the need for par-ticipatory baseline research with war-affected children that highlights spe-cific threats to their well-being, their responses to the many adversities of conflict, and the resources and assistance to which they have access. For example, research in Afghanistan in 2002 provided valuable insights into the vital role that family and immediate community can play in mitigating the impact of conflict upon the psychosocial well-being of the young. For six months, the NGO Save the Children USA worked with groups of children in Kabul to explore their experiences, concerns, and hopes (De Berry, Fazili, Farhad, Nasiry, Hashemi, & Hakimi, 2003). The research team used a num-ber of participatory methods to facilitate group discussions; the richness of the research findings is testament to the strength of qualitative, child-focused research tools and their utility in eliciting young people's own perspectives.

Children involved in the research talked about a number of risks that were having a detrimental impact in their daily life and were causing them distress. Importantly, by the time of the research, few children were experi-encing direct fighting or violence and this was not a major preoccupation for them. Instead their concerns related more to the difficulties of carrying out roles and responsibilities such as supporting their families economically, try-ing to access education, and trying to fulfill simple daily tasks such as fetch-ing water or firewood. They spoke of the challenge of living in a devastated city with only the most basic of infrastructure, where the bombed houses were a constant reminder of the war that had now passed. They highlighted a particular concern about the hazards of increased traffic in the city.

The young people were unanimous in saying that members of their fam-ily were the most important people that they turned to for help in coping with these difficulties. They related how family members gave them practi-cal help. For example, children explained how the assistance of a brother or sister was vital when fetching water—one of their most arduous family responsibilities. More than this, however, children said that they benefited from the moral, spiritual, and emotional support of their families. They gave examples of how caring parents listened to their concerns and prompted them to have the courage and determination to overcome a challenge.

Children stated how prayers and faith, taught to them by their parents, were a source of comfort. They illustrated that having family members around them would help them see the best in a situation, and many attested to how their parents taught them to be thankful and grateful despite their situa-tion. This thankfulness enabled them to be resilient; through it children explained that they were not overcome by what they had to face but that they could keep it in perspective. They explained that without such a family, the world they lived in was a more bewildering and threatening place. Children in Kabul were therefore adamant that a close and protective family was vital to their ability to cope with the myriad challenges encountered day by day.

Studies such as the one conducted in Kabul provide a holistic view in which environmental factors are seen to interact with personal susceptibilities and competencies to influence children's well-being, resilience, and coping either positively or negatively. They thereby enable the development of programs that are consistent with local understandings, values, and practices tailored to children's particular conditions and concerns and supportive of local mechanisms of protection and support. It is our contention that this kind of approach is likely to have greatest benefit for children in the complex and challenging circumstances of war and displacement in South Asia.

References

Bose, A. (2000). *Jammu and Kashmir—Focus on children and women. A statistical profile.* (Briefing report for UNICEF). New Delhi, India: UNICEF.

Centre for Anthropological and Sociological Studies. (1999). *2000 National youth survey, overview report and tables on selected topics and illustrated data—Sri Lanka.* Colombo, Sri Lanka: University of Colombo.

Chakma, K. (2005). Chittagong Hill Tracts. Speaking notes for Ms. Kabita Chakma. Retrieved February 1, 2005, from http://action.web.ca/home/sap/attachchakma1.rtf

De Berry, J., Fazili, A., Farhad, S., Nasiry, F., Hashemi, S., & Hakimi, M. (2003). *The children of Kabul: Discussions with Afghan families.* Westport, CT: Save the Children. Retrieved January 4, 2005, from http://www.savethechildren.org/publications/

Jubilee Action. (2002, May). *Jubilee Action IDP briefing paper.* Retrieved January 3, 2005, from http://www.jubileeaction.co.uk/reports/

Kartha, T. (2000). Management and control of light weapons in South Asia. In D. Banerjee (Ed.), *South Asia at gun point. Small arms and light weapons proliferation.* Colombo, Sri Lanka: Regional Centre for Strategic Studies.

Madhosh, A. G. (1996). *The present turmoil and plight of children in Kashmir.* Srinagar, India: University of Kashmir, Faculty of Education.

Newman, J. (2003, October). *Narrating displacement: Oral histories of Sri Lankan women.* (Refugee Studies Centre [RSC] working paper No. 15). Oxford, UK: University of Oxford, International Development Centre. Retrieved January 3, 2005 from http://www.rsc.ox.ac.uk/index.html?pub_working

Stockholm International Peace Research Institute. (1999). *SIPRI yearbook 1999: Armaments, disarmament and international security.* Oxford, UK: Oxford University Press.

United Nations. (1996, August). *Impact of armed conflict on children report.* (UN document # A/51/308). New York: G. Machel. Retrieved January 4, 2005, from http://www.unicef.org/graca/

———. (2000). *United Nations Population Information Network.* Retrieved January 3, 2005, from http://www.un.org/esa/population/pubsarchive/pubsarchive.htm

United Nations Children's Fund [UNICEF]. (2001, May). *Investing in children in South Asia.* South Asia High Level Meeting on Investing in Children. Kathmandu, Nepal. Retrieved February 1, 2005, from http://www.unicef.org/newsline/01nnkathmanduunderstanding.htm

CHAPTER 5

SERVING THE PSYCHOSOCIAL NEEDS OF SURVIVORS OF TORTURE AND ORGANIZED VIOLENCE

Peter Berliner and Elisabeth Naima Mikkelsen

Introduction

This chapter aims at describing the needs of survivors of torture and organized violence. First, a definition of torture will be presented. Second, we will describe the prevalent sequelae of torture and organized violence. Third, we will describe the treatment approach to survivors suffering from symptoms emerging from the exposure to torture and organized violence. The needs of this group are different from the majority of people, who may be more in need of a community-based approach providing empowerment and development in terms of livelihood and access to social support, while the first group may be in need of treatment in a clinical sense. Finally, a community-based approach will be described in practical terms, which hopefully will be helpful to the practitioner implementing this approach.

The chapter concludes that the community approach is able to reach a large number of people, which makes it useful in war-torn countries with large numbers of traumatized people, and that the community approach therefore can be an inspiration for professionals in the developed countries. But still a small percentage of people will respond to traumatizing events with long-lasting symptoms despite the community-based support system. These people will be in need of treatment in a clinical sense. In the treatment centers we see this particular group of people.

Definition of Torture

The United Nations' Convention against Torture and Other Cruel, Inhuman or Degrading Treatment or Punishment (1984) defines torture in the following way:

> The term "torture" means any act by which severe pain or suffering, whether physical or mental, is intentionally inflicted on a person for such purposes as obtaining from him or a third person information or a confession, punishing him for an act he or a third person has committed or is suspected of having committed, or intimidating or coercing him or a third person, or for any reason based on discrimination of any kind, when such pain or suffering is inflicted by or at the instigation of or with the consent or acquiescence of a public official or other person acting in an official capacity. It does not include pain or suffering arising only from, inherent in or incidental to lawful sanctions.

Torture is an evil and destructive form of human interaction, which involves at least two positions, the victim and the torturer. It is characterized by extreme humiliation, degradation, and dehumanization as the torturer inflicts severe physical or psychological suffering upon the victim. The torturer/victim relationship is highly asymmetric because the situation causes the victim to be completely dependent on and manipulated by the torturer (Doerr-Zegers et al., 1992).

At an individual level, torture is used as punishment with the purpose of destroying the victim as a human being through the systematic infliction of severe pain and psychological suffering. Also, torture is used to destroy the victim's identity by forcing him to become a traitor to his comrades and to his ideology. At a social level, authoritarian governments of all colors have used torture as a political tool to create fear and intimidate dissident groups with the purpose of preventing the population from expressing opposition toward governmental policies. Thus, countries subjected to a climate of terror may contain whole communities affected by violence. In order for such societies to engage in processes of reconciliation and national healing, the social reparation needs to go through the sequential steps of truth, compensation, justice, and reconciliation (Becker et al., 1990; Bronkhorst, 1995; Quiroga & Gurr, 1998).

The Size of the Problem

In 1997, Amnesty International reported torture and maltreatment in 115 out of 215 countries (53.5 percent). In the last 10 years, the medical and psychological service programs for survivors of political or other forms of organized violence have expanded. While Amnesty International identified 100 programs in 25 countries, the International Rehabilitation Council for Torture Victims (IRCT) listed 94 programs in 49 countries, belonging to its network of torture rehabilitation services (IRCT, 1997) and further estimated that as many as 166 programs existed in 81 countries in 1997.

Types of Torture

Torture methods can be divided into physical and psychological methods. The Chilean Human Rights Commission has listed 85 different types of physical torture (Orellana, 1989). Physical torture can be brutal with severe physical damage and a high lethal rate, but often the torturers want to avoid visible body marks. The most common methods of physical torture are beatings, suspension, stretching, electric torture, submersion, suffocation, burns, cuts, and sexual assaults.

The psychological methods of torture will often include induced exhaustion through food, water, and sleep deprivation; isolation of the victims; and monopolization of perception, for example through movement restriction and high-pitch sounds. In some cases, the victims and their families are threatened with death or they experience staged executions. In other cases, the victims witness the torture of another prisoner or of family members.

The Treatment Approach to Helping Survivors of Torture and Organized Violence

The increasing numbers of refugees presenting to mental health services in North America, Australia and New Zealand, and European countries pose significant clinical challenges for heath practitioners. Inevitably, the most challenging and most difficult to engage in a psychotherapeutic context are those who are survivors of torture and political violence. Some will have suffered multiple losses in addition to their torture experiences. The psychological complaints will vary depending on age, cultural, and socioeconomic differences.

There are a number of studies conducted with refugees (Lavik et al., 1996), and survivors of torture (Allodi, 1994; Carlson & Rosser-Hagan, 1994) and political violence (Goenjian, Steinberg, and Najarian, 2000). The prevalence of torture in selected samples of refugees varies depending on nationality, sex, age, and time. For instance, a random sample of 3000 asylum seekers who arrived to Denmark in 1986 showed a torture prevalence of 20 percent. In 2001 it was stated that 50 percent of the refugees suffer from depression and anxiety and 20 percent shows sign of other symptoms related to torture and organized violence (The Ministry for Internal Affairs and Health, 2001). A prevalence of 23 percent was found in a sample of refugees requesting asylum in Sweden (Horvath-Lindberg, 1988). Studies of refugees seeking asylum in Western countries have shown that there is a consistently higher rate of mental distress in the refugee population compared to the general population. The symptoms include depression, anxiety, demoralization, stress, fear, pain, and post-traumatic stress disorder (PTSD) (Silove, 2004; McFarlane, 2004).

The psychological well-being of refugees is threatened not just by their experiences prior to and during their flight, but also by their experiences in the host country. They may face a number of stressors:

- Family separation and violence in refugee camps, including rape and humiliation
- Fear and uncertainty about the future, especially while waiting for a decision on their asylum claim, in a political context, where it is increasingly difficult to be granted asylum
- Loss of economic basis and social status
- Changing of roles within the family
- Isolation due to difficulties with the language of the host country and separation from the local population
- Racism and discrimination

Symptoms and Reactions

Torture survivors often develop symptoms of major depression, obsessive-compulsive disorders and psychoses, and there can be sexual dysfunctioning whether or not the person was subjected to sexual torture. Studies have shown that many torture survivors experience changes in their identity (Somnier & Genefke, 1986; Barudy, 1989) and have a high level of co-morbidity (Cunningham & Cunningham, 1997; Somnier et al., 1992). The torture survivor may have lost body parts and the accompanying loss of normal bodily function. They may have lost family members, work, or credibility and status. If the torture survivor migrates to seek asylum, the losses can be compounded to include the breakdown of marriages, cessation of a planned course of education, and degradation of wealth and status (Turner & Gorst-Unsworth, 1993; Skinner, 1997). Research reviewed by Charney, Deutsch, and Krystal (1993) and Southwick, Bremner, Krystal, & Charney (1994) has established a psychobiological mechanism for PTSD. This could explain the persistence of the PTSD symptoms, and why current treatments are only partially effective, thereby having significant implications for the treatment of PTSD patients and survivors of torture.

Torture is associated with severe pain, and knowledge about pain is vital for the understanding and alleviation of pain in torture survivors. In addition, chronic pain (long-term pain) in torture survivors is the most reported problem, and because chronic pain is associated with physical, mental, and social decline, it remains to be an obstacle to rehabilitation. A study (Roche, 2002) showed that young males from the Middle East with a history of torture living in exile had notably higher incidence of chronic pain compared to similarly aged populations in developed countries. It concurred with the conclusions made in other studies regarding the epidemiology of torture pain (Amris, 2005), which found that typical methods of torture, such as beatings, suspension by limbs, and falanga (foot whipping), are consistent with a high incidence of musculoskeletal symptoms of pain.

A focal question is whether the evidence on pain shows a higher incidence of chronic pain in torture survivors compared to normal populations in developed countries. In a survey (Roche, 2002), using the sample of a normal population, chronic pain was defined as the experience of everyday pain during a minimum of three months. The respondents were asked to rate how much their pain was interfering with daily activities. The results revealed significant associations between the prevalence of chronic pain and people with lower socioeconomic status, poorer health, and low employment status, as well as older people and females, thus establishing that people with chronic pain were more likely to be unemployed or to be receiving a pension. In addition, the study confirmed conclusions about a strong relationship between chronic pain and psychological distress made in previous studies, as they demonstrated an important association between daily pain interference and higher levels of psychological distress.

Research of associated risk factors for chronic pain is an important step toward successful post-torture rehabilitation in exile. The poor identification and management of chronic pain in torture survivors may prolong and even exacerbate pain-related disability and passivity, leading to chronic psychosocial and economic disadvantage. A survey of torture survivors from communities in Vietnam, Cambodia, Spain, Iran, and Iraq indicated that between 21 and 40 percent reported chronic pain (Roche, 2002).

Essential risk factors in torture survivors' coping are avoidance, passive strategies, and negative beliefs and behaviors based on fear. During the last decades, a significant amount of research has confirmed a consistent relationship between negative coping strategies (beliefs and behaviors), in particular "catastrophizing," passivity, chronic pain, and poor adjustment to the current life situation (Amris, 2005). Symptoms of trauma are strongly associated with avoidance, causing restricted behavior and movement dysfunction.

There are similarities between emerging psychological symptoms in torture survivors and the main constellation of symptoms corresponding to those collected in the syndrome labeled as post-traumatic stress disorder, or PTSD (Cunningham & Cunningham, 1997). However, labeling torture survivors as having PTSD is partly insufficient because of the complexity and magnitude of the effects of torture (Reeler, 1994). A widespread theme in the testimonies given by survivors of genocide and organized violence is that many experience the feeling of having survived their own death, a symptom similarly described in relation to Holocaust survivors (Langer, 1997).

In the World Health Organization's (WHO) diagnostic manual ICD-10, the above problem is taken into consideration by mentioning that exposure to torture and organized violence may lead to lasting changes in the attitude and coping of the survivor. This includes two of the following: (1) hostile or distrustful attitude; (2) tendency toward social isolation; (3) feeling of emptiness or hopelessness; (4) chronic tension and alertness; (5) feeling alien. These symptoms have a profound effect on daily functions, condition, or surroundings.

Torture survivors express their suffering in many ways and two survivors' stories are rarely alike; however, some statements about their experiences, which commonly seem to appear in their narratives, describe feelings of survivor guilt, hopelessness, inadequacy, and isolation:

"It would be better if I was dead," "I have lost my taste for life," "I am nothing and I have no value."

The torture survivors express that they are not in contact with life, they feel like a "walking dead," and they have no ability to interact with others. The survivor has been so close to death for extended periods of time and has seen other people get killed while waiting for his own death. According to the torture survivors, these experiences cause the feeling of being a "living dead" (Berliner et al., 2005).

One survivor tells the story of waiting for his execution for eight months in a prison cell with some other men. Several times a week people were taken out of the cell to be executed, but not him. He never knew what was going on or why this was happening. Every day he expected his execution and finally he could not stand being in this situation anymore. Consequently, he volunteered to clean the gallows that were used to hang the prisoners because it made him feel more secure, knowing in depth about the instrument that he believed would eventually kill him. Another survivor explains how he feels alienated and different from other people. He does not feel respected or accepted as a human being, and he is afraid to share his feelings with others.

Survivors of torture and organized violence often are afraid that if other people hear about their experiences, they will become overwhelmed, so they often feel that they cannot talk to anyone about the terrible things they experienced. The survivor often expresses feelings of guilt about what has happened and a sense of guilt about the death of other people. The aim of torture is to remove the feeling of being human and to destroy the survivor psychologically and physically for life. The torture is meant to destroy the survivors' trust in other people and in themselves, as shown in the example above.

Interventions

When treating the torture survivor it is not only necessary to assess the various symptoms listed above, but it should also be considered of equal importance that a trusting relationship between the torture survivor and his/her therapist develops. Treatment progress cannot be made without this trusting relationship. Similarly, cultural understanding is essential when choosing the methodology of the social assessment of the torture survivors, as a standard Western psychiatric interview can be highly counterproductive (Mollica, 1988). There are good arguments for a bio-psycho-social approach to treat and rehabilitate torture survivors, as this approach provides long-term flexible involvement to cope with relapses, thereby endorsing increased functionality for the torture survivors to achieve personal goals. As a result, increased functionality becomes the main outcome objective for the therapy, rather than symptom reduction, though that may also be a goal in treatment.

The torture survivor probably has a combination of psychological, social, medical, and legal problems, which explains why numerous programs of psychological treatment have adopted multidisciplinary approaches. Supportive methods may in some cases be more useful than pushing the survivors to talk about their experiences of torture. Relaxation therapy and sensitive physical techniques can relieve some of the legacies of severe pain, dysfunction, and stress (Berliner et al., 2004). Moreover, psycho-social treatment of torture survivors may be more effective when it is focused on the daily activities in which the person participates, as it is based on the understanding that body, mind, and social relationships exist in a unified process, consisting of three dimensions: the body/mind, activities/participation, and the environment (WHO, 2001).

Psychotherapeutic Approaches to the Treatment of Torture Survivors

Research has demonstrated that cognitive behavioral therapy (CBT) is effective with a variety of anxiety disorders, including PTSD, yet there is little in the literature to document its use with survivors of torture. In a meta-analysis of studies on effects of psychotherapeutic treatments for PTSD (Sherman, 1998), the author states that psychotherapeutic treatment reduces PTSD and general psychiatric symptomatology, and that these effects are maintained even after the treatment has been terminated (p. 4). The predominant psychotherapeutic modalities in the studies were behavioral and cognitive behavioral interventions. In a meta-analysis of studies in the comparative efficacy of treatments for post-traumatic stress disorder (van Etten & Taylor, 1998), it is suggested that in symptom reduction, psychological therapies were more effective than drug therapies, and both were more effective than controls. And among the psychological therapies, behavior therapy and EMDR were most effective, and generally equally so. CBT operates on a multi-layered understanding of cognition, behavior, and context. The therapy reflects and impacts on the daily practice of the patient and sustains enhanced functioning in that context. Thus, there is strong support for the assumption that therapies that invite the client to act in new ways during the therapeutic sessions and outside in their daily life—rather than just talk about the possibility of doing so—have a better outcome than therapies without this component.

Common features in the clinical presentation of torture survivors are poor coping strategies, negative self-beliefs, and escape avoidance behavior stemming from their experiences. The method holds a focus on the "here and now" and the specification of realistic, measurable, and achievable treatment goals, negotiated and agreed with the patient to bring about the desired changes in their life and the use of collaborative strategies between the patient and therapist (Hackman, 1993). The survivor needs to construct values and assumptions about themselves, others, and the world, to enable the development of trust, meaning, and more functional behaviors. This is done in interaction with other people, which means that the integration of the survivor into the community is crucial (Regel & Berliner, 2005).

In the construction of values fostering a changed view of oneself, others, and the challenges of living in exile, the narrative approach may be used even though the theoretical framework of this approach differs markedly from the one of CBT. At the practical level both methods emphasize the context; that is, problems must be solved through action. The idea of the narrative approach is that a particular situation can be understood through many different narratives. The role of the psychologist becomes to walk together with the client into different landscapes, created by different narratives in order to co-construct a narrative, open for problem solving, and thereby create possible "exits" to the client's present situation. The principles of the narrative approach are closely associated with those of social constructionism and post-structuralism, in which language and performance are perceived to be constructing the meanings by which lives are understood. According to these approaches, language is perceived as capable of creating social and individual realities. Consequently, the narrative approach focuses on how the survivor talks about his life and how he performs accordingly to the stories he lives by. However, whether or not a particular narrative is acceptable to a particular torture survivor depends partly on larger, dominant narratives in the community and society about being a survivor, a refugee, and a citizen in general.

A young torture survivor from Iraq complained about not being a good father and husband, because he suffered from insomnia during nighttime and consequently had to rest during the late afternoon every day. At that time his wife was busy with their child and chores in the house. The torture survivor used a narrative of being without agency—that is, the ability to act in the way he would prefer, namely, helping the wife and playing with the child. He said that he was able to sleep in the afternoon, but that he woke up with nightmares. In the therapy, another narrative stating the good intentions was produced, and he agreed to try to perform the intentions by refraining from sleeping in the afternoon and instead spending the time with his family. This was very difficult for him, as he felt extremely tired after a period of time; however, he benefited from the changed attitudes toward him within the family.

Another survivor of torture told about being unable to support his family, because he could not get a job. He opposed living on social welfare and suffered from severe headaches, which started whenever he thought about his present position. During his history of torture, he was exposed to electrical maltreatment to his head. By focusing on his wish for a better future and his good intentions (his will) to support his family, a narrative of being capable of getting a job emerged. The social worker at the center managed to get a job for him, and his social position was changed by this.

In a country in Latin America a young man was referred for individual support. Fifteen years earlier he had survived a massacre in his village. One Sunday morning the military attacked the village during church time, where all the inhabitants gathered for the church service. The soldiers came on big trucks and started to shoot people. The young man, who at the time was a small boy, survived because an old man grabbed him by the hand and ran into the forest with him. They did not dare to go back to the village, so he grew up in another part of the country and did not know if members of his family had survived the massacre. As an adult he began to suffer from hearing the roaring of the motors of the vehicles that had brought the soldiers into the village. This symptom increased and became unbearable for him. In treatment the roaring sound was seen not as a symptom, but as a honoring of lost family members and as a wish to meet with the rest of his family. A trip was arranged to his village of origin and when he came to the village, he was immediately recognized by the surviving villagers, even though fifteen years have passed. He was greeted by people and met with the few surviving family members. He decided to stay in the village.

In another massacre in a village, a young boy was captured by the soldiers and forced to kill some women. Later the soldiers dropped him on a road near the capital. Twenty years later he was referred for treatment, because he suffered from severe flashbacks and nightmares about the killings. During treatment he decided to visit the village in which he had committed the atrocity against the women. He was recognized in the village and attempts of reconciliation were organized. But even though the people in the village accepted the fact that he had killed the women because he was just a scared little boy, he could not accept himself and left and never returned. So even though present problems are being addressed and practical solutions are tried, the impact of torture and organized violence may be very difficult to ameliorate.

As a practical tool, the model shown in Figure 5.1 has been developed in the support program for survivors of torture and organized violence. Arrow 1 signifies how the present life situation may contain problems and challenges, for instance economic problems, housing problems, and difficulties getting a job. The person in question will react to these problems in order to find useful and effective strategies to solve them (arrow 3). But in clinical cases the coping is impacted by bodily stored, implicit triggered reactions, which force the survivors to react in manners that were applicable to the torture situation—that is, dissociation and avoidance behavior. To reprocess these responses one must extinct the stored reactions by acting otherwise. This means that focus must be on actively addressing present problems in the present context of daily life (arrow 2). The only way to reinforce a new set of behavioral reactions is to start practicing these—and then to integrate

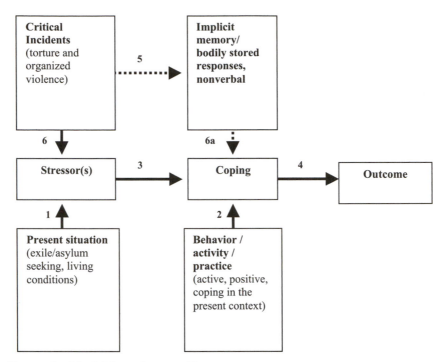

Figure 5.1 Model for a Support Program

the experience into an understanding, which integrates behavioral activities and verbal processing.

Torture/Organized Violence and Community Interventions

Wars today are often civil wars directed against poor segments of the population by terrorizing people through massacres, torture, and other forms of violent oppression, including rape, kidnapping, and execution of local leaders or arbitrarily picked people. Since World War II more than 165 wars have harried a variety of countries, most of them developing countries, where the wars have taken a great toll on already scarce resources. Millions of people—the vast majority civilians—have been killed or injured or have lost family members and homes. Millions have been forced to leave their homes and their countries, seeking asylum in other parts of their country or in a foreign country.

Above we described the clinical approach to helping individuals impacted by torture and organized violence. As stated previously only a certain percentage of the impacted people will develop symptoms in a pathologic way. The PTSD diagnosis is based on a strong individualistic approach to human life, which may cause challenges in non-Western contexts where different notions about the self and interpersonal relations exit (Bracken, 1998; Bracken, Giller, & Summerfield, 1995; Summerfield, 1999, 2001). Accordingly it is a challenge to the clinical approach to include contextual factors in terms of social, political, and cultural realities, which are central in shaping the experiences and responses to trauma. Cultural realities refers to cultural identity, spiritual or religious involvement and ontological beliefs, which strongly influence particular dominant concepts of self and community, illness, and healing. As results of political realities such as war, state oppression, and political violence, the social realities are often dispersed families and social networks, destroyed local economies and productions, and destroyed social values such as inter-human trust and faith.

In this section we will describe the community-based approach to *psychosocial rehabilitation* in war-torn communities. A community may be defined as a social entity with some degree of cohesion consisting of different interest groups that are motivated by economic, political, and religious motives and by specific values and cultural perspectives. Community-focused frameworks go beyond studying interpersonal dynamics by reflecting on practical and participatory solutions to people's problems. To understand problems and resources at the community level is to perceive them as embedded in practices, which employ and expand the material, communicative, and discursive context of the community.

The notion of social trauma may serve as a theoretical background for a conceptual framework about community-based rehabilitation. The idea behind community-based rehabilitation is that psychological problems and psychological processes need to be understood in relation to specific contexts of life—the specific circumstances of life experienced by a particular person or group. This means that problems are not understood as something inherent in the person, but rather as something embedded in the person's particular contexts of life, which are driven, influenced, and shaped by particular social, political, economical, religious, and cultural discourses and practices.

One of the main ideas behind the approach of community-based rehabilitation is that since people belonging to a particular community have particular living conditions in common, some of the problems experienced by the community members must be interlinked with their living conditions. This can be applied to war-torn communities, where a number of people suffer from the same contextual circumstances. Interventions directed toward such communities can be through the traditional support systems; however, often these systems have been destroyed and the interventions should then be aimed at reintegrating people into the community, identifying and transforming community networks, and the formation of a new normality of a supportive social fabric.

In postconflict societies, community-based interventions are about making use of resources in the community in order to provide support for affected people in the aftermath of the violence. Community resources of support and care may be used in an active and collaborative way, empowering the individual participating community members and the community as a whole. This may emerge in processes of collaborative decision making, the formation of support groups for people who share the same problems, and including vulnerable groups in the community.

Community-based development projects seek to generate changes, in that local groups become capable of gaining power to control decisions, and organize and control their own lives. The key initiative for community-based rehabilitation and development efforts is to create a set of values and practices conducive to peaceful coexistence through non-violent conflict resolution, capable of reducing the alarming levels of violence emergent in the communities. Hence, the approach of community-based rehabilitation focuses on real-life problems connected to violence and loss.

Example 1: A Community Program in Guatemala

From 1960 until 1996 Guatemala was subjected to civil war between the military and FAR (Fuerzas Armadas Rebeldes), a part of URNG (Unidad Revolucionaria National Guatemalteca). The effects on the civil population of the URNG insurgency strategy and in particular the government's and the military's counterinsurgency have been estimated to be more than 150,000 casualties, more than 50,000 people missing, approximately 1 million people internally displaced, and more than 100,000 external refugees. More than 440 villages were destructed. The war left many women as widows and many children as orphans.

The main psychosocial problems emerging from the civil war include mistrust, fear, insecurity, pain, guilt, grief, religious and moral confusion, and violent behavior (rape, robbery, domestic violence), absence of accepted leadership, and alcoholism. The communities are characterized by a loss of trust and hope, and by the mentioned symptoms of apathy and violent behavior, which continue the destruction of the social fabric (Anckermann et al., 2005).

ODHAG (Oficina de Derechos Humanos del Arzobispado de Guatemala) is a part of the Catholic Church's office of Social Services of the Archbishop of Guatemala. ODHAG was created in 1990 by an Archbishop decree on human rights violations against the most vulnerable part of the population. In the community-based psychosocial rehabilitation program, the organization endeavors to create actions aimed at supporting empowerment and economic and social development of communities impacted by the atrocities during the civil war.

The goal is to reinstate and construct a community-based story of what happened as a dominant narrative with a potential to include the individual narratives into a shared understanding. This leads to a strengthening of a social support system emerging from participation in communicative and practical activities. The importance of the social support is understood in developmental terms, which means that the social support system is seen as an integral component of a development of the living conditions in the community (i.e., production and distribution of supplies). This formulation of the goal consequently involves a shift in focus from symptoms of psycho-traumatology to real-life problems connected to torture, genocide, and violent oppression. These include substance abuse, domestic violence, criminality, marginalization (isolation and loneliness), lack of human rights and dignity, and lack of political and economic participation and options.

The overall goal of the program is to engage people in a shared striving for moments of happiness, where people rejoice in the joy of living. This concept is embedded in a spiritual and religious belief, and happiness is understood as being together in mutually giving and supportive social relationships. The good life with moments of happiness is thereby seen as connected to the sense of community and not to the idea of the psychology of the individual. This elucidates the focus on the community, where the individual is seen as embedded in the community as a participant, who gets their position and options (and constraints) from and by the community. Through this process the individual may be given the possibility to contribute in a unique way to the shared activities, communicative as well as practical.

The methodological idea of the project is the notion that social problems in a community must be solved at a practical level. In the slipstream of a war or genocide, the social order and the social identity of people and communities are disturbed or even destroyed. Due to the killing of friends, family members, and acquaintances, the social tissue of the community is riddled with losses of relations, trade, and meaning. The community is imbued with fear, anger, and despair, which emerge from the breakdown of the social fabric. The social, discursive, and practical activities, which beforehand ascribed social identity and power to the individual, are gone and replaced with violence and a lack of a shared narrative. On top of this they are strained by the sheer harshness of winning the daily bread and a place to live. These questions and problems are related to the community level and can only be solved at this level.

ODHAG's program starts with an assessment of the needs of the community. This is done through a process of collecting testimonies in the communities. In this process, focus is on the witnessed distortion of the social fabric of the community, and the individual stories are perceived and used as a contribution to the overall narrative about the distortion of the social tissue. In answer to an expressed need for help in the community, the program provides sessions in which the participants can reflect on and negotiate their present situation. This leads to community growth through a shared learning process, in which the participants discuss plans and how to implement these plans. It empowers the community to act in new ways of problem solving and development-oriented activities. Embedded in this endeavor is an ongoing striving for the promotion of human rights.

The response to the needs of the impacted community is implemented through the establishment of different support groups in the community. There are S*elf-help Groups*, where people with similar problems discuss how to solve the problems, and *Life Project Groups* with a practical assignment such as the building of a community house or the restoration of the water supplies. Third, there are *Formation Groups* with a focus on the overall developmental plans of the community, and finally are the *Reflection Groups* with a focus on psychosocial problems within the community. The groups are all interconnected and supportive of each other. Through the participation in these groups, the *social fabric* is organized through sharing of goals, practices, and activities.

In the first phases of the program, the collection of testimonies was predominant. The reflection groups were established as a forum for integration of the individual stories into a shared and commonly accepted narrative about what happened during the civil war. This provided the survivors of organized violence and torture with a new perspective on the individual suffering and strengthened the mutual understanding.

Through the telling and retelling, the plot of the narrative is changed. In the beginning of the telling, the individual positioned themselves by telling a story that produces shame, fear, and humiliation. Through the retelling, the narrative was changed—by the responses of the listeners and thus co-constructors of the story—to a story about human dignity, suffering, and possibilities for the future. This is done with respect for the suffering of the individual, through recognition of similarities between the individual stories. People recognized the suffering and were able to support others, practically and socially, from this understanding. They regained their dignity in this active and participatory process, where they reinterpreted their experience into a coherent story, which was comprehensible, thus making them recognizable as members of the community. Through this process, focus is gradually turned toward the production of a hope for a better future, which is actively gained through the solution of local problems. The pivotal point of the discussion eventually becomes planning of projects for the increase of the political power of the community and its plans for economic development and growth. An essential part of this is the continuous struggle against violence—organized as well as in relations within the community.

The specific objectives of the program are to

- Encourage a sense of belonging to the community
- Promote co-responsibility and full participation of everyone
- Favor respect for and practice of human rights
- Produce shared plans and commitments for the future
- Develop the capacity of listening, dialoguing, and reflecting on the reality
- Promote and strengthen a network of social relationships
- Achieve a sense of self-esteem and respect for others
- Establish a culture of peace, promoting reconciliation

In one particular program for widows, the organization managed to provide small houses and means for a production of handicrafts. The women survived on this. In a session, 22 women gathered in a community house joined by a psychologist and a priest. The psychologist showed a poster with a picture of the historical phases of the civil war (before, during, and after). Inspired by the picture, one of the women began to tell her story of the war:

> I lived in a village together with my husband and my children. We had eight children, three boys and five girls. One day the soldiers came. They started to shoot people. It was chaotic; they just killed everyone they saw. My husband and my sons were outside, working in the forest, but they were found and killed. I tried to save my daughters, but they were killed, so I ran to the forest with my 14–year-old daughter. In this way we survived, but we didn't dare to go back to the village, so we traveled to the capital, where I tried to get a job as a maid in a house. I succeeded in getting such a job, but I was not allowed to let my daughter stay in the house as well. They gave me a small room next to the kitchen to live in, but I never got any money, only a room to stay in and food from the kitchen. So I arranged that my daughter could work for some relatives, who lived in the capital. As the years went by we lost contact and my daughter later moved to another part of the country. In more than ten years I stayed in the house as a maid. I had lost everything—my family, my hope, my trust in other people. One day I decided to go back to my old village, even though it was without any real purpose. I just wanted to leave. Then I heard about this program, and I came here. Now I have been here for two years and I feel better now, because we work together here and we support each other. It is a bit like having a family.

At this point, another woman started to comment on the story:

> Your story is very much similar to mine. And I agree with you on that coming here was like a new beginning, because you have people to talk with and to laugh with. Now I can laugh again, which I couldn't for a very long time. But I feel that we are losing it a bit. In the beginning we were better at supporting each other. Now, if someone is ill, we cannot be sure that someone will visit her and help her if needed. It is like we are more selfish now.

A long discussion about this began, and it included an analysis of the possible background for the changes and a decision on becoming better at providing social support to each other, including practical help and even material help when someone needed that. Some of the younger women had small children, and it was pointed out that they needed help to look after the children. The meeting ended in a good atmosphere with sharing of anecdotes about situations where the needed help was given in ways that afterwards seemed funny. So people laughed and enjoyed the companionship of the others.

Example 2: Social Trauma in the Philippines

Balay is an organization in the Philippines that provides psychosocial development and rehabilitation to communities affected by torture and organized violence (Anasarias et al., 2005). The focus is on the community as a whole and rehabilitation is aimed at the attainment of healing, empowerment, and development in the communities that Balay serves. In the island of Mindanao where Balay currently focuses its attention, several violent conflicts have happened over the past decades that involve disagreements between what is referred to as the Tri-people. The three peoples are the Moros (Moslems), the Settlers (Christians), and the indigenous people. This conflict affects civilians because it triggers mistrust and tension among the peoples. Organized political violence characterized by coercion, deprivation, and physical and psychological assaults, such as armed conflicts, have produced generations of traumatized communities of displaced peoples.

The work of Balay focuses on helping people become active participants in the rehabilitation process of their own communities through various intervention strategies that include curative, preventive, and proactive elements. The strategies range from community planning, community dialogs, local rituals, peace camps, capability building, psychological processing, and education to participation in actions for social change.

In the context of conflict-affected civilians in Mindanao, experiences of organized political violence and forcible displacement may bring about collective suffering. As such it affects not only individuals and families but also entire communities. When the armed conflict started, it brought fear, anxiety, and loss to survivors, and it also caused damage to livelihood and environment of affected populations. Moreover, it tore away sociocultural institutions and social support, and fostered mistrust, social tension, and discord. The results of the organized political violence included dispersed families and destroyed social networks, ruined local economies, and loss of social values. In Mindanao, organized political violence has resulted in profound psychosocial effects at the community level, where many communities experience social dysfunction due to the destruction of the domains of community resources and dynamics, aggravating social tensions and climates of mistrust and fear, prejudice, and animosity toward the other group as well as among people.

In 2000, more than one million people were affected by the total war policy declared by the government against the Moros. In February 2003, armed conflict broke out again and this time the fighting, which lasted for four months, produced 400,000 internally displaced people. During this period of emergency, Balay focused on the needs of the people and adopted a survival response, providing medical and food supply and establishing temporary places for worship. Whenever it was needed, Balay would establish alternative schools for children on the evacuation site. Later when the families had settled down in the evacuation centers, Balay would introduce stress management for the children in the form of play activities. Group debriefing, stress management activities, and food preparation committees were likewise organized for adults.

The majority of the psychological processing conducted by Balay would be in the form of mass interventions in large groups of people who were gathered and encouraged to speak out, and express their feelings by crying or being angry. The groups would either be comprised of people from different ethnic backgrounds or they would be comprised of people from the same ethnic background. Most groups would start off as a homogenous group and after having worked with Balay for awhile, it would begin to participate in sessions with a group from a different ethnic background. Through this process, people were encouraged to try to make sense of what has happened and discover where their feelings of anger and resentment come from. Usually they come to the point of understanding that all the people of the community, regardless of their ethnic and religious background, are victims and survivors of violence, conflict, and war. Also, rituals for healing and for resuming the good relationships are practiced.

This community-based strategy for psychosocial rehabilitation may provide conditions that will reduce conflicts, tensions, and misunderstandings, eventually improving the mental health and the psychosocial well-being of individuals. The objectives of the community-based psychosocial rehabilitation approach is to achieve healing in the communities, in individuals and families, and to achieve empowerment and community mobilization, enabling communities to act for peace and human rights promotion.

To rehabilitate a community displaying *social trauma* requires a perspective, which incorporates political, cultural, and social realities as essential components of its perspective as well as its priorities, viewing the psychological processes in a context of the actual social and political circumstances and factors, thereby making inequalities and oppressions visible.

Balay focuses almost entirely on the community as a whole and on members participating in the process of restoring their own community on an interpersonal as well as on a practical level. The interventions of Balay emphasize very concrete and practical interventions, such as bridging cultural misunderstanding, providing livelihood support, community capability building, or working for future peace. Among the intervention activities agreed upon by Balay and community partners are: creating peace camps, arranging economic support and educational assistance for youth and children, restoring farming activities, human rights seminars, and making psychological processing available for those members who are severely traumatized and in need of individual attention.

Summary of the Community Approach

Communities who have been subjected to trauma through wars and violent conflicts are in need of rehabilitation and healing. The programs may start during the time of disaster and continue in the years following the end of the war, genocide, torture, and organized violence. In Guatemala, ODHAG's community-based program includes three levels of intervention:

- Community *healing* addresses the social and individual reactions to the violent oppression, such as mistrust, fear, destructive behavior, and lack of identity and self-esteem—all leading to a disruption of the social fabric in the community. The overall objectives of community healing are to support the community members and develop appropriate knowledge and skills useful for the healing process in the affected community. Such processes incorporate that the participants express their problems and opinions and that these are reflected upon in the group in a positive manner. This way of using the group process to actively build up a trustful social support system also (re)-establishes the links between the individual and the other members of the community.
- Community *empowerment* intends to strengthen community members' social and organizational participation in decision-making processes in local and national politics, thereby creating a social structure within the community capable of preventing violence. The overall objectives of community empowerment are to support positive changes in interpersonal attitudes, which convey new practices supportive of participatory community development. This includes the promotion of awareness of community interests as interpreted by the community members. The methods for community empowerment include communication and participation, accomplished through group sessions. Empowerment springs from the development of new ways of communicating and acting together.
- Community *development* aims at engaging people in participatory social actions, leading to locally based economic development and community welfare. The process encompasses joint activities, labeled as community *life projects*, which revolve around shared initiative and collaboration in a present–future perspective, leading to sustainable community development. The life projects provide a factual improvement in the living condition in the community. This includes that the reflection group has developed into an integral part of the community and has become a forum for discussion and planning of development projects in the community.

The key message of the community approach is that psychosocial healing and community empowerment are necessary as parts of strengthening community capacities for participation in political and economic development. The key initiative for community development efforts is to create a set of values and practices conducive to peaceful coexistence through nonviolent conflict resolution, capable of reducing the alarming levels of violence. The fundamental idea behind the community development approach is to build and strengthen local resources and volunteer spirit within a multiplication and knowledge sharing strategy. Such efforts may contribute to a much more fundamental reconciliation in postconflict societies with very limited resources and numerous poor, socially excluded, and traumatized people.

Conclusion

Activity and participation are important components in individual treatment as well as in community-based support of survivors of torture and organized violence. A recent study of 80 files of cases of rehabilitation at the Rehabilitation and Research Centre for Torture Victims (RCT; Berliner & Mogensen, 2004) showed that a positive outcome was related to the level of meaningful activities in daily living, social networking (social support), and a decreased level of felt pain (the impact of pain on the functioning in daily living). The challenges of meaningfulness, social support, and lowered pain may be addressed through different methods of interventions in psychotherapy and in the community approach.

The treatment approach may be relevant for torture survivors, who do not have the options of participating in meaningful activities with other people or do not benefit from such activities. The vast majority of survivors of torture and organized violence may be best supported by community programs in which they partake in the process of community healing, community empowerment, and community development—because these activities comprise participation in meaningful activities propelling processes of reconciliation, democratic debates fostering social justice and promotion of human rights, and development of living conditions through economic and institutional development (schools, hospitals, transport).

Activity and participation seem to be the outcome of good rehabilitation programs—and it may be seen that efficient programs start out by providing options for people to participate as the very core of the program itself, because the atrocities of torture and organized violence embody cruel intentions of oppressing the dignity and basic human rights of the surviving communities and fellow human beings.

Acknowledgments

The treatment approach section of this chapter emanates from an inspiring cooperation with Stephen Regel, Director at the Nottinghamshire Health Services Centre for Trauma Studies and Trauma Services. Psychologist Pernille Ianev and psychotherapist Lone Jacobsen have contributed to the development of the concept of psychotherapeutic treatment methods at RCT as presented in this chapter.

The concept of the community approach has been developed with developmental economist Finn Kjaerulf and through profound discussions with Ernesto Anasarias, Head of the Research Unit at the Balay organization in the Philippines and medical doctor Sonia Anckermann and psychologist Manuel Dominguez at ODHAG in Guatemala.

References

Allodi, F. A. (1994). Post-traumatic stress disorder in hostages and victims of torture. *Psychiatric Clinics of North America, 17*(2), 279–288.

Amnesty International. (1997). Report 1997. U.S.: Amnesty International Publications.

Amris, S. (2005). Chronic pain in survivors of torture—psyche or soma? In P. Berliner, J. Arenas, & J. O. Haagensen (Eds.), *Torture and organized violence: Contributions to a professional human rights response* (pp. 31–70). Copenhagen: Danish Psychology Publishers.

Anasarias, E., Berliner, P., Ianev, P., & Mikkelsen, E. N. (2005). Social trauma in the Philippines. In P. Berliner, J. Arenas, & J. O. Haagensen (Eds.), *Torture and organized violence: Contributions to a professional human rights response*. Copenhagen: Danish Psychology Publishers.

Anckermann, S., Dominguez, M., Soto, N., Kjaerulf, F., Berliner, P., & Mikkelsen, E. N. (2005). Psychosocial support to large numbers of traumatised people in post-conflict societies: An approach to community development in Guatemala. *Journal of Community and Applied Social Psychology, 15*(2), 136–152.

Barudy, J. (1989). A programme of mental health for political refugees: dealing with the invisible pain of political exile. *Social Science and Medicine, 28*, 715–727.

Becker, R., Haidary, Z., Kang, V., Marin, L., Nguyen, T., Phraxayavong, V., & Ramathan, N. (1990). The two-practitioner model: Bicultural workers in a service for torture and trauma survivors. In P. Hosking (Ed.), *Hope after horror: Helping survivors of torture and trauma*. Sydney: Uniya.

Berliner, P., Jacobsen, L., Ianev, P., & Mikkelsen, E. N. (2005) Psychotherapy with torture survivors—Solution oriented methods. In P. Berliner, J. Arenas, & J. O. Haagensen, (Eds.), *Torture and organized violence: Contributions to a professional human rights response*. Copenhagen: Danish Psychology Publishers.

———, Mikkelsen, E. N., Bovbjerg, A., & Wiking, M. (2004). Psychotherapy treatment of torture survivors. *International Journal of Psychosocial Rehabilitation, 8*, 85–96.

———, & Mogensen, L. (2004). *The practice of rehabilitation—a study of case files at RCT.* A working paper, RCT, Copenhagen.

Bracken, P. J. (1998). Hidden agendas: Deconstructing post traumatic stress disorder. In P. J. Bracken & C. Petty (Eds.), *Rethinking the trauma of war* (pp. 38–50). London: Free Association Press.

———, Giller, J., & Summerfield, D. (1995). Psychological responses to war and atrocity: the limitations of current concepts. *Social Science and Medicine, 40*, 1073–1082.

Bronkhorst, D. (1995). Truth and reconciliation. Obstacles and opportunities for human rights. Amsterdam: Amnesty International Dutch Section.

Carlson E. B., Rosser-Hagan, R. (1994). Cross-cultural response to trauma: a study of traumatic experiences and posttraumatic symptoms in Cambodian refugees. *Journal of Traumatic Stress. 7*(1), 43–58.

Charney, D. S., Deutsch, A. Y., & Krystal, J. H. (1993). Psychobiological mechanisms of post-traumatic stress disorder. *Archives of General Psychiatry, 50*, 294–305.

Cunningham, M., & Cunningham, J. D. (1997). Patterns of symptomatology and patterns of torture and trauma experiences in resettled refugees. *Australian and New Zealand Journal of Psychiatry, 31*, 555–565.

Doerr-Zegers, O., Hartman, L., Lira, E., & Weinstein, E. (1992). Torture: Psychiatric sequelae and phenomenology. *Psychiatry, 55,* 177–184.

Goenjian, A. K., Steinberg, A. M., & Najarian, L.M. (2000). Prospective study of posttraumatic stress, anxiety, and depressive reactions after earthquake and political violence. *American Journal of Psychiatry, 157*(6), 911–916.

Hackman, A. (1993). Behavioural and cognitive psychotherapies: past history, current applications and future registration issues. *Behavioural and Cognitive Psychotherapy, 21* (supplement 1), 1–75.

Horvath-Lindberg, J. (1988). Victims of torture. The Swedish experience. Chapter 4. Torture and the infliction of other forms of organized violence. In D. Miserez (Ed.), *Refugees—the trauma of exile. The humanitarian role of the Red Cross and Red Crescent.* Geneva: Martinus Nihoff Publishers.

International Rehabilitation Council for Torture Victims (IRCT). (1997). Need for international funding of rehabilitation services for torture victims. *Torture, 7,* 41–42.

Langer, L.L. (1997). The alarmed vision: Social suffering and holocaust atrocity. In A. Kleinman et al. (Eds.), *Social Suffering.* Berkeley: University of California Press.

Lavik, N. J., Hauff, E., Skrondal, A., & Solberg, O. (1996). Mental disorder among refugees and the impact of persecution and exile: some findings from an outpatient population. *British Journal of Psychiatry, 169,* 726–732.

McFarlane, A. C. (2004). Assessing PTSD and comorbidity: Issues in differential diagnosis. In J. P. Wilson & B. Drozdek (Eds.), *Broken spirits. The treatment of traumatized asylum seekers, refugees, war and torture victims.* New York: Brunner-Routledge.

The Ministry for Internal Affairs and Health. (2001). *Report from the working committee on rehabilitation of traumatized refugees.* Copenhagen, Denmark.

Mollica, R. F. (1988). The trauma history: The psychiatric care of refugee survivors of violence and torture. In F. M. Ochberg (Ed.), *Post traumatic therapy in victims of violence.* New York: Brunner/Mazel.

Orellana, P. (1989). *Violaciones a los Derechos Humanos e Información.* Colección Documentos. Fundación de Ayuda Social de las Iglesias Cristianas. Santiago, Chile.

Quiroga, J., & Gurr, R. (1998). Approaches to torture rehabilitation: A desk-study, covering effects, cost effectiveness, participation and sustainability. Copenhagen: RCT.

Reeler, A. P. (1994). Is torture a post traumatic stress disorder? *Torture,* 59–63.

Regel, S., & Berliner, P. (2005). Cognitive behavioral therapy with torture survivors: A case report. In P. Berliner, J. Arenas, & J. O. Haagensen (Eds.), *Torture and organized violence: Contributions to a professional human rights response.* Copenhagen: Danish Psychology Publishers.

Roche, P.A. (2002). *Evidence based reasons for conducting long-term and multidisciplinary research into the management of post-torture pain: A review of the international scientific literature on pain and application to pain management in survivors of torture.* Copenhagen: RCT.

Sherman, J. J. (1998). Effects of psychotherapeutic treatments for PTSD: A meta-analysis of controlled clinical trials. *Journal of Trauma Stress, 11*(3), 413–435.

Silove, D. (2004). The global challenge of asylum. In J. P. Wilson & B. Drozdek (Eds.), *Broken spirits. The treatment of traumatized asylum seekers, refugees, war and torture victims.* New York: Brunner-Routledge.

Skinner, D. (1997). Torture survivors in the long term after liberation. *Torture, 7*(1), 4–8.

Somnier, E., & Genefke, I. K. (1986). Psychotherapy for victims of torture. *British Journal of Psychiatry*, 149, 323–329.

———, Vesti, P., Kastrup, M., and Genefke, I. K. (1992). Psychosocial consequences of torture: Current knowledge and evidence. In M. Basoglu (Ed.), *Torture and its consequences. Current treatment approaches.* Cambridge, UK: Cambridge University Press.

Southwick, S. M., Bremner, D., Krystal, J. H., & Charney, D. S. (1994). Psychobiologic research in post-traumatic stress disorder. *Psychiatric Clinics of North America*, 17, 251–264.

Summerfield, D. (1999). A critique of seven assumptions behind psychological trauma programmes in war affected areas. *Social Science and Medicine, 48,* 1449–1462.

———. (2001). The invention of post traumatic stress disorder and the social usefulness of a psychiatric category. *British Medical Journal, 322,* 95–98.

Turner, S., & Gorst-Unsworth, C. (1993). Psychosocial sequelae of torture. In J. Wilson & B. Raphael (Eds.), *International handbook of traumatic stress syndrome,* New York: Kluwer Academic Publishers.

United Nations. (1984). Convention against Torture and Other Cruel, Inhuman or Degrading Treatment or Punishment. UN. Doc. A/39/51.

van Etten, M. L., & Taylor, S. (1998). Comparative efficacy of treatments for post-traumatic stress disorder: A meta-analysis. *Clinical Psychology and Psychotherapy, 5,* 126–144.

WHO. (2001). *International classification of functioning, disability and health.* Geneva: WHO.

CHAPTER 6

MANAGING STRESS IN HUMANITARIAN AID WORKERS: THE ROLE OF THE HUMANITARIAN AID ORGANIZATION

John H. Ehrenreich

Humanitarian aid work is intrinsically stressful. Humanitarian aid workers often live and work in physically demanding and/or unpleasant conditions, characterized by heavy workloads, long hours and chronic fatigue, and lack of privacy and personal space. They are often separated from their families for extended periods. They complain of inadequate time, resources, and support to do the job asked of them and of inadequate recognition for the job they do. They face conflict within their work team, created or intensified by prolonged close proximity and intimate interdependence. They experience conflict with local authorities and moral anguish over the choices they often have to make (Who to help and who not? Deal with corrupt or vicious warlords or militias or not be permitted to provide aid at all?). They face chronic danger. They are repeatedly exposed to tales of traumatization and personal tragedy or to gruesome scenes and they may, themselves, have horrific experiences.

While stress can be a source of growth and although many humanitarian aid workers withstand the rigors of their work without adverse effects, many others do not. Both anecdotal reports (see, among others, Britt & Adler, 1999; Danieli, 1996, 2002; Holtz, Salama, Lopes Cardozo, & Gotway, 2002; McFarlane, 2004; Smith, 2000; Smith, Agger, Danieli, & Weisaeth, 1996; and Stearns, 1993) and several recent empirical studies (Eriksson, 1997; Eriksson, Bjorck, & Abernethy, 2003; Eriksson, Snider, deJong, Carr, & Lopes Cardozo, 2002; Eriksson, Vande Kemp, Gorsuch, Hoke, & Foy, 2001; Holtz, Salama, Lopes Cardozo, & Gotway, 2002; Lopes Cardozo & Salama, 2002) have abundantly documented the negative emotional consequences of humanitarian aid work. As many as one-third or more of recently returned expatriate staff of humanitarian aid organizations show clinically significant signs of emotional distress. Similar levels of distress have been found among national staff of international and local humanitarian aid organizations and among human rights workers. The adverse emotional effects of work in the humanitarian aid field may include post-traumatic stress syndromes (resulting from direct exposure to or witnessing traumatizing experiences), "vicarious" or "secondary" traumatization (resulting from repeated exposure to the stories and witnessing the suffering of direct victims of trauma), depression, pathological grief reactions, anxiety, and multiple psychosomatic complaints.

The Impact of Stress on Humanitarian Aid Workers

One common reaction of both humanitarian aid agencies and aid workers themselves to the evidence of the adverse effects of stress on aid workers is to deny its significance. In the face of the overwhelming needs of recipients, they argue, the relatively minor distress experienced by aid workers is of minor concern. However, the consequences of adverse responses to stress on the part of humanitarian workers go far beyond the distress experienced by the staff members themselves. Stress adversely affects the ability of aid workers to carry out the humanitarian aid agency's goals of providing services to those directly impacted by a disaster or other humanitarian emergency.

Although there is only anecdotal evidence for this from the humanitarian aid world itself, there is an abundance of evidence from other industries (including commercial sectors such as transportation and non-profit sectors such as education and health care). The evidence indicates that, regardless of industry, chronic stress and burnout have significantly negative impacts on the ability of the employing agency to carry out its purposes. (For a review of the negative impact of burnout on work performance, see Maslach, Schaufeli, & Leiter, 2000; more severe forms of reaction to stress are even more disabling.)

1. Staff members suffering from chronic stress and burnout have less commitment to their employing agency and show higher rates of turnover. This leads to a loss of skilled, experienced staff in the field as well as increased recruitment and training costs.
2. Staff members suffering from chronic stress and burnout have higher accident rates and higher rates of illness, resulting in more absenteeism and increased health services utilization (and with the latter, increased health insurance costs).
3. "Stressed out" staff members are poor decision makers and may behave in ways that place themselves or other members of the team at risk or disrupt the effective functioning of the team.
4. Chronic stress and burnout are directly associated with lowered efficiency and effectiveness in carrying out their assigned tasks.

Distressed staff members may become "over-involved" or "over-identify" with beneficiary populations or, conversely, become callous and apathetic toward beneficiaries. They may engage in self-destructive behaviors such as drinking and dangerous driving and interpersonal conflict with co-workers or with family members may increase.

Managing Stress: The Organizational Role

Fortunately, although humanitarian aid worker stress has adverse effects on the ability of the agency to carry out its mission, at least some stressors can be prevented or lessened, and the effects of stress on individual staff members can be mitigated by actions undertaken by individual staff members, by managers and supervisors, or by the agency as a whole.

There is a large literature addressing stress management by individuals. Several recent publications specifically address the issue of actions that can be taken by individual humanitarian aid workers to reduce their exposure to stressors and lessen the likelihood of adverse reactions to the remaining stressors (Ajdukoviç & Ajdukoviç, 2000; Centre for Humanitarian Psychology, 2004; Ehrenreich, 2004; Fawcett, 2002, 2003; United Nations High Commissioner for Refugees [UNHCR], 2001). Less attention has been given to actions that can be undertaken by the agencies that employ aid workers to reduce the stress experienced by their staff and its adverse consequences for both staff and the organization. (See, however, Antares Foundation, 2004, also reprinted in Ehrenreich, 2004; Fawcett, 2003; Quick, Quick, Nelson, & Hurrell, 1997.) This topic is the focus of the remainder of this chapter.

Managing stress in staff of humanitarian aid organizations is an essential ingredient in enabling the organization to fulfill its field objectives, as well as necessary to protect the well-being of the individual staff members themselves. We will consider four essential elements of an effective organizational response:

1. Developing a general organizational commitment to creating a culture of stress management
2. Providing appropriate effective leadership and efficient management at all levels of the organization
3. Promoting team cohesion
4. Developing specific organizational policies and practices that reduce stress and its effects

These elements overlap considerably, but for expositional purposes will be treated separately.

General Organizational Commitment

The first step in an organizational response is for the agency to make a *commitment* that stress management is important. Many returned humanitarian workers report that their organizations are not very sympathetic to or supportive of staff that experience work-related emotional distress. They also describe a "macho" culture of denial among aid workers themselves in terms of the negative psychosocial impact of exposure to the stresses of humanitarian work. "If you can't stand the heat, get out of the kitchen." "If you go out in the rain, expect to get wet." Many aid workers feel (possibly correctly) that reacting emotionally to their work will expose them to the ridicule of other workers and interfere with their career prospects.

Several surveys have provided a more nuanced view. Although most agencies employing aid workers are aware that adverse stress reactions are a risk for relief workers, psychosocial support mechanisms for staff in their organizations are "underdeveloped" (Ehrenreich, 2004; MacNair, 1995; McCall & Salama, 1999; World Health Organization, 1998). There is little effort to screen potential staff with respect to risk of adverse responses to stress; pre-assignment training in stress management and conflict resolution is generally minimal or omitted altogether; support for stress management in the field is spotty and occurs on an "as-needed" basis; and few organizations provide any formal support for staff after the end of their assignment. Even fewer organizations report systematic organizational efforts to address potential sources of stress rooted in the practices of the organization itself.

As will be discussed below, a wide variety of organizational practices have the potential to either help protect employees from stress or increase the distress staff experience. The organization that is committed to reducing stress self-consciously examines the stress implications of both existing and newly proposed policies and practices. Formally or informally, it makes an analysis analogous to an "environmental impact statement." It asks, "What will the effects of this policy or practice be on the stress experience of our staff?" The answer to this question is only one factor in decision making, of course, but the mechanisms should be in place to assure that it is not ignored altogether.

The organization also seeks to establish an organizational culture in which stress prevention and mitigation is a priority. It makes it clear, explicitly and through practice, that *failure* to engage in appropriate stress management practices will be a blot on the record of individual staff members, supervisors, and managers.

Leadership and Management

Leadership is probably the single most important element in reducing staff stress. One dimension of leadership, "leadership style," has to do with how the leader treats staff, how decisions are made and communicated, and how staff are motivated, encouraged, assisted in doing their jobs, and rewarded. A second dimension, "moral leadership," includes how the leader acts, inspires staff, creates a sense of vision, and transmits his or her own personality, vision, and values to the organization. A third dimension, "management skill," comprises the practical abilities needed to organize and carry out the programs, policies, and activities of the organization.

A large body of organizational research has established that "leadership style" and quality of "moral leadership" have a major impact both on work effectiveness and on the work-related stress experienced by a wide variety of workers, including operating room staff (doctors and nurses), teachers, high school guidance counselors, social workers, and residential mental health workers. (For recent examples, see, *inter alia,* Bell & Carter, 2004; Gellis, 2002; Harris, Day, & Hadfield, 2003; Langner, 2002; Lubofsky, 2002; Remy, 1999; Rome, 2000.)

Both the highest work effectiveness and the lowest employee stress come from leaders whose leadership style inspires trust and confidence:

- Good leaders are technically proficient in their own jobs and understand the work of staff members.
- Good leaders are good problem solvers and decision makers. The degree to which a leader consults with staff and involves them in decision making may vary, depending on the amount of information available to the leader, the motivational level and experience of staff, the specific situation, and time pressures. However, to the extent that the specific conditions permit (and they usually do), a participatory (consultative) style is usually associated with lower staff stress.
- Good leaders are good role models. Leaders lead not only by what they say, but also by what they do.
- Good leaders look out for the well-being of staff and are concerned about their human needs as well as their task performance. They encourage staff to take responsibility and develop their technical skills and personal capacities, and they praise and reward success.
- Good leaders treat each employee as an individual and provide individual personal and psychological support, on an "as-needed" basis, without being intrusive.
- Good leaders keep staff informed (and keeps informed of what staff are doing). They communicate the organization's overall vision and goals and how employees can contribute to realizing these.
- Good leaders seek to build team cohesion and encourage teamwork.

"Bad" leadership is itself a source of stress, amplifying any external sources of workplace stress. The author recalls one of his own bosses who, when resources were plentiful, insisted on making all hiring decisions and other resource allocation decisions himself, with no consultation with staff, but who, when cutbacks were in order, asked the staff to make the decisions as to who and what should be eliminated. Needless to say, good staff morale did not result!

"Good" leadership not only prevents the stress *caused* by bad leadership, but also *helps protect staff from stress originating outside the organization itself.* A widely publicized recent example was the leadership provided by New York City Mayor Giuliani in the days immediately following 9/11. Despite his more generally autocratic leadership style (which, following my earlier discussion, may not provide a positive model for most humanitarian aid organizations), in the post-9/11 crisis his strengths appeared. What was significant about Giuliani's role was not the specific programs he established or the specific actions he took, but rather the example of calmness and courage and hopefulness he provided, his ability to express the collective feelings of grief without being overwhelmed, the sense of "we can handle this" that he helped to create, and the encouragement and support he provided for people to resume normal routines.

The concrete management skills of the leader also have an impact on staff stress. The principal risk here is bad management practices and inept management skills on the part of supervisors, field managers, country directors, and others in the organizational chain. Badly run meetings, unclear job descriptions or assignments, poor prioritizing of tasks, confused or conflicted lines of authority, confusion as to who reports to whom, failure to obtain supplies that are needed, incompetence in making budget requests and managing funds, hiring inappropriate local staff, and inconsistent supervision all create stress for staff. By contrast, good management creates an environment in which staff members are able to do their jobs effectively.

Despite clear evidence that leadership plays an important role in both increasing team efficiency and protecting workers against the adverse effects of stress, leadership abilities are often not a major factor in agency hiring decisions. Most operational leaders (e.g., country directors, project directors) were initially field staff. Few advertisements recruiting for such positions indicate any requirement for formal training in management and leadership skills, and, in most instances, if a potential team leader has good field experience and technical skills, lack of clear evidence of leadership skills is not an obstacle to selection. The advantage of this in terms of ensuring that leaders have the technical skills and experience needed for their job is obvious, but it contributes to neglect of the leadership role.

Fortunately, while it may be that some people are "naturally" good leaders, basic leadership skills can be taught. Managerial and supervisory staff can be trained to be good leaders. In recruiting and hiring managerial and supervisory staff, organizations should assess their leadership qualities as well as what positions a person has held or what their technical competencies are. Leadership training should be required for all staff expected to lead teams. Such training should include a focus on interpersonal skills, group dynamics, team functioning, and conflict resolution, as well as instruction in practical management skills. A hands-on component, under the supervision and guidance of a training specialist, should be part of this training. Specific training in recognizing signs of individual and team distress, in judging how stress is affecting individual and team function, and in basic stress management interventions should be part of this training (Fawcett, 2003). Numerous schools, organizations, and consultants can assist in providing leadership training for individuals or for organizations, and online training programs are also readily available.

Team Building

Even after highly traumatic experiences, the personal capacities and activities of the individuals directly experiencing the stress account for much less of the psychological outcome than factors within the control of the organization, such as leadership and social (team) support.

The amount of social support people have is a key variable in determining their responses to stressful events. (For a review of studies of the impact of social support on vulnerability to post-traumatic stress disorder [PTSD], an extreme stress reaction, see Resick, 2001.) While an individual aid worker may (and should) have many sources of social support, including family, friends, professional associations, church groups, and community or recreational organizations, his or her *work team* is of special importance. The members of the work team share a common goal—work—and often live in close proximity to each other, and share hardships, dangers, successes, and failures. At its best, the team provides an enormously powerful level of protection against the stresses of humanitarian work. At its worst, it becomes itself a source of stress.

Team building starts with central organizational policies and practices. The agency identifies team skills as part of the qualifications they are looking for in prospective employees and seeks to assess these in interviewing and other selection procedures. It provides training in teamwork as part of its orientation process. It seeks out ways to build team cohesion as a by-product of other activities (e.g., providing a common safety and security training experience for the members of a team). It makes team-building skills an *essential* requirement in selecting people for leadership positions. It trains supervisors and mangers in conflict management and other skills needed for maintaining team cohesion. It systematically attends to and reviews team functioning at every level of the organization. It has policies in place for addressing the problem of dysfunctional teams and for addressing the problem of an individual staff member who has good skills but is having difficulty functioning in his or her team.

At the level of the team leader, several practices enhance team cohesion:

- The team leader fosters communication among team members. He or she ensures team members know what the other members of the team are doing, the difficulties and dangers they face, and the successes they have.
- The team leader builds bonds among team members by creating opportunities for team members to work with one another, to meet together, and to share common experiences. He or she encourages opportunities for team members to get to know each other personally, outside of work as well as at work, and personally know each team member (though not necessarily intimately).
- The team leader creates an atmosphere in which problems, concerns, and worries can be voiced in a non-judgmental atmosphere and without

fear of negative consequences, and he or she enlists team members in support of one another and in collective problem solving.

- The team leader is alert to evidence of cliques, bickering, envy, and backbiting, and responds promptly to address any of these and to analyze their underlying causes. He or she is careful to treat all team members equitably, fairly, justly, and reasonably, and if any team member does not feel this is the case, the issue is addressed.

- The team leader is alert to any evidence of sexual, racial, or ethnic harassment or any other form of harassment. He or she moves promptly to protect the victim(s) of any harassment and to make it clear that such behavior is unacceptable.

- The team leader does not seek a false show of unity, where unity does not in fact exist, but creates an atmosphere in which differing opinions are valued. At the same time, the leader creates mechanisms that permit reaching decisions, even if differences persist, in a way that lets all members of the team feel they can accept the decisions.

- The team leader is alert to signs of stress in individual staff members. He or she monitors staff, formally or informally (on a routine basis, as well as in the wake of crises), and urges upon staff adherence to basic stress management routines (e.g., taking adequate time off, taking breaks, maintaining reasonable hours, maintaining good nutrition, adhering to safety and security procedures, and engaging in stress-reduction exercises). The team leader is prepared to provide team members with basic support in the wake of unusually stressful incidents and to request help from the central organization when levels of stress appear that cannot reasonably be handled. The leader models good individual stress management practices.

One particular set of issues that the team leader recognizes as a potential threat to team cohesion consists of tensions in the relationships between national and international staff. The expatriate is a guest in the receiving culture, but often plays the role of a dominant guest, who insists that his or her own efficiency and interaction rules must be followed within the work group. Expatriates are usually paid far better, have more job security, and have a clearer career path both within their agency and in the humanitarian enterprise as a whole. The expatriate will eventually leave; the national staff member will remain behind, often without the financial support of the currently employing agency. At a deeper level, many of what are now the poorer countries of the world were, not very long ago, colonies or dependencies of the same countries that now are sending humanitarian assistance, and even now they remain in an economically dependent relationship. Europeans and North Americans, even those whose home country did not directly colonize the land of their humanitarian work, may share skin color and certainly share culture with people from the country that did. From the perspective of the recipients of assistance, long histories of disempowerment and heavily inculcated feelings of cultural inferiority and expectations of deference and dependency complicate any relationships, however superficially benign, with those from outside. There are no simple formulas for dealing with these issues of power, but a conscious awareness of them (for both expatriates and national staff) and a self-conscious effort to base interactions on humility, mutual respect, transparency, and true partnership is a good starting point.

Specific Organizational Policies and Practices

Most of the policies discussed above involve direct interactions between the individual worker, the team, and local supervisors and managers. There are additional organizational policies and programs relevant to reducing stress in aid workers that are carried out at the level of the whole humanitarian aid organization or that do not fit neatly into the categories discussed above.

- The organization itself has a clear structure. Lines of authority and reporting are transparent and unambiguous. Every staff member has a clear job description and is clear as to his or her organizational responsibilities. Stress management is part of the job responsibilities of supervisors and managers. More generally, the organization's human resources policies and practices are in conformity with the industry standards described in the InterAction (1997) *Private Voluntary Organization (PVO) Standards* and the People in Aid (2003) *Code of Good Practice.*
- In recruiting, hiring, and assigning staff, the organization matches the prospective staff member's skills and expertise to the task demands of the proposed assignment. It also assesses the prospective staff member's experience of stress and trauma and his or her ability to cope with the expectable stresses of the assignment, and it advises, makes assignment decisions, and provides training taking this into account.
- Before the organization sends a staff member to the field, it provides the employee with a clear operational orientation. This includes making sure staff understand the organization's mission, both in general and in the specific project to which the worker will be assigned; making sure staff understand the risks they are likely to encounter and training them in safety and security procedures; teaching staff about stress reactions and providing training in personal stress management; and providing training in conflict management and team functioning. The orientation is repeated when an experienced worker is being sent to a new assignment.
- The agency periodically scrutinizes its own "routine" practices for the effect they will have on employee stress and undertakes to modify them to lessen stress. It reviews its paperwork and other bureaucratic procedures and requirements to reduce them as much as possible. It undertakes to provide adequate facilities in the field for employees to eat, wash, rest, and have some privacy. It ensures that staff will have adequate

access to health services, including mental health services. It makes sure that it has clear and adequate safety and security procedures in place and that it has procedures to make sure that these are observed.

- The agency has a clear policy of supporting staff members' individual activities that lessen stress. For example, it understands the adverse impact of prolonged periods of sustained work in individuals and *insists* (not just permits) staff members limit working hours, take at least a day off each week, and take longer rest and recreation breaks and vacations periodically. One especially important set of organizational policies focuses on supporting the ability of staff members to maintain their social support systems. As part of this, the agency facilitates frequent communication between staff members on assignment and their families back home, even if this entails some short-term costs to the organization (see Fawcett, 2003).
- The organization has arrangements in place to provide outside psychological support for staff, on an "as-needed" basis, in the wake of highly stressful or traumatic events.
- The organization has clear policies in place concerning potential evacuation. Evacuation is extremely stressful and the situation in which a worker is evacuated directly to his or her home should be avoided. Provisions should be made for a several day stopover before a worker is returned home to allow the worker to process what has happened in the company of their team. The organization should also be clear as to its policy with respect to evacuating national staff, before the situation creating a potential need arises.
- The agency has clear policies forbidding sexual harassment, racial or ethnic or national harassment, and any other form of harassment, and has grievance procedures in place to enforce these policies.
- The organization provides staff members with both an operational debriefing and a personal psychological debriefing at the end of an assignment. An operational debriefing is aimed at improving the functioning of the agency. Thus, it focuses on what staff members did in their assignments, what happened, what was done well and what not so well, and what can be improved. By contrast, personal psychological debriefings are aimed at helping the staff members process their personal reactions. These focus on how the staff members experienced their assignments, how they are dealing with the thoughts and feelings created by these experiences, and what their ongoing needs for support are. The operational debriefing should come first. While the pressures of transitioning out of an assignment make it easy to miss or skip this step, not having an adequate operational debriefing is often felt as a major stressor. But an operational debriefing alone is not sufficient; the personal psychological debriefing should also be carried out.
- The organization is aware that different workers and different *groups* of workers may have somewhat different needs, with respect to stress

management, and does not insist on a "one size fits all" policy. In particular, there may be differences between national and international staff and, within each group, differences among those of different ethnicities/nationalities, between men and women, between professionally trained and less skilled workers, and between workers with more direct contact with beneficiaries and those with less.

With respect to all of these differences, it is well to recall the observation of Clyde Kluckhohn and Henry Murray (1953, p. 53) that "Every man is in certain respects like all other men, [in certain respects] like some other men, [and in certain respects] like no other man." For example, while most of the observations in this chapter apply equally to both national and international staff, the two groups may have some different stressful experiences. What is experienced as stressful to one group may not be identical to what is experienced as stressful by the other. Stress may be manifested differently in different cultural settings (e.g., in somatic reactions rather than clear emotional expressions). And the organizational behaviors that are experienced as supportive may differ (e.g., for some national staff, time off to take care of family needs may be more "relaxing" than "vacation" time spent sitting on a beach).

Conclusion

Humanitarian aid agencies have a dual responsibility with respect to reducing staff stress. They must effectively carry out their primary mission and, at the same time, they must protect the well-being of their own employees. These responsibilities are not in conflict with one another.

From a purely utilitarian perspective, staff stress and burnout have an adverse impact on the ability of the humanitarian aid agency to provide services to the recipients of its work. Workers suffering from the effects of stress are likely to be less efficient and less effective in carrying out their assigned tasks. They become poor decision makers and they may behave in ways that place themselves or other members of the team at risk or disrupt the effective functioning of the team. They are more likely to have accidents or to become ill. From the standpoint of the humanitarian aid agency, staff stress and burnout may impede recruitment and retention of qualified staff, increase absenteeism, decrease staff morale and efficiency, increase health care costs, and create legal liabilities.

The agency's role with respect to stress goes beyond a mere duty to shield employees from harm and ensure that they are "good workers," however. The agency has a positive responsibility, growing out of and consistent with their overall humanitarian mission, to enhance growth and development among staff. The agency should be committed to encouraging staff to develop their own skills and knowledge and to enhancing their expertise, which will increase the likelihood of the agency achieving its field-based objectives.

For the most part, attempts by humanitarian aid agencies to lessen stress or mitigate the effects stress has on their staff, have focused on activities that can be undertaken by the aid workers (e.g., agencies provide staff with training in "stress management"). Less attention has been given to actions that can be undertaken by the agencies themselves. Developing a general organizational commitment to creating a culture of stress management, providing appropriate effective leadership and efficient management at all levels of the organization, promoting team cohesion, and developing general organizational policies and practices that reduce stress and its effects do not depend on the individual activities of staff members; however, implementing these practices may be the most effective and the most cost-effective way of lessening the adverse impact of stress on staff members and the aid organization.

References

Ajdukoviç, D., & Ajdukoviç, M. (Eds.). (2000). *Mental health care of helpers.* Zagreb, Croatia: Society for Psychological Assistance.

Antares Foundation. (2004). *Managing stress in humanitarian workers Guidelines for good practice.* Amsterdam: Antares Foundation. Retrieved February 3, 2005, from http://www.idealist.org/psychosocial/resources/field_mgr_bestpractices.html

Bell, J., & Carter, A. (2004, January). Does your team leader lessen or increase your stress? Paper presented at the Annual Conference of the Division of Occupational Psychology, British Psychological Society, Stratford-upon-Avon.

Britt, T. W., & Adler, A. B. (1999). Stress and health during medical humanitarian assistance missions. *Military Medicine, 164*(4), 275–279.

Centre for Humanitarian Psychology. (2004). Management of extreme stress and of crisis in humanitarian work [Interactive CD-ROM]. Geneva, Switzerland: Centre for Humanitarian Psychology. Available at http://www.humanitarian-psy.org/pages/training_form.asp

Danieli, Y. (1996). Who takes care of the caretakers: The emotional consequences of working with children traumatized by war and communal violence. In R. J. Apfel & B. Simon (Eds.), *Minefields in their hearts* (pp. 189–205). New Haven, CT: Yale University Press.

———. (2002). *Sharing the front line and the back hills: International protectors and providers: Peacekeepers, humanitarian aid workers and the media in the midst of crisis.* Amityville, NY: Baywood Press.

Ehrenreich, J. H. (2004). *The humanitarian companion: A guide for staff of humanitarian aid, development, and human rights projects.* London: ITDG.

Eriksson, C. B. (1997). *Traumatic exposure and reentry symptomatology in international relief and development personnel.* Unpublished doctoral dissertation, Fuller Theological Seminary, Pasadena, CA.

———, Bjorck, J., & Abernethy, A. (2003). Occupational stress, trauma and adjustment in expatriate humanitarian aid workers. In J. Fawcett (Ed.), *Stress and trauma handbook* (pp. 68–100). Monrovia, CA: World Vision International.

———, Snider, L., deJong, K., Carr, K., & Lopes Cardozo, B. (2002, November). *International perspectives on humanitarian aid worker support.* Paper presented at the annual meeting of the International Society of Traumatic Stress Studies, Baltimore, MD.

Eriksson, C. B., Vande Kemp, H., Gorsuch, R., Hoke, S., & Foy, D. W. (2001). Trauma exposure and PTSD symptoms in international relief and development personnel. *Journal of Traumatic Stress, 14*, 205–212.

Fawcett, J. (2002). Preventing broken hearts, healing broken minds. In Y. Danieli (Ed.), *Sharing the front line and the back hills: International protectors and providers: Peacekeepers, humanitarian aid workers and the media in the midst of crisis* (pp. 223–232). Amityville, NY: Baywood Press.

———. (2003). *Stress and trauma handbook.* Monrovia, CA: World Vision International.

Gellis, Z. D. (2002). Coping with occupational stress in healthcare: A comparison of social workers and nurses. *Administration in Social Work, 26*(3), 37–52.

Harris, A., Day, C., & Hadfield, M. (2003). Teachers' perspectives on effective school leadership. *Teachers & Teaching: Theory & Practice, 9*(1), 67–77.

Holtz, T. H., Salama, P., Lopes Cardozo, B. L., & Gotway, C. A. (2002). Mental health status of human rights workers, Kosovo, June 2000. *Journal of Traumatic Stress, 15*(5), 389–395.

InterAction. (1997). *InterAction's Private Voluntary Organization (PVO) standards.* Washington, D.C.: InterAction. Retrieved February 3, 2005, from http://www.interaction.org/pvostandards/#10.0%20Guidelines

Kluckhohn, C., & Murray, H. A. (1953). Personality formation: The determinants. In C. Kluckhohn, H. Murray, & D. M. Schneider (Eds.), *Personality in nature, society, and culture* (2nd ed., pp. 35–48). New York: Knopf.

Langner, D. E. (2002). Burnout and leadership styles in residential mental health workers (Doctoral dissertation, Chicago School of Professional Psychology, 2002). *Dissertation Abstracts International: Section B: The Sciences and Engineering, 62*(8-B), 3807.

Lopes Cardozo, B., & Salama, P. (2002). Mental health of humanitarian aid workers in complex emergencies. In Y. Danieli (Ed.), *Sharing the front line and the back hills: International protectors and providers: Peacekeepers, humanitarian aid workers and the media in the midst of crisis* (pp. 242–255). Amityville, NY: Baywood Press.

Lubofsky, D. J. (2002). Supervisor leadership style and counselors' burnout (Doctoral dissertation, University of San Diego, 2002). *Dissertation Abstracts International: Section B: The Sciences and Engineering, 63*(3-B), 1598.

MacNair, R. (1995). *Room for improvement: The management and support of relief workers* (Relief and Rehabilitation Network Paper No. 10). London: Overseas Development Institute.

Maslach, C., Schaufeli, W., & Leiter, M. (2000). Job burnout. *Annual Review of Psychology. 52*, 397–422.

McCall, M., & Salama, P. (1999). Selection, training, and support of relief workers: An occupational health issue. *British Medical Journal, 318*, 113–116.

McFarlane, C. A. (2004). Risks associated with the psychological adjustment of humanitarian aid workers. *The Australasian Journal of Disaster and Studies.* Retrieved February 7, 2005, from http://www.massey.ac.nz/~trauma/issues/2004-1/mcfarlane.htm

People in Aid. (2003). *The People in Aid code of good practice.* London: People in Aid. Retrieved February 7, 2005, from http://www.peopleinaid.org/code/code01.htm

Quick, J. C., Quick, J. D., Nelson, D. L., & Hurrell, J. J. (1997). *Preventive stress management in organizations.* Washington, D.C.: American Psychological Association.

Remy, M. N. (1999). The relationship of principal leadership styles and school-site conditions to stress levels of elementary school teachers (Doctoral dissertation, University of San Diego, 1999). *Dissertation Abstracts International: Section A: Humanities and Social Sciences, 60* (5-A), 1414.

Resick, P. A. (2001). *Stress and trauma (Clinical Psychology: A modular course)*. East Sussex, United Kingdom: Taylor & Francis Group.

Rome, K. P. (2000). The palliative effect of leadership agents on reactions to workplace stressors (Doctoral dissertation, University of Sarasota, 2000). *Dissertation Abstracts International: Section A: Humanities and Social Sciences, 60*(11-A) 4091.

Smith, A. (2000). Lessons from Western Kosovo for the documentation of war crimes. *Psychiatry, Psychology & Law, 7*(2), 235–240.

Smith, B., Agger, I., Danieli, Y., & Weisaeth, L. (1996). Health activities across traumatized populations: Emotional responses of international humanitarian aid workers: the contribution of non-governmental organizations. In Y. Danieli, N. S. Rodley, & L. Weisaeth (Eds.), *International responses to traumatic stress: Humanitarian, human rights, justice, peace and development contributions, collaborative actions and future initiatives* (pp. 397–423). Amityville, NY: Baywood Press.

Stearns, S. D. (1993). Psychological distress and relief work: Who helps the helpers? *Refugee Participation Network, 15,* 3–8.

United Nations High Commissioner for Refugees [UNHCR] Staff Welfare Unit. (2001). *Managing the stress of humanitarian emergencies.* Geneva, Switzerland: UNHCR. Retrieved February 7, 2005, from http://www.the-ecentre.net/resources/e_library/index.cfm

World Health Organization. (1998, July). *Consultative meeting on the management and support of relief workers.* Geneva, Switzerland: Author.

CHAPTER 7

PSYCHOSOCIAL CRISIS INTERVENTION WITH MILITARY AND EMERGENCY SERVICES PERSONNEL

Erik L. J. L. De Soir

What makes you, breaks you and . . . what breaks you, makes you!

Introduction

Over the past decade there has been a constantly increasing interest in the psychosocial consequences of long-term deployment in conflict areas and the multiple impacts of large-scale accidents and disasters throughout the world. Particular attention was directed at frontline personnel, in military operations or emergency response services, who developed psychological injuries related to their professional duties. These personnel may either have been directly injured (i.e., physically) or witnessed their fellow soldiers or colleagues being harmed or killed. Such "line-of-duty" hazards are predictable consequences of choosing a dangerous occupation, and so the personnel involved were expected to absorb these events without psychological harm being done. After all, having chosen these careers and duties, weren't they then sufficiently toughened and prepared to absorb such shocks? And yet evidence repeatedly suggested that people in these highly stressful occupations were vulnerable to "burnout" and other forms of psychological injury.

Mental health professionals, civil authorities, and top-level management at military and emergency services organizations have turned to the various domains of victimology, crisis psychology, and psychotraumatology for answers. Consequently, most basic training courses for fire, rescue, emergency, police, and military services personnel now invest considerable effort toward introducing aspects of stress and trauma specific to the field of crisis intervention and disaster response. And yet, there still seems to be a lot of confusion with regard to the potentially traumatizing impacts of crisis response operations or emergency response and the necessary help and support the different categories of victims should receive.

In Europe, it is only since most of the armed forces became involved in a new type of risky peace support operations in postmodern (intrastate) conflicts, and since several large-scale accidents and disasters took place in the beginning of the 1990s, that multidisciplinary coordination and co-operation became more organized in a broader operational framework. The objective of these psychosocial disaster plans and/or psychosocial support models was to assure the necessary psychosocial support, both as an immediate response to crisis and as a psychosocial follow-up in the long term.

A major step in the whole process was the creation of postgraduate courses in *disaster medicine* and *disaster response* in which the key personnel of the several disciplines working together at grassroots level were trained to use the same psychosocial framework and to allow them to use the same concepts in times of crisis. The next step was the development of joint regional psychosocial disaster plans for hospitals, industry plants, and risk areas, and the organization of special follow-up training for disaster response networks of doctors, nurses, fire and rescue personnel, psychologists, psychiatrists, social workers, clergy, and so forth. The same evolution took place in the armed forces, where prior to, during, and after long-term deployment, a whole set of support measures was proposed to the soldiers and their families. Some problems remain unresolved, since successful psychosocial intervention in military operations, crisis situations and disasters also requires a successful integration of the intervening disciplines resulting in a common conceptual basis with respect to the immediate and long-term psychosocial needs of trauma victims.

This chapter will discuss the possibilities for psychotrauma support, from the immediate post-impact psychosocial intervention to the long-term professional trauma therapy, reviewing respectively: (1) the potentially traumatizing core of emotionally disturbing events; (2) the impact of these kinds of events on various categories of victims; (3) the support activities one can expect from peers, coordinated by peer support officers and supervised by mental health professionals; and, finally, (4) the transition from peer support to professional aid (including the different stages of the trauma therapy).

Acute Reactions

I would like to start by putting aside the widespread and overgeneralized concepts of *traumatic event* and *traumatic stress,* thus trying to reserve these terms for events that are really traumatizing, and to watch over the restricted use of these terms. The traumatizing character of an emotionally disturbing event is always the result of a personal and subjective interpretation of this event by the individual struck by the event and not merely dependent from objective cues in the given event. Both in the literature and the spoken language, the use of the term *trauma* is too widespread; these days, everything seems to become a trauma. This conceptual lack of clarity influences the practice of psychosocial crisis intervention and early intervention.

A good illustration of this problem is the whole psychological debriefing controversy about whether or not critical incident stress management (CISM) techniques are effective. While the techniques of psychological defusing and debriefing (Mitchell & Everly, 1993; Raphael, 1986) were originally developed to support emergency personnel—such as deployed troops, firefighters, rescue workers, and the personnel of police or emergency medical services—they have also been widely used (and researched upon) to support all kinds of victims of critical events. One problem with this is that the definition of a critical incident has always been very vague and these CISM techniques, which are supposed to help the direct trauma victims and their significant others as well as all the other involved categories of stricken people, have rapidly conquered the whole trauma field. Both critical incident stress debriefing (CISD)—being an integral part of CISM—and the latter concept of early intervention became a container concept of various kinds of interventions for various kinds of victims.

In the meanwhile, a whole disaster business has been developed, and professional caregivers or high-risk organizations (e.g., banks, petrochemical industry, rescue services, army, police) were urged or legally forced to "do something" to support their personnel exposed to various kinds of emotionally disturbing and potentially traumatizing events. For further in-depth discussion, I would like to orient the reader of this chapter toward the extensive review and discussion work on stress, trauma, and early intervention in recent European publications (De Clercq & Lebigot, 2001; De Soir & Vermeiren, 2002).

In this chapter, I classify an event as *emotionally disturbing*, when it is abrupt and shocking, and involves disturbing feelings of anxiety and/or depression, followed by guilt and/or shame and/or sadness and/or rage. By its sudden impact, the event temporarily (and more or less severely) disrupts the emotional and/or physical and/or cognitive equilibrium of the individual and their significant others, being struck by the secondary impacts of the event. Examples of this kind of event are the painful or sudden death of a friend or a relative, seeing severely injured or dead people, and other important losses. These events are shocking, instead of directly traumatizing, if they did not lead to a subjective and/or objective confrontation with death in the mind of the stricken individuals or if they did not involve a fight to survive during which the stricken individual(s) was confronted with a state of psychological terror, frozen fright, and unspeakable experiences that are impossible to symbolize or verbalize.

In Antwerp (Belgium), there has been a very sudden and severe hotel fire at New Year's Eve in which more than 10 people lost their lives and 150 people were injured (approx. 30 people were severely burned and remained in a burn treatment center for months). The surrounding people, living in the same neighborhood could also have been traumatized, but I tend to consider this event as emotionally disturbing (i.e., temporarily disruptive impact) for the involved firefighters, police personnel, and emergency medical services.

If the secondary (e.g., significant others) or tertiary victims (e.g., professional caregivers and emergency personnel) did not get personally involved during the aforementioned hotel fire or if they did not go through a mental process in which they identified themselves with the stricken victims, I do not consider this event to be potentially traumatizing for these categories of "exposed" persons. Nevertheless, traumatization can result from a process of strong identification with victims or through on-scene contact with friends or relatives (or victims looking like friends or relatives) and especially children, always considered to be the ultimate victims. In other cases, such an event can also trigger[1] earlier trauma and thus lead (again) to post-traumatic sequelae, aggravating the already damaged mental structure of the stricken individual.

I would like to qualify an emotionally disturbing event as traumatic if this event satisfies the following criteria: (1) the event is sudden, abrupt, and unexpected; (2) involves feelings of extreme powerlessness, horror and/or terror, disruption, anguish, and/or shock; (3) implicates vehement emotions of anxiety and fear of death, due to; (4) the subjective (feelings) or objective (real, direct) confrontation with death (i.e., the real or felt severe threat to one's physical and/or psychological integrity or the integrity of a significant other). What I consider to be central in this definition is the confrontation with death in which the illusionary state of predictability and security are replaced with a situation characterized by deep physical or psychological injury, irreversible damage, humiliation, and irreparable destruction. The overwhelming impact of this close encounter with death typically involves a condition of frozen fright and psychological terror that is difficult to relieve.

Traumatic events shake the very foundations of the human being; you cannot expect anybody to cope with these kinds of events without suffering long-term psychological damage. Besides the feelings of extreme powerlessness and helplessness, and the overwhelming impression of deep penetration into one's own physical and psychological integrity, trauma survivors will have to cope with the potentially ego-destructive emotions of permanent uncertainty, survivor guilt, anxiety, shame, and loss of control. The more severe the physical injury, the longer the recovery and working-through process will last, and the more likely we are to be pessimistic about the long-term prognosis. Traumatic events also result in the loss of connectedness with the surrounding significant others and the life environment in general.

During the traumatogenic (potentially traumatic) event—in what we will call the peritraumatic stage—the direct victims act in a way that is very significant for their survival and very comparable to what we find in animals being threatened by a predator (Nijenhuis, 1999). In most trauma accounts we can easily find the following successive stages: (1) immobility—in nature this kind of immobility (cf. concepts such as animal hypnosis, tonic immobility, frozen fright) sometimes means "survival" and "escape from death"—and total inhibition; apparently, this freezing happens in a state apprehension of danger and attempts to find the right or most adequate survival response; (2) flight, if there is enough time and space for escape, otherwise numbness and freezing might return, or even the opposite reaction pattern—panic and senseless activation; (3) fight, for as long as the fight to survive has a sense and offers a chance to survive in the stage of the traumatization process; (4) total submission—the moment on which the stricken victims experience overwhelming power and violence, of the predator, the perpetrator, technology, or simply nature; it seems as if they understand that fighting death has no more sense; it is at that moment that dissociative behavior—alienation, depersonalization, anesthesia, analgesia, narrowing of attention, tunnel vision, out-of-body experiences, derealization, and so forth. (cf. Infra)—sets in, as if this would allow the victims to die without feeling pain or without even knowing consciously that they are on the way to die; and finally, the last stage in this traumatization sequence, if the danger or death threat disappears; (5) recovery, recuperation and return of pain sensitivity, partial consciousness of what happened, widening of attention (e.g., behaviors that are typical for a return to reality).

It seems as if adequate early trauma intervention and support can lessen the suffering over trauma survivors, but will never prevent them from developing long-term sequelae or chronic post-traumatic stress disorder. Once the traumatization has taken place, the damage is done and nothing can reverse this. As I will describe in what follows, I think that at least in some cases, there is a possibility for on-scene (peritraumatic) primary prevention of post-traumatic sequelae, but these chances are rare and often unexploited.

Operational Stress and Trauma among Emergency Personnel

Life-threatening events and large-scale accidents, calamities, or disaster situations are not only potentially traumatic for the direct victims and their significant others, but they can also traumatize the involved caregivers. Even military troops, deployed as peacekeepers in a crisis response operation in which the core business is about humanitarian assistance of the stricken population or war relief activities, can be confronted with the same types of problems. Instead of acting as fighting troops, they behave as military caregivers and frequently suffer from what one could call vicarious traumatization.

Everyone who starts out as a firefighter or a paramedic may reasonably expect to be confronted sooner or later with emotionally distressing, shocking, and potentially traumatic events. As in all high-risk and vocational professions, military or police personnel, money couriers, prison guards, emergency medical personnel, it is to be expected that these persons as well as their employers be well armed to deal with these impacts. In fact it is generally assumed that the consciousness of having to work with living, injured, or dead victims of fire or serious accidents, natural disasters, violent crimes, hostage situations, or shootings automatically leads to good psychological assimilation. This is absolutely untrue! I have led several field studies (De Soir 1995, 1996, 1997), based upon semi-structured clinical interviews with military personnel, firefighters, and paramedics, which have shown that one in 10 firefighters or ambulance personnel have not come to grips with earlier traumatic experiences incurred during an intervention. The short- and long-term effects of intense and sudden stress as well as the slowly accumulating stresses appear to have a very destructive effect on the rescuers' and caregivers' well-being.

Without noticing it, they get hard hit medically, psychologically, socially, and relationally. The virile world of firefighters and emergency medical personnel is a very particular and closed one, to which an outsider is only reluctantly admitted. The same is true for highly trained military units in which one needs enough field credibility to be allowed in the group. Many earlier effects at mending the detrimental effects of post-traumatic stress disorder in firefighters, emergency medical services, police departments, or military units have failed because the projects had little ecological validity or because the initiators approached their potential "victims" on the wrong assumption that they would ask for and accept psychological support. Nowadays, it is common knowledge that non-embedded psychologists, trying to work with rescuers, emergency personnel, law enforcement, or the military, as specialists do with their patients, are seen more as intrusive spies than as welcome helpers.

Firefighters, paramedics, emergency medical nurses, police personnel, or soldiers, for example, want to be heard, supported, and helped by someone who is as similar to them as possible, who shares the same meanings, and who lives in a similar world. The problem with many organizations is that they suffer from what we like to call the "not-invented-by-technicians-syndrome." Traumatic stress is not easy to calculate or to express in a mathematical model. The fact that the management of many large and semi-large organizations is in the hands of technicians and managers, who have had a minimum of training in interpersonal relationships, human resources management, and leadership, considerably complicates the introduction of the so-called soft values. Many staff members automatically become officers because they have a certain level of training or expertise; they occupy themselves mainly with very technical issues with respect to accident prevention, risk management, techniques, or procedures. Therefore empathy with the purely human problems at grassroots level—where the average educational level is usually lower but the average number of emotionally destabilizing interventions higher—is not always easy.

Firefighters, police officers, soldiers, and/or masculine emergency medical personnel usually consist of men who have been educated to believe that crying is a sign of weakness and/or for girls. They have become experts at stifling pain and hiding emotions with black humor and cynicism as the only outlet. As a matter of fact, it was this "outlet" of safety valve that permitted these men and women to maintain a workable psychological distance from the victims. During their work, often in grueling circumstances, they have learned to concentrate on technical or operational manipulations, and to suppress their emotions. In the past, this behavior has often been explained as insensitivity, but the way in which firefighters deal with their feelings appears to be very functional. Yet this John Wayne–like behavior, when the excitement of the intervention is over and the armor is dropped and the firefighters/paramedics wake from their functional tunnel vision, leads to a host of problems.

The uniformed individual is typically very action- and goal-oriented, dedicated, very motivated, ambitious, and prepared to take calculated risks. The word "failure" is not in this person's dictionary. For caregivers and rescuers, deceased victims are equaled with failure (or coming too late). The often overwhelming powerlessness coupled with the inability to reflect on emotions turn many firefighters into prospective burnout victims, and in many elder firefighters, emergency medical nurses, and paramedics, the symptoms of burnout are evident. Unwillingness or inability to talk about impressions and accumulating emotions inevitably leads to problems in the long run. Some leave emergency medicine or rescue work after a few years, startled and scarred by what they had to go through. Five years of service in fire fighting or emergency medicine—certainly for volunteers—seems to be a critical period.

If they succeed in finding a balance with regard to traumatizing interventions and the time they invest in voluntary aid within those five years, the chances of remaining with the corps for a longer period increase. One of the first important hurdles is learning to deal with feelings of guilt and impotence. Firefighters have to learn to accept that they should not be too harsh on themselves because there just is no coping with some situations. Others leave their jobs with a bitter feeling of failure after a long and strenuous grapple with a passion got-out-of-hand for violence and loss. Many firefighters and caregivers are in fact "trauma junkies" who do not like periods of inactivity. The escape valve appears to be black humor, irony, and cynicism.

Within these firefighters and caregivers we can imagine the physical, mental, and emotional exhaustion as an ever-increasing chaos. The person concerned has to invest more and more energy in avoiding confrontation with his proper experiencing of past traumatic interventions. Alcohol and hyperactivity (often in occupations that increase social isolation) are common ways of realizing this escape. They spend a lot of time in the fire department, occupy themselves with odd jobs, play cards and drink together, go through past interventions in the pub—in their own language, which is a mix of humor and bitter seriousness—and keep outsiders at a safe distance. In this way, they share an important amount of time together. There is a strong mutual bond among firefighters and paramedics of this kind. They remain, albeit from the sideline, and even when retired, very involved with everything the corps organizes. That is to say, crisis responders are doers rather than thinkers and talkers and once they start talking, it is difficult to stop or modulate the destabilizing release of tension.

Firefighters and paramedics do not tolerate busybodies and do not want to feel a victim. In this environment it feels as if the counselor himself needs to have "a little cancer" to be able to deal with cancer. Counseling by a psychiatrist, psychologist, therapist, social worker, or mental health worker in general from a viewpoint of power and degree-based knowledge does not work with firefighters and crisis responders. As stated before, it will be important to treat the fire fighting and emergency medical personnel as equals to obtain a mandate of equality and from there on to start a discussion about an emotionally disturbing (potentially traumatizing) intervention. This insight recently led to the creation of the *European Association of Fire Psychologists*, an association reuniting mental health professionals who are both a trained and experienced firefighter or paramedic, and a clinical psychologist or psychiatrist.

Firefighters and paramedics realize that the borderline between success and failure, between saving and not being able to save, and therefore between being a hero or a "victim" is very thin indeed. First-line counseling will therefore have to be oriented toward creating an atmosphere of confidentiality and mutual understanding to be able to discuss everybody's feelings about the intervention, followed by legitimizing and normalizing possible reactions. Using the time-honored phrase on them, that they are having "*normal reactions to an abnormal situation*" (but without using this phrase to stop them from further open expression of emotions) does them good.

In the group the following emotions usually surface: often overpowering impotence, a hated feeling of helplessness, a paralyzing grief about the suffering of the victims, the intense guilt of not having been able to do more, and the anger generated by all this. This is not what they joined the fire brigade or the ambulance service for, whatever the average person may think about it. But what is important to note is that their emotional intervention-based experience is primarily seen as a depressing one rather than one belonging to the category of life-threatening and traumatic experiences. It is quite obvious that different kinds of interventions need different kinds of post-intervention support. This is an element that seems to be underestimated in the current trauma research, in which no difference is made between emotionally shocking and depressing events, grief about the losses suffered is an essential part of the working-through process, and in the life-threatening, high-anxiety, and high-arousal events, immediate arousal reduction and physical recuperation seem to be much more important than immediate emotional coping. Before treating the sequences of crisis psychological assistance and going into the details of what will be called the psychosocial matrix of crisis psychological assistance, it is important to consider the emotionally disturbing intervention as a difficult puzzle, from which the pieces have to be put back together again, to allow the stricken firefighters and paramedics to fully understand the context in which the intervention took place.

Psychological Shock Assimilation after a Large-Scale Intervention

The acute psychological experience of a disturbing and potentially traumatizing event is one of extreme powerlessness and loss of control. Through accidents with children and/or acquaintances, the illusion of invulnerability—"*accidents only happen to careless or unknown people*"—is seriously compromised and may lead to intense feelings of guilt, shame, fear, anger, and the like. The stricken caregiver can, in many instances, no longer maintain his or her image of the world. The basic assumptions and expectations about life are no longer valid. Everything, even in the practice of fire fighting, becomes dishonest, unjust, unpredictable, and dangerous. There is danger behind every corner. Training no longer stands for controllability. Every intervention means "danger" and every call-up is fraught with fear.

> Peter had been involved in the rescue operations for the Switel fire from the first moments. He had helped dozens of shocked and burned victims (e.g., by sprinkling them with water till the evacuation from the disaster scene). Peter was a very experienced firefighter of about 50 years of age. After the rescue operations, he was convinced of his good work. He did not feel the need to tell about his experiences nor to participate in the post-intervention debriefing sessions. He did not want to dwell on this one big intervention and just wanted to let everything rest. A few years later he was confronted with a series of emotionally disturbing experiences in his own private life, all this happening in just a three-month period: he lost his mother and father, his wife was diagnosed with breast cancer, and his oldest daughter attempted suicide. Peter was not able to cope with both the regular disturbing experiences from his fire practice and his personal experiences. He asked for help—contacting me by e-mail, telling that he started to have nightmares, and that in each nightmare he saw his own family sitting at a table in the Switel hotel fire and being suddenly burned by the fire. While his relatives were screaming for help he was looking for them with his full fire equipment and oxygen mask, being completely lost and disoriented by the heat and the smoke.

This example clearly demonstrates that potentially traumatic events that have not been worked through or integrated, and which have been blunted in the post-immediate stage, can accumulate in the psyche and cause trouble in a much later life stage and often at a very unexpected moment.

This demonstrates clearly that psychological group debriefing with all the participants in a major intervention is a must, even if nobody should participate in psychosocial crisis intervention on a mandatory basis, so that the minds of the caregivers concerned can be put to rest as quickly as possible. In some cases, support activities will have to include both the victims and their caregivers. Caregivers will already start on the site of the accident with their first psychological support for the dazed and shocked trauma victims. They will be supported themselves, on-scene, by their own well-trained peers. And in many cases, after the intervention, when suffering their own post-fact collapse, they will make contact again with the stricken victims (or the victims' families), inviting them to the emergency department or fire brigade to talk about their experiences and to work through the event together.

The CRASH Model

The psychosocial matrix of the CRASH model for crisis psychological support forms a 3 × 3 matrix: (1) the *primary, secondary,* and *tertiary victims,* belonging to one of these three categories depending of the type of potentially traumatizing impact they suffered; and, (2) the *primary, secondary,* and *tertiary prevention,* depending on the time at which the trauma support takes place. The concrete realization of the complete framework for psychosocial and crisis psychological support consists, on the one hand, of a kind of emotional triage to sort out the different kinds of victims, dividing them in three different categories, and on the other hand, the selection of the right support technique, at the right moment and carried out by the right people, thus trying to realize an optimal fit between victims and the kind of support they get.

At first, the model might seem too simplistic, being too much a reduction of a very complex reality, but my field experience with this model, which has been implemented in several European countries and which has been in application for the management of numerous large-scale accidents, disasters, and critical incidents in military operations, clearly demonstrates that this hands-on model leads at least to much better results than the one-size-fits-all approach of most critical incident stress management protocols.

The *primary victims* in this model are the directly stricken victims of the calamity or disaster, which means those who have to be rescued and/or medically saved, and those who have been directly confronted with the life-threatening potentially traumatic stimuli. For instance, the people who were celebrating New Year's Eve at the Switel hotel, which was destroyed by fire in some 30 seconds, and who escaped, needed to be rescued, or received medical treatment belong to the category of primary victims. The same thing is true for soldiers being struck in heavy gunfire or a police officer involved in direct shooting.

The *secondary victims* are the significant others, closely related to the primary victims or playing a significant role as bystanders, in the first rescue attempts (before the emergency services arrive) or providing the first assistance to the primary victims and their families. The *social tissue* of significant others—relatives, family members, friends, colleagues, and so forth—creates a victim's dendrite of people who can be considered to be secondary victims. A quick calculation in numbers leads to the insight that for each primary victim, we have approximately 10 to 15 secondary victims.

The *tertiary victims* are the professionally involved people, caregivers, or law and order personnel—fire and rescue personnel, police, emergency medical services, etc.—who have been in direct contact with the primary and/or secondary victims.

Strictly speaking, *primary prevention* would have to be everything that is done to prevent the traumatogenic impact itself. However, I like to use a broader and less conventional definition of primary prevention, including the whole series of activities of trauma education and preparation, training, and the creation of intervention models and structures. Even the on-scene and peritraumatic psychological support can be considered as a kind of primary trauma prevention. Thus, I personally consider all the support activities aimed at lowering the level of post-traumatic sequelae, to be primary prevention.

In this model, I propose that primary prevention ends when: (1) the fire, rescue, and emergency medical services are demobilized; and (2) the primary and secondary victims, after the initial support and assistance offered to them on the scene of the accident or the disaster, are administered in the hospital or rejoin their own social system or life environment.

The immediate support, both on the scene of the accident or in temporary support centers on the field, carried out by the caregivers of fire & rescue, or ambulance services, or even provided by volunteers from civil defense, Red Cross, or others services, is also considered to be primary prevention. The *on-scene buddy aid* or *peer support—the help for colleagues and from colleagues* on the scene of the accident—then the *initial emotional and physical recuperative talk sessions* (sometimes described as *defusing*) are also considered to be *primary prevention of post-traumatic sequelae in tertiary victims*. As already stated, primary preventive support activities can be carried out by non-professional caregivers or peers.

The *secondary prevention,* in the post-immediate stage, essentially consists of: (1) a quick and adequate detection of post-traumatic sequelae and psychosocial problems; (2) a rapid and adequate intervention, with the right interventions, carried out by the right people and all this at the right moment. Secondary prevention aims at the early detection of problematic responses or coping styles in victims, and an intervention adequately tailored to the needs of the victims, in order to prevent these problems from exacerbating and becoming chronic in the long term. I consider most *early intervention protocols* to be a kind of *secondary prevention (for tertiary victims)*.

These secondary preventive support activities could, in some cases, be carried out by non–professional caregivers, as long as they work under permanent supervision of well-trained and professional mental health specialists. I am convinced that the currently known models of *critical incident stress debriefing* or *psychological debriefing* have been designed as a secondary prevention for tertiary victims, *which should not be used to support or debrief primary or secondary victims*. I argue that the negative publicity on these intervention techniques is not due to these protocols but to the incorrect use of these techniques with people who should not be reexposed to their trauma so soon after the impact or after an insufficient physical, emotional, and psychological recovery period.

The *tertiary prevention*, finally, aims at the full professional curative trauma care, which can become necessary for the different categories of victims after several months during which these victims tried to cope with their experiences without any professional help.

Tertiary prevention can mean psychotherapeutic action from a broad range of perspectives, but in nearly all trauma models, the first stage of the therapy will aim at reduction and stabilization of the current trauma symptoms and complaints, followed by a stage in which there will be a renegotiation of the trauma-related material, mostly using narrative exploration and cognitive reframing techniques, and finally in the last stage, working toward integration of the loss and trauma in the personal life story of the survivor.

In my opinion, it is very important that the on-scene rescue workers and caregivers know how to guide and support the primary victims on their way back to reality, trying to calm these victims down, helping to ground them during and immediately after the rescue operations, and assisting them in their first reorientation attempts after the traumatic impact. Especially the trauma survivors who showed dissociative response need to be grounded on-site in order to prevent them from staying overwhelmed by the life-threatening, and potentially traumatic, stimuli. In this way, the on-scene support of rescue workers, firefighters, and paramedics, or the immediate support in Battle Shock Recovery units in military operations, should be seen as real primary prevention of chronic psychological trauma.

The first signs of post-impact recovery appear when the victims start again to search the surrounding environment for information about what happened. This yearning for information in the immediate post-impact stage makes the primary victims very fragile and suggestible with respect to the first rumors about what happened. The mental reconstruction of what really happened is very difficult for the involved victims since they all suffered more or less from a narrowing of their field of consciousness, focusing on peritraumatic details that were relevant for their own survival or rescue. Lots of trauma-related, essentially preverbal sensations about speechless terror have been registered but need much more elaboration before they can be transformed into senseful traumatic memories. Thus, each kind of support in that stage has to aim at physical recovery and cooling down but not so much verbal expression since it is much too early for the narrative expression of what happened.

The on-scene support for primary, secondary, and tertiary victims can be executed along the same principles. The first psychological help in the peritraumatic and immediate post-impact stage has to aim for absolutely the reduction of the level of arousal and the recreation of basic security and safety around the traumatized victim. One could assume that the natural support a mother provides to a child in a state of anxiety, in trying to secure and calm the child down, is the same kind of support a traumatized victim needs.

Physical Recuperation, Emotional Ventilation, and Emotional Uncoupling

The discussion of emotionally disturbing, shocking, or traumatizing interventions, in group and according to procedure, will be called Emotional Uncoupling (EU) in what follows. EU is in fact an individual or group-oriented intervention—based on the commonly known Psychological Debriefing (PD) process—in which the most important elements of a past emotionally disturbing experience are treated shortly after the events. Lately psychological debriefing—mostly based on the elementary protocol of *Critical Incident Stress Debriefing* (Mitchell & Everly, 1983)—has been generally advised as the best stress-management technique for high-risk professions like the people providing aid in disasters, firefighters, military personnel, police personnel, and so forth. (Bergmann & Queen, 1986; Dunning & Silva, 1980; Griffin, 1987; Mitchell, 1981; Raphael, 1986; Wagner, 1979). At this moment, a number of variants of the original Mitchell-protocol of psychological debriefing are widely used in psychological crisis intervention services. The problem is that in many cases, outcome-expectances of psychological debriefing were too high, and more recently, specialists started arguing about the effects of psychological debriefing.

First, we do not like the term "debriefing" because many of its users do not even fully understand the meaning of it or think they can very easily carry out these debriefings. Second, we think that the outcome criterion (i.e., the prevention of post-traumatic stress disorder) may be the wrong one. I believe that the guided reconstruction of an emotionally disturbing and/or traumatic event appears to be of primary importance.[2] As the most important purpose of EU is the lessening of the (often intense) psychological suffering caused by an emotionally disturbing or traumatic event, it is clear that accurate memories of this event are of primary importance. This in itself poses a problem for large-scale interventions in which different teams of emergency medical personnel, firefighters, or even larger groups of caregivers took part. These individuals often have trouble realizing the larger context of the intervention in which they took part as a small but often important link. The following practical example will illustrate this:

Following a very heavy traffic accident in which four people died, a fireman had to watch from a distance of only a few meters how his colleagues and the emergency medical personnel applied first aid and even attempted to reanimate a victim that was severely trapped in one of the cars. He was there, ready to intervene at the slightest spark with the high-pressure lance. Yet, after the event he felt superfluous and useless. To him this was the worst thing that has ever happened. Having to watch how his colleagues struggled to try and save four people with fatal injuries. During the Emotional Uncoupling Procedure at which his colleagues, the emergency medical personnel, the police, the tow service, and a few other caregivers were present, this fireman exploded in anger and afterwards started to cry. Until the moment that a nurse said that she would not have taken such risks—there was gas dripping from the car on the other side—if he had not been there, ready to intervene. The eye contact she had kept going with him during the intervention, and which he had read as a reproach, had on the contrary meant a lot to her. In fact she was grateful to this fireman for his presence. She also said something else that was very important—she told him that even while they were driving to the scene of the accident, she had heard over the intercom which fire brigade would assist them. It had given her a feeling of "if it's those guys, everything is going to be all right."

This intervention by people from the medical staff meant more to the fireman and his colleagues than any therapeutic intervention could have. In general, these kind of remarks by "outsiders"—witnesses, medical staff, police—all mean a lot to firefighters; it makes them feel useful in their job, which sometimes appears to be very passive and frustrating. We always use this example when a colleague tells us he thinks that psychological debriefing—what we call Emotional Uncoupling in this text—should only take place in small groups and within the proper corps only. In some cases, even the testimonies of witnesses or direct victims can be essential in this reconstruction process.

Further and equally important goals of Emotional Uncoupling include ventilating tensions and frustrations, normalization, comprehension and legitimization of occurring reactions and feelings, replacing negative cognitions by positive ones in the course of the discussion, creating an almost mythical bond among fellow caregivers, and the identification of those participants who may run a high risk of problematic assimilation.

Goals of Procedures for Emotional Uncoupling

Emotional Uncoupling Procedures (EUP) appear to be an effective means of handling the direct and delayed post-fact emotional collapse in caregivers. One should not expect to eliminate or reduce sensationally the risk of long-term dysfunctioning after a traumatic crisis, but this kind of support, which has to take place at the right time and by the right people, will always be very much appreciated by the caregivers and allow them to emotionally uncouple more easily from disturbing and/or traumatic interventions.

The *Big Five of Victimology*, as we call the following five factors, will be essential to ensure a healthy coping with emotionally disturbing events: (1) providing correct and honest information; (2) mobilizing the available natural support systems; (3) ensuring the right rituals; (4) avoiding secondary victimization (by avoiding bad reactions from outsiders); and (5) providing the necessary recognition to the concerned caregivers.

From the above, it becomes clear that the main goals of *emotional uncoupling procedures* aim to help the afflicted gain insight into the fact that both the initial on-scene coping mechanisms and their post-fact psychological suffering are the engine behind the assimilation of the trauma, but that they can

Table 7.1
Goals of Emotional Uncoupling Procedures

First	Together with everyone who took part in the event, establishing a correct reconstruction of what really happened by putting the pieces of the puzzle of each concerned person together.
Second	To give these people ample occasion to ventilate their emotional reactions concerning the events and to establish the intensity of these reactions.
Third	Offer recognition, support, information, and comfort the stricken, by offering a detailed discussion, legitimization and normalization of the symptoms
Fourth	Initiate, stimulate, and catalyze the proper assimilation capacities in each participant in order to help him restore the feeling of safety and trust (and their feeling of predictability and control) in the environment in which they live and work.
Fifth	Take away the feeling of being uprooted by stressing and stimulating the togetherness and the connection among partners in adversity. Also stimulate and support the social environment of the victim.

let this engine work for them instead of letting themselves be flattened by it. In fire and rescue services, these *emotional uncoupling procedures* will normally be extremely well received since most of their impact is rather *depressogenic* (initiating a potentially depressing impact, following the confrontation with grief and bereavement) instead of traumatogenic (meaning the typical high anxiety and high arousal type of event); practical experience teaches me that the more depressing events are, the more they are necessitating early emotional ventilation.

Shock, sorrow, pain, fear, anger, and other intense emotions are useful catalysts to promote a functional assimilation of an emotionally disturbing and potentially traumatic event. Assimilation will be ongoing because a minute stimulus (very often a smell) may impel the victim to relive the whole scene. Emotional uncoupling should not be used to confirm these feelings or to squash them, but to offer recognition for the feelings that surface during the session. They may be present as normal and legitimate reactions to an abnormal situation.

Besides these main goals there are a number of smaller, individually oriented goals. They comprise first the cognitive restructuring through a clear notion of the traumatic event and the reaction of it. The world of the victim can very well be turned upside down for a moment but does not have to remain like that forever. Next the individual and group tensions have to be diminished. Also one has to see to it that feelings of abnormality experienced by the victims of emotionally disturbing and/or traumatic events are lessened by letting the victims share these feelings with more or less like-minded people, and telling them that they are having normal reactions to an abnormal situation. Also an attempt has to be made to increase the support, cohesion, and solidarity of the group. The afflicted have to be prepared for symptoms or reactions that can occur later, and last but not least, who may need help later is identified.

Conclusions

With this chapter, I tried to create the full picture of a framework—the psychosocial matrix of psychosocial crisis intervention—for immediate and post-immediate support after potentially traumatizing events. The illustrations for this chapter were taken directly from my own field practice as a firefighter and paramedic, and from my clinical practice as a trauma counselor in risky military operations and large-scale accidents or disaster situations. From my perspective on psychological trauma, I tried to go beyond the superficial trauma descriptions found in psychiatric manuals and for most of the time we minimalized the use of the concept of post-traumatic stress disorder (PTSD)—still "the reference" with respect to psychological trauma in most Anglo-Saxon countries. I also wanted to provide some extra insights with respect to first psychological support and early trauma intervention instead of using the widespread CISM protocols for all kinds of trauma victims.

An essential point in this discussion was the difference between the directly life-threatening (traumatogenic) events, and the depressogenic (depressing and grief inducing or sad events and bereavement situations) events. Standardized models of how victims respond to extreme stress, and standardized interventions for early trauma support, never seem to make the difference between these various kinds of events and often allow a culturally blind and ideological use of intervention techniques, which may not prevent people from developing chronic trauma and/or complicated grief. Pre-formatted and standardized techniques used in a too-broad variety of situations, the uncritical attitude toward these techniques, and the failure to take into account the differences among various situations in which these victims were involved, made both scientists and clinicians doubt about the effectiveness of their interventions.

Meanwhile, trauma support and critical incident stress management seems to have become an ideology. This ideology of acute trauma management not only conquered large parts of the United States, Europe, Australia, and New Zealand, but the whole world, often paralyzing the minds of lots of practitioners, till the scientific debate and controversy on the effectiveness of psychological debriefing and early intervention exploded less than a decade ago. But, the damage was already done.

I am convinced that we all have to do a part of our homework again, having the moral strength and courage to fully and independently develop our own practice-based trauma concepts, which we get from our basic experience in the trenches, in strong collaboration with trauma researchers, instead of undergoing the tyranny of concepts that are imposed by the high-profile trauma doctors, bio-psychiatrists, and neuroscientists, often heavily sponsored for their laboratory research but lacking field experience or credibility. They claim evidence-based practice to be the only standard in the field; I think that trauma practitioners and clinicians should claim an equal status and respect for practice-based evidence.

Notes

1. The principle of *triggering* is one of the central problems in the working-through process of trauma victims. A psychological trauma is always characterized by a combination of several symptoms clusters, normally; (1) the original, potentially traumatizing event being a more or less direct contact with a life-threatening situation; (2) a cluster of symptoms in which the original event is re-experienced; (3) a cluster of symptoms in which the original event is denied or avoided; (4) a cluster of symptoms characterized by hyperarousal; and (5) a social dysfunctioning of the stricken individual. When trauma victims are confronted by various stimuli that make them remember or think about the original traumatizing event, these stimuli can TRIGGER the same reactions (event dissociative responses) as the original event itself. The human brain does not seem to make a difference between the original event and the re-experienced events with a *neurobiological storm* as a consequence.

2. Why continue to argue on the outcome of Psychological Debriefing (PD) during every scientific congress when nearly all participants (trained and supervised caregivers' peers belonging to the firefighter and medical emergency stress teams already lead more than 200 Emotional Uncoupling Procedures) express themselves as "being glad to have participated," "grateful for the recognition and help provided," and so on? One should simply not expect to "prevent PTSD" in administering PD to trauma victims or traumatized firefighters.

References

Bergman, L. H., & Queen, T. (1986). Critical incident stress: Part 1. Fire Command, pp. 52–56.

De Clercq, M., & Lebigot, F. (2001). *Les traumatismes psychiques.* Paris: Masson.

De Soir, E. (1995). Stress & trauma in fire & rescue services [Unpublished research report]. Leopoldsburg, Belgium.

———. (1996). Stress & trauma in fire & rescue services [Unpublished research report]. Leopoldsburg, Belgium.

———. (1997). Stress & trauma in fire & rescue services [Unpublished research report]. Leopoldsburg, Belgium.

———, & Vermeiren, E. (Eds.). (2002). *Les debriefings psychologiques en question.* Antwerp, Belgium: Garant Uitgevers.

Dunning, C., & Silva, M. (1980). Disaster-induced trauma in rescue workers. *Victimology,* 5, 287–297.

Griffin, C. A. (1987). Community disasters and posttraumatic stress disorder: A debriefing model for response. In T. Williams (Ed.), *Post-traumatic stress disorders: A handbook for clinicians* (pp. 293–298). Cincinnati, OH: American Disabled Veterans.

Mitchell, J. T. (1981). *Emergency response to crisis: A crisis intervention guidebook of emergency service personnel.* Bowie, MD: RIBrady.

————, & Everly, G. E. (1993). *Critical incident stress debriefing: An operations manual for the prevention of traumatic stress among emergency services and disaster workers.* Ellicott City, MD: Chevron.

Nijenhuis, E. R. S. (1999). *Somatoform dissociation: Phenomena, measurement, and theoretical issues.* Assen, Netherlands: Van Gorcum.

Raphael, B. (1986). *When disaster strikes: How individuals and communities cope with catastrophe.* New York: Basic Books.

Wagner, M. (1979). Airline disaster: A stress debriefing program for police. *Police Stress,* 2, 16–20.

CHAPTER 8

HELPING JOURNALISTS WHO COVER HUMANITARIAN CRISES

Elana Newman and Bruce Shapiro

Introduction

Journalists, especially those covering humanitarian tragedies, are directly and indirectly exposed to physically and psychologically dangerous situations as part of their occupational duties. Journalists bear witness daily to war, poverty, natural and man-made disasters, criminal activities, and accidents. Many of the tragedies that they cover may be personal ones, directly affecting their workplace, home, community, and loved ones (Gilbert, Hirschkorn, Murphy, Walensky, & Stephens, 2002). Although the few studies of U.S.-based journalists suffer from sampling problems, initial evidence suggests that nearly all reporters are exposed to dangerous situations and observe the types of events that mental health professionals characterize as traumatic (Feinstein, Owen, & Blair, 2002; Newman, Simpson, & Handschuh, 2003; Pyevich, Newman, & Daleidan, 2003; Simpson & Boggs, 1999). Less is known empirically about the effects upon journalists when covering humanitarian crises, although personal reflections suggest this work is extremely dangerous and emotionally taxing (Danieli, 2002).

For example, when covering humanitarian crises, journalists face complex ethical and moral issues regarding life and psychological risks to informants and translators, as well as other psychological dilemmas. Finally much good coverage about trauma requires empathetic engagement with the pain of others, a task that has been shown in other responder groups to contribute to post-traumatic risk (Regehr, Goldberg, & Hughes, 2002). Unfortunately, journalists are seldom taught how to empathetically engage with others and simultaneously protect themselves psychologically (Newman, 2002).

Resiliency and Journalism

The overwhelming majority of trauma survivors do not suffer from long-standing psychological disorders in the wake of tragedy, although a minority do suffer. Given the high level of traumatic events and pain witnessed, journalists appear comparatively resilient (Newman et al., 2003; Pyevich et al., 2003). A possible explanation is that a commitment to the mission of telling stories of the exploited, the opportunity to put their experiences into narrative form, training, and support from management may assist journalists in resiliency.

Vulnerabilities

Both narrative accounts and an emerging research literature document that a minority of journalists and humanitarian workers are at risk for the development of post-traumatic stress disorder (PTSD) and other mental health issues (Danieli, 2002). For example, a study of international relief and development personnel (Eriksson, Vande Kemp, Gorsuch, Hoke, & Foy, 2001) showed that 10 percent of returning staff who worked in the field with trauma survivors met full criteria for PTSD. Similarly, a subgroup of journalists, particularly war correspondents, appeared to be at risk for PTSD, depression, and substance abuse problems (Pyevich et al., 2003; Newman et al., 2003; Feinstein et al., 2002; Simpson & Boggs, 1999). Clearly, PTSD and related disorders are occupational hazards for journalists who cover stories that involve the pain and suffering of others.

In addition to psychopathology, it is likely that these journalists experience problems that are not in the clinical range, but affect their quality of life, relationships, and their views about the world. Early in our efforts to assist journalists, we focused solely on the "working wounded." However, both the research and our encounters made us recognize that journalists are indeed resilient, and only a minority develop diagnosable mental health problems. Instead, many journalists are challenged or changed by exposure to and engagement with disasters, accidents, and human malevolence. In the clinical field this is the notion of vicarious traumatization (McCann & Pearlman, 1990), the concept that empathetic engagement with survivors of disaster and atrocity cannot help but change any witness' behaviors, beliefs, and emotions. These changes deserve attention and can affect the quality of professional coverage of traumatic events or personal engagement in the world.

Journalists who are professional witnesses to humanitarian crises describe both psychopathology and changes in their worldview and behavior. While many remain grounded in their commitment to publicize atrocity and pain, several depict the psychological costs of this work (Danieli, 2002). Furthermore, collective grief about the numbers of journalists who die in pursuit of this calling may complicate psychological responses to the work, perhaps resulting in survivor guilt.

Mental Health and Journalism

The long-standing culture of American newsrooms poses a significant challenge to contending with the mental health impact of journalistic work. Even more than such traditionally "macho" first-responder professions as police or firefighters, journalists and their managers have been reluctant to reveal, either among themselves or with professionals, the emotional impact of difficult assignments.

Part of this reluctance is perhaps predictable. Like soldiers and police officers, reporters and photographers—even local reporters working in the community—are expected to be able to handle anything. To take one extreme example, at the beginning of the current Iraq war, many local news media throughout the United States availed themselves of new opportunities to embed reporters, photographers, and videographers with combat units. Reporters whose previous experience never extended past city hall and the local police station found themselves shipped out to hostile-environments training and to the war.

Even reporters and photographers who never leave their local communities can expect themselves pulled off a benign beat—sports, education, politics—in the event of a natural disaster, crime spree, terrorist incident, or other major story. In a hurricane or tornado, for instance, all hands will be mobilized, propelling both novice reporters and seasoned veterans alike out to scenes of devastation and into personal encounters with victims and witnesses. Even those who stay in the television studio or newsroom can expect to view unedited video feeds, raw footage, and horrifying photographic images too gruesome for publication. Many journalists who are not in the field covering humanitarian crises, nevertheless, provide technical support to deployed colleagues who are covering such issues.

At all levels of the profession, journalists fear that any exposure of emotional vulnerability will damage their careers. We have interviewed many reporters who feel, rightly or wrongly, that even Employee Assistance Programs pose risk. Editors, for their part, face enormous pressures of their own in making assignments and meeting daily production deadlines—all barriers to compassionate responses to emotional distress. Newspapers and television stations are frequently understaffed and contending with severe budget restrictions. All of this makes the news gatherer's workplace an unlikely environment in which to nurture understanding of emotional vulnerability.

There are other challenges as well. Local journalists in particular may find themselves reporting on stories which threaten their own families or neighbors (Newman, Davis, & Kennedy, in press). During the Washington, DC, sniper spree, for instance, some reporters walked their children to the very schools victimized by rifle fire, then went into the newsroom to follow the story. During the triple Florida hurricanes of 2004, journalists evacuated their families and then returned to the beat or spent 36 hours at a stretch reporting even while their own houses were flooded up to the second story. In humanitarian crises, journalists can be in situations where their own safety is threatened, friends are victimized or harassed, or people they cover or who assist them are at great risk.

At the same time, social support from within the peer community of journalism is eroding. The robust newsroom life portrayed in movies like *All the President's Men* or *The Front Page* is increasingly a thing of the past. Thanks to personal computers, digital cameras, and cell phones, many reporters and visual journalists now spend most of their time working away from their colleagues. Photographers no longer need return to the darkroom to process their images; reporters no longer return to their desk to hammer out copy. Even in the newsroom itself, the casual contact occasioned by reporters handing copy off to editors, or huddling over a typewriter to fix a lead sentence, has been sacrificed to the efficiency of e-mail. The isolation of journalists has grown so extreme that *New York Times* reporter Jayson Blair was able to fabricate stories from his apartment in Brooklyn, calling editors on a cell phone claiming to be on assignment in West Virginia.

Most of all, the mission of journalism involves deadline stresses, reporting techniques, and personal commitments that make journalism a sometimes-insular professional culture—and a culture often at odds with the imperatives of mental health. Mental health professionals may counsel traumatized clients to seek personal safety; but the core mission of reporters involves, at times, running toward danger. Mental health professionals may believe that sleep schedules, predictability of schedule, and other stabilizing factors contribute to well-being, but news events respect no such boundaries. In fact, even the most senior correspondents or photographers have little expectation of a predictable schedule.

Finally, we have found that many mental health professionals share a guarded suspicion of journalists' work, perhaps because of stark contrasts in their professional objectives. For instance, while clinicians are committed to client privacy, reporters must hurry to interview victims to meet deadlines. Clinicians may also recoil from the intrusive stalking of victims by a minority of aggressive reporters.

It should be noted, however, that in humanitarian disasters, journalists and mental health professionals are not always at odds. Publishers and broadcasters often see a civic duty to provide essential mental health information to readers: to interview mental health experts, list hotline numbers, and provide essential information for readers or viewers afflicted by trauma. On a deeper level, journalists share a commitment to forge meaningful narratives from chaotic events, affirm the experiences of victims, and transmit their suffering to a broader public. The challenge is how to cope with the risk of emotional injury without impeding the mission of reporters to bear witness and tell stories about the most difficult human experiences.

Journalists and Psychologists in Collaboration

At the Dart Center we have been experimenting with defining the nature of support for journalists. We have worked with journalists and news organizations contending with a variety of disasters, ranging from the Oklahoma City bombing to the events of September 11, 2001, as well as hurricanes, tornadoes, and many other catastrophic news stories. We have worked with many journalists, some experienced at covering humanitarian crises and others returning from their first professional experience covering such events. A major effort has been made to conduct workshops for journalists in communities across the world, where a free press is just emerging, and journalists who want to tell truthful accurate stories face taxation, harassment, arrest, or even death. For these various groups, we have experimented with a variety of educational, counseling, and institutional approaches, with varying success. Overall, we've found that the best way to help journalists is to share information about trauma and its impact. Information regarding maladaptive and adaptive coping, the language of emotional injury, and PTSD can inform journalists' reporting, or can give them a language to describe their own issues and lead them to seek help—or both. Some reporters may be acutely aware of their own emotional injury and crave direct counseling or help. Others, without desire or inclination to see trauma in personal terms, welcome the chance to broaden their reportorial toolbox in dealing with victims.

Given the culture of journalism described previously, we have found it essential that these efforts are not seen as emanating from the "touchy-feely" ethos of clinicians, but from journalists who augment their knowledge from scientifically based researchers and clinicians. Across all venues, mental health professionals join with journalists and journalism educators collaboratively to conduct trainings and seminars. Wherever possible, respected journalists or journalism educators are invited as the key participants and public face to discuss this, although trauma-focused specialists or victim advocates offer support and information.

Education in the Field

There are many ways to reach journalists coping with the aftermath of humanitarian disasters, and the Dart Center for Journalism and Trauma has tried multiple methods of outreach. In some cases we have simply introduced dialogue of the relationship between psychological trauma and journalism at professional conferences and gatherings, placing award-winning journalists on panels beside experienced clinicians. At various professional journalism conferences in recent years, for instance, the Dart Center has organized panels on reporting on war and human rights, investigating child sexual abuse cases, reporting mental health issues, interviewing victims, creating news photography of trauma, and other subjects. In London, Dart Centre Europe organizes a regular public speaker series at the Frontline Club—a correspondents' watering hole and community forum—as well as periodic private meetings of journalists seeking collegial support in contending with traumatic experiences.

In a few cases, the Dart Center has organized educational events and activities for journalists facing particular challenging stories. For six months in 2001–2002, Dart Center ran Dart Center Ground Zero in New York, which included a series of panels, discussion groups, film screenings, and other events for journalists covering the World Trade Center and Pentagon attacks. In southwest Florida in 2004, reporters at the Tampa Tribune and WFLA-TV—both veterans of the Dart-Ochberg Fellows Program, a mid-career educational fellowship—initiated a regional educational session for reporters and photographers covering the aftermath of hurricanes, with Dart Center staff providing background information and facilitating discussion of reporters' newsgathering practices and self-care. Because a subgroup of journalists are private people who tend to avoid group events but are committed to individual pursuits of knowledge and self-understanding, we offer self-study resources, news articles, samples of journalism, transcripts of discussions, and book reviews on the Internet. Future efforts may involve new forms of computer-based assistance.

Education in Journalism Schools

The Dart Center for Journalism and Trauma has promoted free-standing classes at journalism schools specifically covering trauma as well as integrating this curriculum into existing courses. At the University of Washington, professional actors help students practice skills; survivors of trauma also come to the classroom to talk with students. At other schools, discussions of trauma have entered into ethics courses and reporting classes. For the last two years, the center provided train-the-educator workshops to help journalism teachers integrate trauma-related education into courses. In addition, short seminars for college newspapers have been fruitful for addressing future journalists.

Peer Support

Early in the Dart Center's existence we attempted, with the encouragement of some journalists, to develop a formal peer-counseling system. This proved impractical to organize and difficult to sustain, given geographical distances, the structure of newsrooms, and the culture of the profession. Instead, we've developed peer support based on two general approaches, detailed below.

Building a Network of Journalists Knowledgeable about
Traumatic Stress

Much peer support occurs more organically, with a journalist telling a friend who finds a journalist who was trained by the Dart Center. At the core of this effort is the Dart Ochberg Fellows program, a series of seminars for mid-career journalists interested in trauma issues. The Fellows program is augmented by regional meetings and professional conferences, out of which emerge individuals who serve as informal newsroom mentors on traumatic stress issues. These journalists, with some consultation from mental health professionals they have met through their association with the Dart Center, engage colleagues. Informally we believe that this network of journalists has offered assistance to many journalists and photographers who cover humanitarian events both in the field and once they return home.

Traumatic-Risk Assessment

In the UK Dart Centre Europe has adapted a simple Trauma Risk Assessment Program, a model developed by the Royal Marines. Journalists and newsroom managers are briefed on trauma information and given a system for evaluating colleagues who may be at risk in the wake of a stressful assignment. This is not therapy, but instead gives a structured format for assessing health following deployment to a dangerous or difficult region. This also appears to be a useful technique for reporters covering war or humanitarian catastrophes.

Professional Referral

Legal barriers prevent the Dart Center from providing direct referral services to journalists. However, the Center's extensive network of journalists and allies in the mental health professions provide a useful channel for finding help. We are teaching journalists how to recognize the need for professional referral and how to assess potential therapists' skills as informed consumers.

Educating Mental Health Professionals and Trauma Scientists

We have also been training trauma specialists to consider the needs of journalists who call to interview them. In addition to training them regarding how to be good sources, we also encourage them to ask journalists what they think about the topic, their experiences and reactions as a means of allowing journalists to feel free to contact them in the future for referral information.

Systematic Training within News Organizations

In a number of cases, news organizations themselves have sought the Dart Center's aid in systematically training their news staff and managers. These have ranged from one-time briefings to more systematic approaches. The most promising model has been developed by the BBC's newsgathering and news training divisions. Initially, the BBC sought help from Dart Centre in Europe organizing briefings for news staff involved in coverage of the Iraq war. This program—backed up by an on-site consultant with a background in both journalism and psychology—stimulated significant interest both on the newsroom floor and at top levels of news management. It has since been broadened to cover a wider range of personnel and incorporates the aforementioned Trauma Risk Assessment Program developed by the Royal Marines. In addition, the BBC's news training division now incorporates basic information about trauma risk in its basic news training curriculum.

Summary

There is no simple, singular method for lending psychological support to journalists covering traumatic events, especially those who are involved in humanitarian crises. It is clear, however, that education and training are key both to give journalists information they need about trauma and to develop a network of knowledgeable professional peers. Over time we have developed a series of strategies to support journalists, and we continue to develop strategies to assist various sectors of the news business. We try to implement programs that will help journalists consider these issues both before and after difficult assignments. Organizational and individual programs are likely to be most successful in helping journalists facing humanitarian crises communicate the experiences of victims and transmit their suffering to a broader public.

References

Danieli, Y. (2002). *Sharing the front line and the back hills: International protectors and providers: Peacekeepers, humanitarian aid workers and the media in the midst of crisis.* Amityville, NY: Baywood Publishing.

Eriksson, C. B., Vande Kemp, H., Gorsuch, R., Hoke, S., & Foy, D. W. (2001). Trauma exposure and PTSD symptoms in international relief and development personnel. *Journal of Traumatic Stress., 14*(1), 205–219.

Feinstein, A., Owen, J., & Blair, N. (2002). A hazardous profession: War, journalists, and psychopathology. *American Journal of Psychiatry, 159*, 1570–1575.

Gilbert, A., Hirschkorn, P., Murphy, M., Walensky., R., & Stephens, M. (2002). *Covering catastrophe: Broadcast journalists report September 11th.* Chicago: Bonus Books.

McCann, L., & Pearlman, L. (1990). Vicarious traumatization: A framework for understanding the psychological effects of working with victims. *Journal of Traumatic Stress,, 3*, 131–149.

Newman, E. (2002) Journalists and traumatic stress. In Y. Danieli (Ed.). *Sharing the front line and the back hills: International protectors and providers: Peacekeepers, humanitarian aid workers and the media in the midst of crisis* (pp. 305–315). Amityville, NY: Baywood Publishing.

———, Davis, J. L., & Kennedy, S. N. (in press). Journalism and the public during catastrophes. In Y. Neria, R. Gross, R. Marshall, & E. Susser (Eds.), *September 11, 2001: Treatment, research and public mental health in the wake of a terrorist attack.* New York: Cambridge University Press.

———, Simpson, R., & Handschuh, D. (2003). Trauma exposure and post-traumatic stress disorder among photojournalists. *Visual Communication Quarterly, 10*(1), 4–12.

Pyevich, C., Newman, E., & Daleidan, E. (2003). The relationship among cognitive schemas, job-related traumatic exposure, and PTSD in journalists. *Journal of Traumatic Stress, 16*(4), 325–328.

Regehr, C., Goldberg, G., & Hughes, J. (2002). Exposure to human tragedy, empathy, and trauma in ambulance paramedics. *American Journal of Orthopsychiatry, 72*(4), 505–513.

Simpson, R., & Boggs, J. (1999, Spring). An exploratory study of traumatic stress among newspaper journalists. *Journalism and Communication Monographs,* 1–24.

CONCLUSIONS AND RECOMMENDATIONS FOR FURTHER PROGRESS

Gilbert Reyes

A frequently expressed concern in humanitarian circles is that we are chronically engaged in the inefficient process of "reinventing the wheel." Frustrations regarding this issue seem justified, given the tendency of humanitarian organizations to operate in a more territorial and insular manner than is either necessary or wise. Counterarguments point to frequent conferences among these NGOs, but such meetings seldom result in substantive changes in policies or operations, and cooperative agreements are the exception rather than the rule. A reasonable inference can be drawn that some humanitarian organizations would rather take a proprietary stance toward "wheel development," preferring the autonomy and distinctiveness of creating their own "wheel" to the efficiency and communality involved in working cooperatively with others of their kind. Similar observations can be made regarding mental health professionals, who are sometimes better rewarded for relabeling borrowed "wheels" than they would be for adopting existing wheels with minimal adaptations to suit the particular conditions of their situation. One might say that, rather than reinventing the wheel (i.e., the general model of psychological support), a more efficient procedure is to adapt elements of wheels successfully used by others to fit the characteristics of one's own particular terrain. The responsibility for ensuring that a modified "wheel" (i.e., a situation-specific model) will be culturally congruent rests with the people in the affected areas, who are free to select what to keep or discard and choose the placement and timing of its use. Thus, what gets adopted in any given situation will be generally useful principles, but the operational details and practices will vary in accordance with needs, cultures, and conditions.

A major intention of the *Handbook of International Disaster Psychology* has been to establish a sufficiently diversified base of information on when, where, why, and how disaster psychosocial services are implemented, as well as what is done and by whom. Accordingly, the contributing authors have articulated many of the most important ideas that have influenced the development of psychosocial humanitarian operations over the past decade. They have also shared their own activities and experiences in a transparent manner so that others might learn from their successes and failures. Their descriptions of the practices and principles that have been employed to help heal the psychological and social wounds among populations affected by potentially traumatic events offer a rich resource from which others with similar goals may borrow to formulate their own programs and practices.

Volume 1 provided an overview of the field and addressed the fundamentals issues and principles of concern to those who design and implement psychosocial programs for disaster survivors. Volume 2 described a variety of programs conducted around the world and the recommended practices for promoting effect healing at both individual and collective levels. Volume 3 focused specifically on mental health issues of refugees and the favored approaches to needs assessment and psychosocial care under a complex set of conditions and stages of migration. Volume 4 identified several populations whose special needs and circumstances tend to be overlooked and thus require conscientious consideration to ensure adequate care. The authors, all of whom are experienced members of the international humanitarian community, represent a broad spectrum of nationalities, cultures, and viewpoints. The stories told in these pages should prove instructive and inspiring to anyone concerned with promoting the psychosocial welfare of people who have endured the fear and loss that accompany widespread violence and social upheaval. Readers are encouraged to glean from these works the most useful and inspiring ideas from which they can develop their own skills, practices, and programs.

Politics, Cultures, and Controversies Cannot Be Ignored

International psychosocial support activities have not unfolded without controversy. Some have argued that the humanitarian psychosocial movement reflects Western ideology with a vision of life and its norms that is at odds with native cultures indigenous to those places where catastrophic events are most likely to occur. Critics invoke images of cultural imperialism perpetrated by the former colonial aggressors against the relatively innocent and primitive captives of their misguided ministrations. There is certainly some truth in these accusations, given the asymmetry of a humanitarian community dominated by lighter-skinned people of the Northern Hemisphere "serving" the darker-skinned peoples of the Southern Hemisphere in a present version of *White Man's Burden* (Kipling, 1899). But the comparisons employed by these critics are commonly as dramatic, overwrought, and anecdotal as the claims their adversaries use to compel the forces of "compassionate" action. In the absence of reliable evidence, what poses for truth may be unfounded but persuasive claims which better serve the political or religious agendas of their purveyors than they do the psychosocial needs of their targets.

Cultural differences are often invoked as obstacles to effective helping. Cultures do have expectations and values that set boundaries around actions and influence the effectiveness of our means and the appropriateness of our goals. But that does not mean that intercultural collaboration is all about obstacles (Marsella & Christopher, 2004; Szegedy-Maszak, 2005). Cultures are also resilient and malleable to conditions, and can be understood as resources rather than obstacles. Moreover, because the most prominent voices against disseminating "Western models" of psychological support are often Western intellectuals (Pupavac, 2001; Summerfield, 1999, 2005), the discourse is suspiciously devoid of non-Western voices. That is, it would appear to be an argument among "Western" factions, rather than between Western and non-Western voices. This invites a comparison with the colonial era, during which factions within the dominant powers argued over what was in the best interest of the cultures and people whom they held in subordination. The time for Western speakers to serve as proxies for non-Westerners should be passing, and the fact that non-Western speakers often call for more collaboration casts suspicion on the claims of the anti-Western Westerners.

This state of affairs is not specific to the debates over models or intervention strategies, but instead cuts across almost every issue and area of concern in humanitarian intervention. Representatives of developing nations are shamefully underrepresented in the discourse of assertions, arguments, and deliberations that converge to influence the development of humanitarian psychosocial policies affecting their regions. Moreover, even when governments and ministries from the developing world are somewhat represented, the same cannot be said for less affluent groups with little access to state power. This means that women, religious and ethnic minorities, indigenous tribes, and underclasses may have little say in the planning, implementation, and distribution of psychosocial services. Thus, a strong recommendation is presently expressed for greater inclusion of non-Western voices and perspectives in the discourse over which psychosocial beliefs and practices are appropriate, welcome, or desirable for use among disaster survivors in developing countries. Beyond this, it is also important to seek the insight and wisdom of groups at the margins of national and international power circles. Of particular concern is the muted influence of women from the least developed nations, whose lives (and those of their children) are among those most frequently and severely affected by war and other disasters.

Concerted International Efforts Are Needed

Humanitarian stakeholders share values and interests that should improve their prospects for collaborating toward commonly held aspirations.

Nevertheless, it is a widely held perception that they often function with a greater emphasis on autonomy than on cooperation. While it is understandable and predictable that the social psychology of these organizations would mirror those of governments and corporations, it is unfortunate that humanitarian organizations would rather tolerate waste and duplication than pursue cooperative partnerships that might allow a more efficient division of efforts and responsibilities. For example, psychosocial support for expatriate delegates has received considerable attention, and some, but not all, organizations have the requisite resources to provide mental health care for their field personnel. Cooperative agreements would allow psychosocial delegates from one NGO partner to share their services with personnel from another, resulting in better distribution of preventive care without the need for each NGO to develop its own psychosocial services.

As recently as 2001, the World Health Organization issued a declaration requesting that the international community agree to consensual guidelines for improving cooperation in the best interest of serving the psychosocial needs of refugees and other displaced populations (WHO, 2001). Such cooperation and collaboration would require division of roles and activities, a consequence of which would be to limit the autonomy of any given signatory organization. Unfortunately, the sovereignty of governments and NGOs alike tends to supersede such noble ideals as cooperative action or the placing of a beneficiary's interests above organizational politics. Nevertheless, leaders in the humanitarian community, faced with inadequate funding and an escalating spiral of mission objectives, should take a progressive route toward the forging of collaborative agreements that would improve efficiency and decrease unnecessary duplication of services.

International Standards of Care Are Needed

Psychosocial services have become a staple part of humanitarian relief operations around the world. Much of this progression has been driven by an increasing emphasis on the psychologically "traumatic" impact of war, disasters, and other tragic events. The fundamental propositions of international disaster psychology begin with the belief that extreme psychological distress and trauma predictably follow from events in which death, injury, and massive loss are involved. Specific claims are seldom made regarding the magnitude of the psychosocial consequences, but the impact is expected to include profound distress and substantial impairment of adaptive behavior among a large proportion of the population. A sense of extreme urgency is also evident in the alarming tone of news reports quoting claims by international mental health experts that major portions of populations affected by the 2004 Indian Ocean tsunami will develop trauma or other mental disorders (e.g., WHO, 2005). The responses to these alarms vary, with some ad hoc psychosocial emergency teams responding within the first few weeks (e.g., Kuriansky, 2005), while larger organizations take a more cautious, measured, and deliberative stance (Anderson, 2005).

Given the generally predictable occurrence of disasters, wars, and other catastrophic events, there would seem to be a third alternative in which planned action strategies are prepared well in advance. Once an activating event occurs, the strategy can quickly be reviewed and revised to fit any unanticipated conditions and the action plan can then be implemented without unnecessary delay. In fact, many governmental and nongovernmental organizations do exactly that with regard to material supplies such as food, water, medicines, munitions, and plastic sheeting. Indeed, this policy of preparedness for the unexpected is quite common for most goods that are considered essential to survival or social stability. Countless institutions, from police and fire departments to hospitals and insurance companies, exist to respond quickly when chronic problems arise, and many communities now have emergency mental health response capacities as well. Yet the global community, after more than a decade of experience with international disasters, remains relatively unprepared to respond to the psychosocial aspects of a major disaster in any systematic and concerted manner.

After nearly a decade of discussion regarding "best practices," no widely accepted standards of care have emerged. Contributing to this problem is the paucity of real research in this area. The present author recommends that humanitarian psychosocial organizations and experts (e.g., Psychosocial Working Group, 2004), convene not only to establish consensual endorsement of interventions, but also to develop action strategies for responding with all deliberate speed and coordination to address the psychosocial needs of disaster survivors. Organizations with an historical head start in developing psychosocial programs can help to inform others, and the sharing of lessons learned and approaches to delivering services can be exchanged in the service of all concerned. A more provocative suggestion would include establishing an international NGO dedicated specifically to providing psychosocial support in a manner analogous to that of Médecines Sans Frontières (Doctors Without Borders) in the arena of medical care.

Rapid Assessment of Psychosocial Needs Should Be a Standard Practice

Recent efforts directed toward the rapid assessment of psychosocial needs in disaster-affected populations have been helpful and instructive (e.g., Dodge, 2006; Jacobs et al., 2006), but episodic and limited in scope. The history of medical and psychosocial interventions demonstrates the importance of accurately assessing problems and resources before devising a plan to provide services. In the rush to relieve human suffering after catastrophic events, there is a danger in assuming the nature and magnitude of psychosocial needs while ignoring existing resource capacities in favor of imported experts. Although it is true that some presuppositions based on past experience are likely to prove true, important information may be missed or delayed unless needs assessment is granted a formal role in the overall service plan. To ease the succession from needs assessment to intervention, it is possible to begin assessing very early and in tandem with the deploying and tailoring of services (i.e., listening to the beneficiaries and tailoring the service model). It is also crucial to build an evaluation component into the service model so that the lessons learned are less subject to global appraisals that suit political rather than developmental aims.

Psychological Trauma versus Disaster Psychology

The international humanitarian community must operate on assumptions that are either self-evident or adapted from analogous circumstances. Thus, it is self-evident that supplies of clean water will be critically needed in remote regions where refugees often assemble, and it stands to reason that the emotional needs of people displaced by a wildfire will be analogous to those of people displaced by an earthquake. Historical trends in the mental health fields have elevated the concept of psychological trauma to a position from which it eclipses any other explanatory framework or descriptive terminology. This has led to a condition where psychological trauma is treated as though its existence and importance are self-evident across every type of human catastrophe, from war to flood and famine to disease. In turn, the proper response to these events must center foremost on preventing or alleviating the formation of a traumatic disorder. Evidence to support the proposition that refugees (Fazel, Wheeler, & Danesh, 2005), torture survivors (Silove, 1999), and others who have suffered terribly in disasters often develop trauma-related symptoms and clinical disorders is abundant and convincing. But there are many psychosocial consequences other than trauma that carry great importance and that are often more amenable to change without intrusive interventions that may not be welcomed or valued by disaster survivors. Thus, the emphasis on trauma may inadvertently obscure the importance of less dramatic issues that are not as "sexy," compelling, and provocative in tone. Nevertheless, what is actually provided in many instances is not "trauma-focused treatment," but instead consists of more mundane-sounding approaches such as education, stress management, and crisis intervention, which are often what is most useful for prevention activities and immediate relief of acute stress.

Disaster psychology, while closely connected to traumatology, is also distinct in several ways, including a decidedly normalizing stance toward short-term responses to acute stress and a pronounced emphasis on community-based interventions. In contrast to the clinical therapies typically applied in cases of post-traumatic stress disorder, the techniques preferred by disaster psychologists are more akin to crisis intervention and stress management and emphasize reduction of emotional arousal with brief support for problem solving and other effective coping strategies. Disaster survivors are not referred to as either clients or patients, and no "case" is ever formulated or assigned to a particular provider. Privacy is almost impossible, confidentiality is very limited, and no formal therapeutic relationship is either acknowledged or terminated. Rather, if the disaster psychologist detects the need for "clinical" services, a referral is made to an appropriately skilled provider who need not be experienced in disaster mental health. More often, the approach taken could best be described as a "public health" approach, with the purpose of taking steps to prevent the need for more targeted interventions by reducing the impact of known risk factors. This proactive model is superior in many ways to reactive models, but it requires very different skills and objectives from those needed for working with a more select group of survivors who display symptoms of clinical disorders. Thus, the qualifications for disaster psychologists are substantially different from those of traumatologists, and these areas of expertise are not interchangeable. Therefore, while skilled trauma-clinicians have much to offer in response to disaster survivors, they should also acknowledge the need to develop the pertinent skills for disaster field assignments.

Humanitarian Assistance and Military Aggression Are Incompatible

Interventions can take countless forms, and it is debatable whether the aims are indeed wholly altruistic and compassionate (i.e., humanitarian), or if there is another, more selfish agenda being disguised. The secular humanitarian movement has long been encumbered by the historical example of religious charities that blended compassionate deeds with missionary indoctrination. Selective governmental humanitarian efforts in the late twentieth century were often suspected of being part of a global propaganda struggle between the opposing powers of communism and capitalism during the Cold War. These examples illustrate the fragile credibility of altruistic acts across national and cultural boundaries and should inform true humanitarians of the dangers of blended agendas. In a spate of publications over the past decade, contributors have called the humanitarian community to task over its questionable behavior or suspect motives (Holzgrefe & Keohane, 2003; Moore, 1999; Smillie & Minear, 2004). Concurrently, the rates of intentional violence against humanitarian personnel have reached historically high levels (Sheik, Gutierrez, Bolton, Spiegel, Thieren, & Burnham, 2000), as illustrated by the 2003 bombings of the United Nations and Red Cross offices in Iraq during the American occupation. In such a climate of scrutiny, criticism, and profound security concerns, it is more important than ever that humanitarian motives be kept wholly distinct from partisan politics and military adventures.

Since its inception, the Red Cross/Red Crescent movement has wisely promoted and subscribed to principles of neutrality and impartiality in the pursuit of humanitarian goals. Only the strictest adherence to such principles can possibly serve to shield humanitarian workers and the people they seek to serve from becoming targets of terror, torture, and death. This is not to say that military means cannot be employed in the service of humanitarian ends. Indeed, the ostensible rationale behind many if not most wars is to serve the greater good of humanity while defeating some evil force. But in violence the ends are often believed to justify any means of achieving them, and this includes the resort to instrumental aggression in the service of geopolitical goals of domination, pacification, and exploitation. Conversely, in humanitarianism the means must conform to principles of compassion, dignity, and human rights if the ends are to maintain legitimacy. Anything less threatens to destroy the very foundation upon which the international humanitarian enterprise has been erected.

Psychosocial Issues Need Better Advocacy

In the competition for disaster relief resources, psychosocial concerns are given more lip service than action. Basic survival needs are so clear and compelling that humanitarian mental health advocates find themselves relegated to the margins while central planning concerns are pursued with fervor. This is to some extent a necessary and reasonable situation, since mental health is a relative luxury in the face of mass destruction and death. Nevertheless, if psychosocial interventions are ever to be both timely and effective, they must move from being marginal concerns toward being integral and influential in the overall scheme of disaster response planning.

At present the priorities are such that mental health and psychosocial support activities have more propaganda value than actual influence. This helps to keep the mental health sector in a reactive role, rather than supporting systematic, strategic development of responsive operational abilities and the undertaking of initiatives for building more resilient local capacity . Instead, the current state of affairs allows for a public voicing of compassion and vague claims of action for the anguish and trauma of the affected people, while the pace of response is more timid and tentative. This is to some extent due to legitimate doubts regarding the need for psychosocial interventions and an absence of evidence supporting the effectiveness of what is presently being offered. Thus, disaster mental health advocates will need to consider their steps carefully if they are to advance their cause while avoiding the temptation to overstate their importance at the risk of further undermining their precarious progress.

References

Anderson, N. B. (2005). The APA tsunami relief effort, part 2. *APA Monitor, 36*(4), 9.

Dodge, G. R. (2006). Assessing the psychosocial needs of communities affected by disaster. In G. Reyes & G. A. Jacobs (Eds.), *Handbook of international disaster psychology, Vol. 1. Fundamentals and overview.* Westport, CT: Praeger Publishers.

Fazel, M., Wheeler, J., & Danesh, J. (2005). Prevalence of serious mental disorder in 7000 refugees resettled in Western countries: A systematic review. *Lancet, 365,* 1309–1314.

Holzgrefe, J. L., & Keohane, R. O. (2003). *Humanitarian intervention: Ethical, legal, and political dilemmas.* New York: Cambridge University Press.

Jacobs, G. A., Revel, J. P., Reyes, G., & Quevillon, R. P. (2006). A tool for rapidly assessing the mental health needs of refugees and internally displaced populations. In G. Reyes & G. A. Jacobs (Eds.), *Handbook of international disaster psychology, Vol. 3. Refugee mental health.* Westport, CT: Praeger Publishers.

Kipling, R. (1899, February). The white man's burden: The United States and the Philippine Islands. *McClure's Magazine*, p. 12.

Kuriansky, J. (2005, February 21). Finding life in a living hell. Retrieved March 31, 2005, from http://www.nydailynews.com/front/story/283039p-242333c.html

Marsella, A. J., & Christopher, M. A. (2004). Ethnocultural considerations in disasters: An overview of research, issues, and directions. *Psychiatric Clinics of North America, 27*, 521–539.

Moore, J. (1999). *Hard choices: Moral dilemmas in humanitarian intervention.* New York: Rowman & Littlefield.

Psychosocial Working Group (2004). *Considerations in planning psychosocial programs.* Retrieved February 15, 2005, from http://www.forcedmigration.org/psychosocial/papers/PWGpapers.htm

Pupavac, V. (2001). Therapeutic governance: Psycho-social intervention and trauma risk management. *Disasters, 25*, 358–372.

Sheik, M., Gutierrez, M. I., Bolton, P., Spiegel, P., Thieren, M., & Burnham, G. (2000). Deaths among humanitarian workers. *British Medical Journal, 321*, 166–168.

Silove, D. (1999). The psychosocial effects of torture, mass human rights violations, and refugee trauma: Towards an integrated conceptual framework. *Journal of Nervous and Mental Disease, 187*, 200–207.

Smillie, I., & Minear, L. (2004). *The charity of nations: Humanitarian action in a calculating world.* Bloomfield, CT: Kumarian Press.

Summerfield, D. (1999). A critique of seven assumptions behind psychological trauma programmes in war-affected areas. *Social Science & Medicine, 48*, 1449–1462.

———. (2005). What exactly is emergency or disaster "mental health"? *Bulletin of the World Health Organization, 83*, 76.

Szegedy-Maszak, M. (2005, January 17). The borders of healing. *U.S. News & World Report, 138*(2), 36–37.

World Health Organization (WHO) (2001). Declaration of cooperation: Mental health of refugees, displaced and other populations affected by conflict and post-conflict situations. Author: Geneva.

———. (2005, January 19). Press release (SEA/PR/1384): WHO warns of widespread psychological trauma among Tsunami victims. Retrieved April 25, 2005, from http://w3.whosea.org/en/Section316/Section503/Section1861_8571.htm

Epilogue

Yael Danieli

This impressive, thoughtful *Handbook of International Disaster Psychology* succeeds in conveying and mapping many of the key issues and complex challenges that have confronted the field and influenced the development of psychosocial humanitarian operations over the past decade. The scope and depth of this superb compilation would not have been possible even a decade ago, demonstrating how far we have come as a field. But much of it is also a reminder of how far we have yet to go in a world that has unremittingly produced disasters that, despite growing awareness, are met at best by episodic and inconsistent response and a rather limited commitment to preventing them and their long-term—possibly multigenerational—effects.

Created on the ruins of the World War II, the United Nations (UN) was formed in a spirit of optimism. Never again would the world community permit such a devastating war to take place. The world organization was joined by numerous nongovernmental organizations (NGOs) in its efforts to create a new, intensified impetus to alleviate poverty, eradicate illness, and provide education to shape a better world. But despite 60 years of energetic action, problems abound, and are even increasing. Disasters and their consequences continue to torment individuals and societies, leaving trails of illness, suffering, poverty, and death. Life expectancy has increased in most countries, and the proportion of children in the world has risen dramatically as well, with a corresponding growth in the need for food, health care, and education.

Tragically, trauma is clearly as ubiquitous today as it was during and immediately following World War II, when the UN was created, in the words of the Charter, "to save succeeding generations from the scourge of war, which twice in our lifetime has brought untold sorrow to mankind, and to reaffirm faith in fundamental human rights, in the dignity and worth of the human person, in the equal rights of men and women and of nations large and small, and to establish conditions under which justice and respect for the obligations arising from treaties and other sources of international law can be maintained, and to promote social progress and better standards of life in larger freedom."

The end of the Cold War, and the vanishing of its ideological barriers, has given rise, not to a more peaceful world, but to a world in which nationalist and ethnic tensions have frequently exploded into conflict. International standards of human rights, although largely accepted by states, are discarded in the face of fanaticism and stored-up hatred. In addition, issues between states North and South—developed and underdeveloped—are growing more acute, and call for attention at the highest levels. The most recent recognition of this in the context of the UN is the Secretary-General's report, *In Larger Freedom: Towards Development, Security and Human Rights for All* (United Nations, 2005).

People today know more about what goes on in the world than ever before. Cameras transmit their revelations within minutes to living rooms around the globe. Modern mass communication has erased geographical distance and informs us of suffering immediately as it occurs. But increasing and intense coverage may lead to desensitization and apathy as efforts to cope with ever present, overwhelming news of disturbing events result in a psychological distancing from the suffering (Figley, 1995). With the parallel exposure to fictional film and video, the distinction between reality and fantasy becomes blurred. War and disasters may even become entertainment (note the proliferation of reality shows on television). The worst-case scenario occurs when the world is a helpless eye witness and its efforts merely symbolic, with the sole intention of giving the appearance that something is being done (among Sarajevo's 85,000 children, a symbolic group of 32 injured were evacuated). A contrasting scenario is the unprecedented, overwhelming generosity of pledges and outpouring of philanthropy, likely inspired by its proximity to gift-giving holidays, to the victims of the December 26, 2004, Asian tsunami. However, even if we accept that this response was due to the seemingly inherent political neutrality of natural disasters, how do we explain international neglect in the case of other natural disasters, as in El Salvador? The constant threat of terrorism and the aching persistence of war crimes, crimes against humanity, and genocide—previous, ongoing, and current—with the continued suffering of their victims, keep the international community ashamed.

Because the scars of traumatic stress can be both deep and long-lasting, their treatment is imperative. Such treatment, all too often neglected, is crucial in conflict resolution and in the building of peace—possibly the best preventer of further war and violence—among individuals and groups. Unless treated, the germ of hatred and holding on to the image of the enemy—both consequences of traumatic stress—may give rise to new conflicts and bloody clashes between ethnic or religious groups in an endless cycle of violence. Victims may become perpetrators as individuals, as members of families and communities, or as nations. Genuine peace cannot exist without the resolution of trauma. If traumatic stress constitutes one element in this terrible cycle, its interception could be one way to break the cycle.

The cessation of wanton violence and abuse of power without full multidimensional integration of trauma (e.g., political, psychological, social, legal) will impair a nation's ability to maintain peace, to rebuild so that sustainable development is possible.

International Response

In addition to documenting the ubiquity of exposure to extreme events, history has recorded a wide variety of sociopolitical efforts to intervene in ways that address the needs of those who have been exposed and to prevent or minimize the impact of future exposures. Since the creation of the United Nations in 1945, the response by the organized international community and in particular by the UN system has been largely political. The main political imperatives have been from two opposite poles of conflict in finding political solutions: on the one hand, the continued existence of international concern about human suffering, stimulated by the modern media, and on the other hand, conceptions of state sovereignty that lead states to resist international interference in matters that they consider to be under their control and within their jurisdiction. By and large, the joint arrival of intergovernmental and nongovernmental organizations has been able to bring much relief to many victims of disasters, even though such relief tends to be temporary, may not alleviate all the hardships suffered by the victims, and will frequently not address the psychosocial damage. This book should help in keeping attention focused on remedying this unacceptable situation.

Trauma and the Continuity of Self: A Multidimensional, Multidisciplinary Integrative (TCMI) Framework

In my own attempt to describe the diverse and complex destruction caused by massive trauma such as is examined in this volume, I concluded that only a multidimensional, multidisciplinary integrative framework (Danieli, 1998) would be adequate. An individual's identity involves a complex interplay of multiple spheres or systems. Among these are (1) the physical and intrapsychic; (2) the interpersonal—familial, social, communal; (3) the ethnic, cultural, religious, spiritual, natural; (4) the educational/professional/occupational; and (5) the material/economic, legal, environmental, political, national, and international. These systems dynamically coexist along the time dimension to create a continuous conception of life from past through present to the future. Ideally, the individual should simultaneously have free psychological access to and movement within all these identity dimensions.

Trauma Exposure and "Fixity"

Trauma exposure can cause a rupture, a possible regression, and a state of being "stuck" in this free flow, which I (Danieli, 1998) have called *fixity*. The intent, place, time, frequency, duration, intensity, extent, and meaning of the trauma for the individual, and the survival strategies used to adapt to it (see, for example, Danieli, 1985) as well as post-victimization traumas, will determine the degree of rupture and the severity of the fixity. Fixity can be intensified in particular by the *conspiracy of silence* (Danieli, 1982, 1998), the survivors' reaction to the societal indifference (including that of health care and other professionals), avoidance, repression, and denial of the survivors' trauma experiences (see also Symonds, 1980). Society's initial emotional outburst, along with its simultaneous yet unspoken demand for rapid return to apparent normality, is an important example. This *conspiracy of silence* is detrimental to the survivors' familial and sociocultural (re)integration because it intensifies their already profound sense of isolation from and mistrust of society. It further impedes the possibility of the survivors' intrapsychic integration and healing, and makes the task of mourning their losses impossible. Fixity may increase vulnerability to further trauma. It also may render *chronic* the immediate reactions to trauma (e.g., acute stress disorder), and, in the extreme, become lifelong *post-trauma/victimization adaptational styles* (Danieli, 1985, 1997). This occurs when survival strategies generalize to a way of life and become an integral part of one's personality, repertoire of defense, or character armor.

Viewed from a family systems perspective, what happened in one generation will affect what happens in the next, though the actual behavior may take a variety of forms. Within an intergenerational context, the trauma and its impact may be passed down as the family legacy even to children born *after* the trauma. The awareness of the possibility of pathogenic intergenerational processes and the understanding of the mechanisms of transmission should contribute to finding effective means for preventing their transmission to succeeding generations (Danieli, 1985, 1993, 1998).

The possible long-term impact of trauma on one's personality and adaptation and the *intergenerational* transmission of victimization-related pathology still await explicit recognition and inclusion in future editions of the diagnostic nomenclature. Until they are included, the behavior of some survivors, and some children of survivors, may be misdiagnosed, its etiology misunderstood, and its treatment, at best, incomplete.

This framework allows evaluation of each system's degree of rupture or resilience, and thus informs the choice and development of optimal multi-level interventions. Repairing the rupture and thereby freeing the flow rarely means going back to "normal." Clinging to the possibility of "returning to normal" may indicate denial of the survivors' experiences and thereby fixity.

Exposure to trauma may also prompt review and reevaluation of one's self-perception, beliefs about the world, and values. Although changes in self-perception, beliefs, and values can be negative, varying percentages of trauma-exposed people report positive changes as a result of coping with the aftermath of trauma (called "post-traumatic growth," by Tedeschi & Calhoun, 1996). Survivors have described an increased appreciation for life, a reorganization of their priorities, and a realization that they are stronger than they thought. This is related to Danieli's (1994) recognition of competence vs. helplessness in coping with the aftermath of trauma. Competence (through one's own strength and/or the support of others), coupled with an awareness of options, can provide the basis of hope in recovery from traumatization.

Integration of the trauma must take place in *all* of life's relevant dimensions or systems and cannot be accomplished by the individual alone. Routes to integration may include reestablishing, relieving, and repairing the ruptured systems of the survivor and his or her community and nation, and restoring the surviving community's or nation's place in the international community. For example, in the context of examining the "Right to restitution, compensation and rehabilitation for victims of gross violations of human rights and fundamental freedoms" for the United Nations Centre for Human Rights (1992), some necessary components for integration and healing in the wake of massive trauma emerged from my interviews with victims/survivors of the Nazi Holocaust, interned Japanese-Americans, victims of political violence in Argentina and Chile, and professionals working with them, both in and outside their countries. Presented as goals and recommendations, these components are organized from the following perspectives: (A) individual, (B) societal, (C) national, and (D) international.

   A. **Reestablishment of the victim's equality, power, and dignity—the basis of reparation.** This is accomplished by (a) compensation, both real and symbolic; (b) restitution; (c) rehabilitation; and (d) commemoration.
   B. **Relieving the victim's stigmatization and separation from society**. This is accomplished by (a) commemoration; (b) memorials to heroism; (c) empowerment; (d) education.
   C. **Repairing the nation's ability to provide and maintain equal value under law and the provisions of justice**. This is accomplished by (a) prosecution; (b) apology; (c) securing public records; (d) education; (e) creating national mechanisms for monitoring, conflict resolution, and preventive interventions.
   D. **Asserting the commitment of the international community to combat impunity and provide and maintain equal value under law and the provisions of justice and redress**. This is accomplished by (a) creating ad hoc and permanent mechanisms for prosecution (e.g., ad hoc tribunals and ultimately an International Criminal Court); (b) securing

public records; (c) education; (d) creating international mechanisms for monitoring, conflict resolution, and preventive interventions.

It is important to emphasize that this comprehensive framework, rather than presenting *alternative* means of reparation, sets out necessary *complementary* elements, to be applied in different weights, in different situations and cultures, and at different points in time. It is also crucial that victims/survivors participate in the choice of the reparation measures adopted for them.

To fulfill the reparative and preventive goals of psychological recovery from trauma, perspective and integration through awareness and containment must be established so that one's sense of continuity, belongingness, and rootedness are restored. To be healing and even potentially self-actualizing, the integration of traumatic experiences must be examined from the perspective of the *totality* of the trauma survivors' and family members' lives.

With survivors it is especially hard to draw conclusions based on outward appearances. Survivors often display external markers of success (e.g., occupational achievement or established families) that in truth represent survival strategies. Clearly, such accomplishments may facilitate adaptation and produce feelings of fulfillment in many survivors. Thus, the external attainments do represent significant adaptive achievement in their lives. Nevertheless, even survivors in the "those who made it" category (Danieli, 1985) still experience difficulties related to their traumatic past, suggesting that overly optimistic views of adaptation may describe defense rather than effective coping. In fact, it is within this category that we observe the highest rates of suicide among survivors as well as their children. Furthermore, these optimistic views and accounts may cause survivors, who may have already felt isolated and alienated from those who did not undergo similar traumatic experiences, to see themselves as deficient, especially when compared to their "supercoper" counterparts, and deter them from seeking help.

The finding that survivors have areas of both vulnerability and resilience is not paradoxical when viewed within a multidimensional framework for multiple levels of post-traumatic adaptation. And tracing a history of multiple traumas along the time dimension at different stages of development reveals that, while time heals ills for many, for *traumatized* people time may not heal but may magnify their response to further trauma and may carry intergenerational implications.

Future Directions

In the context of prevention, an absolutely necessary precondition is the creation of a network of early warning systems, which necessitates thorough familiarity with, understanding of, and genuine respect for the local, national and regional culture(s) and history (Danieli, 1998). The United Nations and its related organizations have developed such systems concerning environmental threats, the risk of nuclear accident, natural disasters, mass movements of populations, the threat of famine, and the spread of disease. It is now time to include the potential effects of traumatic stress in preparing to confront these and other events.

Comparing this book's conclusions with our conclusions of "International Responses to Traumatic Stress: Humanitarian, Human Rights, Justice, Peace and Development Contributions, Collaborative Actions and Future Initiatives" (Danieli, Rodley, & Weisaeth, 1996), I felt delighted with the editor's assertion that psychosocial services have become "a staple part of humanitarian relief operations around the world" (Reyes, 2006, p. XX). But I must agree with him that, despite this progress, psychosocial issues still need further and greater advocacy. We have a long way to go toward ensuring that mental health concerns become integral and influential in the overall architecture of disaster response planning, in order to support systematic, strategic development of operational capabilities and initiatives to build more resilient local capacity.

I am saddened by the inefficient process of "reinventing the wheel" that persists among both national and international humanitarian organizations. It might be helpful for humanitarian psychosocial organizations and experts, without sacrificing their diversity and richness, to endorse core, evidence-based standards of care and interventions. It would also be useful to develop coordinated action strategies for flexibly available psychosocial preparedness to enable speedy, systematic responses that address the psychosocial needs of disaster survivors.

Although mostly Western, the authors are experienced members of the international humanitarian community, representing a broad spectrum of nationalities, cultures, and viewpoints. I agree with the editors that the time for Western speakers to serve as proxies for non-Westerners should be passing and that *all* voices and perspectives—not only those of the imported experts—must be included in the discourse over which psychosocial frameworks and practices are appropriate for use among disaster survivors in developing countries. The resources, insight, and wisdom of groups at the margins of national and international power circles must be included as well.

Concurring with the guidelines generated by the Task Force on International Trauma Training of the International Society for Traumatic Stress Studies (Weine, Danieli, Silove, van Ommeren, Fairbank, & Saul, 2002), the editor argues for rapid assessment of psychosocial needs to become standard practice, and for building an evaluation component into the service to assess its effectiveness. Such assessment and evaluation practices will guarantee that lessons learned are less subject to appraisals that suit political rather than developmental aims. The concern over the incompatibility of humanitarian assistance, partisan politics, and military aggression is repeated in this book as well, and reinforced by the recognition of the cost paid by humanitarian aid workers and others on the front line (Danieli, 2002).

The five Cs of disaster work—Communication, Cooperation, Collaboration, Coordination, and Complementarity—apply here, too. So does the need for leadership strategies, such as compassionate articulation (Spratt, 2002), that can reduce chaos and terror and thereby diminish the effectiveness of terrorism.

Nongovernmental organizations must improve their efforts at coordination. The greatest obstacle still seems to be competition for visibility and credit, which is essential if they are to compete effectively for increasingly scarce resources. At both the organizational level and in the field, the desire to have highly visible, quantitatively impressive programs can lead to competitiveness and jealousies that work against unified efforts.

There is a risk that the uncritical use of concepts such as coordination, which creates the impression of easy, quick solutions irrespective of the complexities of traumatic stress, may result in the loss of an operational meaning for these concepts. For example, the result may be too many coordinators and too few doing the work, or the actual work may be being reserved to nonprofessional and insufficiently trained volunteers. Such volunteers may serve for short periods of time, with traumatic detriment to themselves, and without contributing to the pool of accumulated knowledge that ought to move the field forward.

It is essential for UN agencies and programs, and for NGOs, to further define and develop complementary roles in their responses to traumatic stress. Complementarity involves the tolerance of, respect for, and capitalizing on the differing strengths of the various partners—UN bodies, governments, NGOs, and the communities they serve.

Some of the programs described in this work are inspiring in their excellence. But what comes through most of all is that, however superb some programs are, they are too few, and the challenges they must face are overwhelming. Each of the noble examples of programs is dwarfed by the needs with which our world is faced. In fact, the most striking theme that keeps emerging in the field is the enormous gulf between what needs to be done and the resources available to do it with. Although difficult in the short term, providing the international community with this needed expertise will lessen long-term costs, and possibly prevent intergenerational effects and the resulting much larger costs—both human and financial.

Another resource-related issue is that available funds tend to be used for emergency shipments of food, medicine, housing, and the like in reaction to situations that have been widely publicized by the media. Once the emergency is no longer new, and the dramatic pictures are no longer on the nightly news, funds usually dry up and are not available for sustaining the short-term gains or for long-term care.

The work in this area radiates good will, idealism, and commitment, despite cynicism and despair, and despite the realization—emerging from situations such as those in the former Yugoslavia, Rwanda, Kosovo, East Timor, Democratic Republic of Congo, and Darfur/Sudan—that humanity has failed to learn the lessons and honor the commitments made after World War II.

The same world that created the circumstances for the crime, the victimization, has also created the circumstances for good and kind and compassionate people to be there for each other, for the victims in time of need. Viewing our work through the prism of traumatic stress, within the multidimensional, multidisciplinary integrative (TCMI) framework, should thus have not only a healing, but also a humanizing, effect on the victims and on society as a whole.

We must pursue primary, secondary, and tertiary prevention. We must continue efforts to reduce the stigma that still exists against the field of mental health while broadening its reach to join hands with other disciplines. We must partner with others in fields at and beyond the boundaries of mental health and extend our investigations and preventive suggestions also to the root causes of disasters.

The danger of bioterrorism, with medically unexplained physical symptoms challenging patients, clinicians, scientists and policy makers, necessitates special training for all public health professionals. Its psychological casualties far outweigh the physical ones (Flynn, 2004), and its long-term social and psychological effects are likely to be as damaging as the acute ones, if not more so (Wessely, Hyams, & Bartholomew, 2001). The threat of bioterrorism also calls for revamping the health/mental health systems on all levels/dimensions—before, during, and after such attacks.

Despite growing awareness and the accumulated body of knowledge, there are still policy makers who either deny the existence of the invisible, psychological wounds, or feel that they have a lesser priority in an era of dwindling resources. At every level, government policy has yet to fully comprehend and embrace the centrality of psychosocial issues in understanding and responding to disasters, particularly to terrorism. For any nation to become optimally prepared to cope, homeland security must include, integrate, and adequately fund psychosocial security (Danieli, Brom, & Sills, 2005) and the full participation of the social sciences in all aspects of preparedness. This book should certainly advance this undertaking.

References

Danieli, Y. (1982). *Therapists' difficulties in treating survivors of the Nazi Holocaust and their children.* Dissertation Abstracts International, 42(12-B, Pt 1), 4927. (UMI No. 949-904).

———. (1985). The treatment and prevention of long-term effects and intergenerational transmission of victimization: A lesson from Holocaust survivors and their children. In C. R. Figley (Ed.), *Trauma and its Wake* (pp. 295–313). New York: Brunner/Mazel.

———. (1992). Preliminary reflections from a psychological perspective. In T.C. van Boven, C. Flinterman, F. Grunfeld & I. Westendorp (Eds.), *The Right to Restitution, Compensation and Rehabilitation for Victims of Gross Violations of Human Rights and Fundamental Freedoms.* Netherlands Institute of Human Rights [Studie-en Informatiecentrum Mensenrechten], Special issue No. 12.

————. (1993). The diagnostic and therapeutic use of the multi-generational family tree in working with survivors and children of survivors of the Nazi Holocaust. In J. P. Wilson & B. Raphael (Eds.) *International handbook of traumatic stress syndromes* [Stress and Coping Series, Donald Meichenbaum, Series Editor]. (pp. 889–898). New York: Plenum Publishing.

————. (1994). Resilience and hope. In G. Lejeune (Ed.), *Children Worldwide* (pp. 47–49). Geneva: International Catholic Child Bureau.

————. (1997). As survivors age: An overview. *Journal of Geriatric Psychiatry, 30* (1), 9–26.

————, Rodley, N.S., & Weisaeth, L. (Eds.) (1996). *International responses to traumatic stress: Humanitarian, human rights, justice, peace and development contributions, collaborative actions and future initiatives.* Amityville, NY: Baywood Publishing.

————. (1998). *International handbook of multigenerational legacies of trauma.* New York: Kluwer Academic/Plenum Publishing.

————. (2002). *Sharing the front line and the back hills: International protectors and providers, peacekeepers, humanitarian aid workers and the media in the midst of crisis.* Amityville, NY: Baywood Publishing.

————, Brom, D., & Sills, J. (Eds.). (2005). *The trauma of terrorism: Sharing knowledge and shared care. An international handbook.* Binghamton, NY: The Haworth Press.

Figley, C. R. (Ed.). (1995). *Compassion fatigue: Coping with secondary traumatic stress disorder in those who treat the traumatized.* New York: Brunner/Mazel.

Flynn, B. W., (2004) Letters to the Editor: Behavioral Health Aspects of Bioterrorism. *Biosecurity and Bioterrorism: Biodefense Strategy, Practice, and Science, 2,* 232.

Green, B. L., Friedman, M. J., de Jong, J., Solomon, S. D., Keane, T. M., Fairbank, J. A., Donelan, B., & Frey-Wouters, E. (Eds.) (2003). *Trauma interventions in war and peace: Prevention, practice, and policy.* New York: Kluwer Academic/Plenum Publishers.

Reyes, G. (2006). Conclusions and recommendations for further progress. In G. Reyes & G. A. Jacobs (Eds.), *Handbook of International Disaster Psychology.* Westport, CT: Praeger Publishers.

Spratt, M. (2002, August 28). 9/11 media may comfort, terrify. Retrieved on August 29, 2002, from http://www.dartcenter.org/articles/headlines/2002/2002_08_28.html

Symonds, M. (1980). The "second injury" to victims. *Evaluation and Change* [Special issue], 36–38.

Tedeschi, R. G., & Calhoun, L. G. (1996). The posttraumatic growth inventory: Measuring the positive legacy of trauma. *Journal of Traumatic Stress, 9,* 455–471.

United Nations (2005). *In larger freedom: Towards development, security and human rights for all. Report of the Secretary-General.* Retrieved May 31, 2005, from http://www.un.org/largerfreedom/contents.htm

Weine, S., Danieli, Y., Silove, D., Van Ommeren, M., Fairbank, J. A., & Saul, J. (2002). Guidelines for international training in mental health and psychosocial interventions for trauma exposed populations in clinical and community settings. *Psychiatry, 65*(2), 156–164.

Wessely, S., Hyams, K., & Bartholomew, R. (2001). Psychological implications of chemical and biological weapons. *British Medical Journal, 323,* 878–879.

APPENDIX: PROFILES OF INTERNATIONAL HUMANITARIAN AGENCIES

Many of the psychosocial services delivered following disasters and other international humanitarian emergencies depend on support from nongovernmental organizations (NGOs). These groups vary greatly in their size, countries of origin, resources, and stated missions and priorities. Some are secular or nonsectarian, while others are rooted in religious faiths. Several are part of the United Nations (UN) system, making them "nongovernmental" in the sense that they are not agents of any particular government, but they are nevertheless answerable to the member states that make up the UN. All, however, share a dedication to compassionate principles of humanitarian action and are committed to relieving the suffering of others and supporting improved quality of life for the beneficiaries of their activities.

The headquarters of these "international" organizations are mostly located in the major capitals of Europe and North America. Similarly, the majority of their administrative personnel are drawn from Europe and the United States, though this is perhaps less so within the UN system. Many of the people serving on international "missions" are citizens of the most developed nations and are referred to as "expatriates" (or "ex-pats") because they live for long periods outside their native countries. Some of these are the people most often seen on television broadcasts as spokespeople for the relief operations. The majority, however, are unknown but hardworking humanitarians who labor long hours under taxing conditions far from the comforts (and responsibilities) of home. These people are deserving of admiration for their ideals, altruistic deeds, and rugged perseverance under hardship conditions that their fellow citizens are unlikely ever to experience. Nevertheless, they do not make up the majority of humanitarian personnel at most disasters. Rather, it is the people who are native to the affected region who often perform most of the duties necessary to recovering the dead, saving lives, relieving pain, and the countless tasks involved in rebuilding their communities. Some work for wages, others are volunteers, and many go home to domiciles lacking most of the basic utilities and comforts that ex-pats still receive even on hardship assignments. They may also be victims of the very disaster or conflict situation that precipitated the relief operation, perhaps having been victimized or fearing for their lives or even losing the lives of family. And yet they find the strength to persevere and to lend a hand to others. If there are unsung heroes to be found in these endeavors, they are these.

Given the importance of international humanitarian organizations in the implementation of psychosocial services, an understanding of these stakeholders and their functions is crucial for those wishing to comprehend this complex field of endeavor. The following profiles of several major humanitarian organizations were mainly compiled by the editors and their staff from documents available on the Internet. All of the agencies were contacted and asked to provide their own profiles, but most declined. This is understandable, given their shoestring budgets, small numbers of available staff, and the countless crucial priorities with which they are faced. We are therefore grateful both to those who were able to respond by providing or editing their profiles and to those who referred us to their Web sites. In that regard, it must be noted that much of the text in these profiles was compiled from public information Web sites and therefore no authorship is claimed by the editors of this volume or their staff members, nor are authorships attributed to any particular staff members of the NGOs. That said, we regret if there are any errors in the public information that have been carried over into the present manuscript.

Christian Children's Fund (CCF)

Address:	821 Emerywood Parkway
	Richmond, VA 23294
Telephone:	(800) 776-6767

Also Known As:

Australia:	CCF of Australia
Canada:	CCF of Canada
Denmark:	BORNEfonden
France:	Un Enfant Par La Main
Germany:	CCF Kinderhilfswerk e.V
Ireland:	CCF Ireland
Korea:	Korea Welfare Foundation
New Zealand:	CCF of New Zealand
Sweden:	BARNfonden
Taiwan:	Taiwan Fund for Children & Families

Organizational Identity

Christian Children's Fund (CCF) is an international child development organization that works in 31 countries, assisting 7.6 million children and family members regardless of race, creed, or gender. CCF works for the well-being and protection of children by supporting locally led initiatives that strengthen families and communities, as well as helping them overcome poverty and protect the rights of their children. CCF programs are comprehensive—incorporating health, education, nutrition, and livelihood interventions that sustainably protect and nurture developing children. CCF works in any environment where poverty, conflict, and disaster threaten the well-being of children.

Brief History

Founded by a Presbyterian minister who had witnessed first-hand the devastation arising out of events leading to World War II, Christian Children's Fund began helping the children of China in 1938. Using the then-unique appeal of "child sponsorship," Dr. J. Calvitt Clarke dedicated his life to improving the lives of children throughout Asia. During more than 60 years of service CCF has broadened its range of assistance to children around the world. CCF currently assists children in 31 countries, including the United States.

Main Activities

Christian Children's Fund works in the United States, the Caribbean, Latin America, Africa, Asia, and Eastern Europe, focusing its comprehensive programs in six main areas of proven expertise: Early Childhood Development, Education, Emergency Relief, Health and Sanitation, Micro-Enterprise Development, and Nutrition. The overriding goal in each of these activities is to establish long-term programs that counter the effects of poverty.

Emergency Relief: In disasters, both natural and man-made, CCF mobilizes temporary Child Centered Spaces, offering basic education, primary health services, and psychosocial interventions. CCF also promotes reintegration, normalization, and community development that is child-focused. During emergencies, CCF works to help alleviate crisis while establishing long-term solutions such as food security and provision of clean water. Other efforts include providing adequate health care systems and educational training; empowering vulnerable women with literacy and advocacy training; setting up schools and training teachers; providing shelters; and establishing income-generation programs.

Health & Sanitation: CCF supports community-based health interventions, including immunization programs, diarrhea and malaria prevention, access to clean water and proper sanitation, and innovative community-based approaches to the HIV/AIDS pandemic.

Nutrition: CCF promotes growth monitoring of children to ensure proper development through adequate nutrition; promotes best feeding practices, including exclusive breast feeding; and addresses food security needs on the community level through animal husbandry and increased agricultural production.

Early Childhood Development: CCF helps children get the best start in life through programs that support integral growth and development, stimulating learning from birth through age five. CCF's Early Childhood Development work is designed to address holistic needs of children by fostering cognitive, social, and emotional development while ensuring that good health is maintained. Because active parent involvement is crucial, CCF has developed a Guide Mothers program that promotes good child-rearing practices, provides training materials, and offers hands-on and remote training for early childhood development practitioners. Additionally, the organization uses a Universal Monitoring Scale to track children's progress in specific areas of growth.

Micro Enterprise Development: CCF helps families and communities become self-sufficient through a three-pronged development approach. This includes micro credit loans and income-generating activities, as well as vocational and business training. CCF's micro-enterprise programs provide working capital to people who already have a trade but do not have access to the necessary start-up funds. The loans enable individuals to purchase large items (ovens, boats, etc.) so that their businesses can get off the ground. CCF believes that micro-enterprise programs lead to stability for families and makes lasting changes in children's lives.

Education: CCF works in collaboration with communities and local government authorities to ensure adequate classroom space and well-trained teachers in primary schools. CCF supports many innovative programs such as nontraditional education for children who must work to help support their families, special school programs for girls at risk of dropping out, peace curricula in schools in countries plagued by war and violence, and after-school tutorial programs and job training for young adults. Development of new schools, establishment of youth literacy programs, provision of condensed educational opportunities for older youth, and apprenticeships for former child soldiers are further examples of how CCF promotes education.

Psychosocial Programming

Psychological health, not just physical health, is addressed by CCF. CCF's "Grannies" program provides young women with opportunities for interaction with older generations. These grannies give information about reproductive health, maternal health, and psychological well-being, in order to increase the health for both babies and mothers. CCF also has programs based on home visitation so that trained personnel may monitor children's immunizations and general health, while teaching parents how to improve the lives of their children.

CCF also addresses the emotional and social impact of HIV/AIDS as a component of their larger response to HIV/AIDS. Families are taught how to protect and take care of their community through in-home care, community-based interventions, and educational outreach programs. Additionally, traditional healers are incorporated into many of these programs due to their importance in developing countries. The psychological impact of HIV/AIDS is addressed in these communities and opportunities for counseling of at-risk populations are made available. Psychological programs have also been implemented in Angola to treat 140,000 children affected by war trauma and in Bathore, where some 30,000 inhabitants migrated from the rural Northeast Albania when the communist system collapsed.

CCF is highly active in advocacy and policy formation issues related to child protection and psychosocial well-being both in the United States and in countries abroad where programs are implemented. In emergency situations in countries such as Afghanistan, Chad, Northern Uganda, and Angola, CCF works to make the psychosocial and protection needs of children and families highly visible and to stimulate donors and governments to provide holistic, community-based, culturally grounded support for children. In Washington, DC, CCF is highly active in venues such as InterAction and co-chairs the InterAction Protection Working Group and the Uganda Working Group. In these arenas, CCF works with policy leaders and U. S. government agencies to integrate child protection into their priorities and ongoing programming. CCF is also active in New York, serving as Co-Chair of the UNICEF NGO Committee and consulting on diverse issues concerning the psychosocial well-being of children in armed conflict.

CCF is active in psychosocial research. In fact, CCF is a core member of the Psychosocial Working Group that was initially convened by the Andrew W. Mellon Foundation. Through funding provided to the group, CCF is conducting research on the impact of large-scale psychosocial programs in Afghanistan in collaboration with Oxford University and Queen Margaret University. Also, CCF recently completed a major research project on children's experiences of poverty. The research indicated that for children, psychosocial dimensions, such as exclusion and depersonalization, are at the heart of their experience of poverty. Also, in Angola CCF conducts extensive research on girls who have been abducted by armed groups. On an ongoing basis, CCF's child protection and psychosocial staff conduct research on the cultural definitions of children's well-being, sources of vulnerability, methods of strengthening children's resilience, and impact of psychosocial programs.

CCF is in the process of integrating psychosocial and protection dimensions into its work in all sectors such as education, health, HIV/AIDS, and micro-credit. Its emphasis is on strengthening children's resilience, increasing local capacities to support children, and building strong child protection networks. The organization is also working to provide help for the helpers using culturally grounded methods.

Publications and Resources for Further Information

CCF provides public access to a variety of publications through its official website: http://www.christianchildrensfund.org

> *ChildWorld*—current and past issues including information on CCF programs and events are available for free download at http://www.christianchildrensfund.org/pubs/
> *ChildWire*—free monthly e-newsletter: http://www.christianchildrensfund.org/pubs/
> CCF Emergency Division: http://www.christianchildrensfund.org/emergency/default.aspx
> CCF's major study on poverty is contained in a three-volume series: *A Review of Contemporary Literature and Thought on Children and Poverty; Shaping A Response to Poverty; and Voices of Children.* The series is available in hard copy.

Church World Service (CWS)

Address: 475 Riverside Dr.
                New York, NY 10115
Telephone: (212) 870-2061
Fax: (212) 870-3523
Email: info@churchworldservice.org

Organizational Identity

Church World Service (CWS) is a faith-based organization affiliated with the National Council of the Churches of Christ in the United States working worldwide in over 80 countries to help communities in need. According to its mission statement, the organization is "Christians working together with partners to eradicate hunger and poverty and to promote peace and justice around the world." These goals are accomplished by working ecumenically with members' communions. A continual focus is put on promoting people's dignity and rights, while meeting their basic needs. Unlike many other voluntary agencies that rely solely on others' donations to fund their programs, CWS is funded through community appeals, U.S. governmental support, member communions, donated materials, and investments.

The Church World Service Emergency Response Program was established as a means to incorporate faith and religion into disaster mitigation, preparedness, and response efforts in vulnerable populations. Following a natural or man-made disaster, the CWS Emergency Response Program helps survivors recover from the physical and psychological effects of trauma. A unique function of this program is the inclusion of a spiritual recovery component following a disaster.

Brief History

Following World War II, many religious denominations joined in a collaborative effort to respond to the needs of those most affected by the war. They worked to provide food, shelter, medicine, clothing, and support to these individuals. These guiding principles remain today. Currently, there are 36 denominations that have partnered with indigenous churches to promote programs of emergency response, capacity building, long-term development, education, and assistance to refugees. In 2003, CWS was active worldwide. Programs were carried out in the United States, Mexico, South America, Asia, Africa, and Eastern Europe.

Main Activities

When disasters occur within the United States, qualified volunteers from CWS are sent to serve as Disaster Resource Consultants. CWS also works to provide disaster preparedness training and technical resources to governmental and nongovernmental agencies. CWS gives priority to particularly vulnerable populations such as women, children, elderly, and disabled persons. Assistance efforts may take the form of emergency kits, direct financial aid, material resources, or trained personnel.

CWS uses an integrated approach when examining the needs of a community to ensure that all people are cared for in a multidisciplinary fashion. In addition to providing material assistance, CWS works to address the poverty and injustices that may be the underlying cause of problems. In addition to disaster work, CWS is involved in ending hunger, advocating for issues such as international debt relief, landmine bans, the HIV/AIDS pandemic in Africa, and landmine use in Palestine.

Psychosocial Programming

Spiritual work is central to CWS psychosocial programs. The organization believes that during the initial period of time following a traumatic event, an active faith-based recovery program can provide crisis intervention to survivors. Not only can this type of spiritual guidance be reassuring to the survivors, it can also serve to redirect feelings of anger and provide new meaning and value to life. This work has also proven to be beneficial for rescue workers in these operations and can play a large role in the prevention of burnout.

CWS helped establish the Seminar in Trauma Awareness and Recovery (STAR) program with the Conflict Transformation Program of Eastern Mennonite University. This program was established in 2002 as a response to the terrorist attacks of September 11, 2001. The seminars are designed to provide training on trauma, healing, justice, security, and peace building to community leaders including, but not limited to, religious leaders whose congregations have been affected by traumatic events and mental health professionals. Training is provided by a multidisciplinary team including, but not limited to, mental health care professionals, professors, massage therapists, and experts in self care. Participation in these seminars allows community leaders to be more closely attuned to the trauma-specific needs of their members. STAR trainings in the United States have been expanded to include international members from countries who have experienced trauma to bring unique and new perspectives to the educational environment. Since the trainings began, 683 community leaders have completed STAR training in the United States. Further, in 2003, CWS expanded the STAR program to Africa and have now trained 121 community leaders internationally. Eastern Mennonite University continues to be actively involved in the STAR trainings and research regarding the program.

CWS also recognizes the importance of staff care as one of its psychosocial aims. Currently, CWS works in conjunction with the Headington Institute on a program that responds to the needs of staff in many locations of the world by providing services such as confidential counseling and monthly self-care newsletters. These services are available to CWS staff in the United States, and field responses to staff members on assignment are also provided. CWS is actively involved in campaigning advocacy and policy formation for the rights of populations who do not have adequate resources. Tips for effective advocacy and educational materials are also available to interested advocates on the CWS Web site.

Publications and Resources for Further Information

The CWS Emergency Response Program maintains an online resource list on its official Web site. Included in this listing are downloadable resources for developing disaster plans for churches, emergency planning guides for congregations, and accounts of recovery efforts for trauma-affected churches.

> Church World Service: http://www.churchworldservice.org
> Church World Service Emergency Response Program: http://www.cwserp.org
> Church World Service Online Resource List for Congregations: http://www.cwserp.org/congregations/
> Coping With Disasters Within the Faith Community: http://www.nmha.org/reassurance/coping_faith.cfm

Headington Institute

Name: Lisa McKay
Address: 200 East Del Mar Blvd., #119
            Pasadena, CA 91105

Telephone: (626) 229-9336
Fax: (626) 229-0514
Email: jguy@headington-institute.org

Organizational Identity and Brief History

The Headington Institute is a nonprofit organization, based in Pasadena, California, that is primarily financed by private donations and foundation grants. The organization also charges cost-recovery fees for some of its professional services. The Institute was established in 2001 to provide psychological and spiritual support for humanitarian aid and disaster relief personnel worldwide. The organization provides a collaborative network of mental health professionals offering preventive education and training, counseling services, and organizational consultation to humanitarian organizations. By providing direct services, information, referrals, and funding, the Headington Institute is a partner to aid organizations in the provision of support for the emotional well-being of their personnel. Since its inception, the Institute has provided hundreds of hours of training and consultation services to over 1000 individuals representing nearly 100 different relief organizations, more than 30 religious denominations, and over 50 countries.

Main Activities

The Headington Institute believes psychological distress is one of the main causes of operational dysfunction in humanitarian organizations. Thus, its guiding philosophy is that ongoing psychological support can help to reduce the stress related to this type of service. In line with this philosophy, the Headington Institute believes that psychological and spiritual support for humanitarian and disaster relief personnel should be routine practice for ethical, financial, and risk management reasons. To implement this philosophy, the Institute currently employs three full-time professional staff and one part-time administrative assistant. Preferred qualifications for professional staff include MSW, PhD, or PsyD in psychology, and some degree of international or cross-cultural experience. The Institute has also collaborated with a number of consultants. Although headquartered in Pasadena, staff frequently travel nationally and internationally to provide onsite services to humanitarian organizations. At this time, most of the international work performed by the Headington Institute is focused in Africa. In the course of its work, the Institute serves humanitarian workers, and disaster relief personnel worldwide, as well as the psychologists, directors, and pastors who care for these individuals.

Psychosocial Programming

Psychosocial services are the core mission, and an integral part of the structure, of the Headington Institute; therefore, three full-time employees devote their time to the provision of such services. The Institute provides services to humanitarian workers with the core goal of fostering and promoting well-being and resilience strategies to help them deal with the stress and trauma inherent in the profession. Direct services include the provision of a variety of counseling services for humanitarian workers as well as a number of training workshops that focus on various aspects of stress and trauma management. Indirectly, the Institute supports humanitarian workers by consulting and educating directors, human resource professionals, and managers of humanitarian organizations as well as by providing a variety of free education resources on the Internet. Additionally, the organization trains providers through workshops for psychologists and pastors who provide direct care for humanitarian workers in the field, and through the provision of continuing education modules for mental health professionals interested in work with those providing humanitarian service. Of these services, training workshops on stress, trauma management, and self-care; counseling; trauma debriefing; and continuing education for mental health professionals are emphasized.

Regarding advocacy, the United Nations has approved the Headington Institute for association with the UN Department of Public Information. The Headington Institute will be associated with the nongovernmental UN Committee on Mental Health. The Committee works with the United Nations and its specialized agencies to promote psychosocial well-being, improve mental health services, and advocate and educate for the prevention of mental illness. It aims to include mental health issues within a broader context of concerns such as vulnerable populations, human rights, poverty, violence, the environment, peace, and well-being.

While the Headington Institute is not currently involved in research regarding mental health or psychosocial issues, the organization plans to continue to develop programs in these areas. Specifically, the Headington Institute is dedicated to maintaining the same focus on services in the future, but anticipates growing as demand increases. The Institute will also expand its international work to focus on Asia and other regions of the world.

Publications

The Headington Institute has many free educational materials available that can be downloaded from the organization's Web site. These resources can be found in the Headington Learning Center; they include, but are not limited to, articles regarding stress and humanitarian work, and resources regarding self-care. A Web page containing links to other sites that may be of interest, such as information on reactions to trauma and organizations with similar missions, is also available through the Headington Institute Web site. Finally, the Institute has continuing education materials for mental health professionals that can be ordered for a fee.

Resources for Further Information

Headington Institute: http://www.headington-institute.org
Headington Learning Center: http://www.headington-institute.org/learning/index.htm
Headington Links of Interest: http://www.headington-institute.org/webdocs/links.htm

International Committee of the Red Cross (ICRC)

Address: 19 avenue de la Paix
                CH 1202 Geneva, Switzerland
Telephone: +41 22 733 20 57
Fax No.:   +41 22 734 60 01
Email: press.gva@icrc.org

Organizational Identity

The ICRC is a Swiss-based humanitarian organization working globally with international legal status. Its work in armed conflicts and other situations of violence is neutral, impartial, and independent. By promoting and strengthening humanitarian law and universal humanitarian principles, the organization strives to assist in the prevention of further suffering.

Brief History

Established nearly a century and a half ago, the ICRC is at the origin of the International Red Cross and Red Crescent Movement. With its distinctive emblem of a red cross on a white background, the ICRC is arguably the most notable humanitarian organization in the world. The ICRC was founded in 1863 to preserve humanity during times of war and crisis. Its primary mission is to serve as a strictly neutral party working to protect and assist people affected by armed conflicts and internal disturbances. This work involves visiting prisoners of war and security detainees, searching for missing persons, transmitting messages between separated family members, reuniting dispersed families, providing safe water, food, and medical assistance to those in need, promoting respect for international humanitarian law, monitoring compliance with the law, and contributing to the development of the law.

Main Activities

Although the ICRC is the product of a private Swiss initiative, its work and scope are international. ICRC activities are funded entirely through voluntary contributions. These donations come courtesy of states party to the Geneva Conventions (governments), National Red Cross, and Red Crescent societies, supranational organizations such as the European Union, and public and private sources. The organization has delegations in some 60 countries around the world, has activities in more than 80, and employs a staff of around 12,000 people, most of them nationals of the countries in which they work. About 800 people provide the essential support and backup to the ICRC's field operations from its headquarters in Geneva, Switzerland.

Within the ICRC exist two separate delegations with differing functions: operational delegations and regional delegations. Operational delegations mainly perform protection, assistance, or preventive activities for the victims of an existing or emerging situation of armed conflict or violence. Regional delegations cover almost every country not directly affected by armed conflict. These delegations have specific tasks that concern operational activities on the one hand and "humanitarian diplomacy" on the other. Their presence in a region enables them to keep a close watch on potentially dangerous developments and to function as an early warning system, making it possible for the ICRC to prepare for rapid humanitarian action.

Psychosocial Programming

Often during crises, civilian populations are exposed to traumatic circumstances such as hostage situations, sexual violence, looting, and massacres. The ICRC works to ensure that these populations not be attacked or otherwise harmed. According to specific provisions in the Geneva Convention, these people and their property are protected. The ICRC remains present in areas where civilians and their property are at risk of being harmed by opposing forces.

The ICRC has programs to train local volunteers and other professionals to deal with the psychosocial impact of crisis situations. These programs focus on conflict-related stress management, recognizing the signs and symptoms of stress, and identifying instances where referrals should be made. The ICRC attempts to incorporate local professionals into the training so that cultural considerations may be made for the specific population.

The ICRC also realizes the importance of family unity, and its Central Tracing Agency works to re-establish familial connections during times of crisis. These include connections among refugees, displaced persons, and missing persons. These services are also made available to detainees and prisoners of war so that they may maintain contact with family and loved ones whenever possible.

Publications

The ICRC offers various materials regarding the work of the organization and humanitarian law. Available resources include printed and online publications (books, brochures, and periodicals), photographs, and audiovisual materials. These materials can be accessed through the ICRC Web site, which also provides access to humanitarian law databases, historical archives, and a library and research center. Most of the online resources are available to the public free of charge. The *International Review of the Red Cross*, both current and back issues, is also available on the Internet. This journal focuses on the activities of the ICRC and related humanitarian issues. The editorials, articles, reports, and other features are available in downloadable PDF format.

Resources for Further Information

ICRC Web site: http://www.icrc.org
ICRC Information Resources: http://www.icrc.org/web/eng/siteeng0
.nsf/iwpList2/Info_resources?OpenDocument
International Review of the Red Cross: http://www.icrc.org/Web/
Eng/siteeng0.nsf/html/section_review_2004_855?OpenDocument

International Federation of Red Cross and Red Crescent

Address: International Federation of Red Cross and Red
    Crescent Societies
    PO Box 372
    CH-1211 Geneva 19
    Switzerland
Telephone: +41 22 730 42 22
Fax: +41 22 733 03 95
Email: secretariat@ifrc.org

Organizational Identity

The International Federation of the Red Cross and Red Crescent (IFRC), based in Geneva, Switzerland, is the world's largest humanitarian organization. The IFRC consists of 181 member Red Cross and Red Crescent societies, a Secretariat in Geneva, and over 60 strategically located delegations, which provide assistance without discrimination on the basis of nationality, race, religious beliefs, class, or political opinions throughout the world. In many Islamic countries, the Red Crescent is used in place of the Red Cross.

The IFRC works through its National Societies, with the International Committee of the Red Cross, and with many other organizations in order to carry out its work more effectively. Due to the Observer status that the IFRC has with the United Nations General Assembly, the Federation is able take part in high-level international debates and access negotiations and deliberations within most international organizations.

In order to integrate services at local and national levels, the National Societies of the IFRC form partnerships with community groups, businesses, government ministries, and intergovernmental agencies. Support at the regional level is obtained through the Federation's representational activity including the UN regional organization, the League of Arab States, and the Organization of American States. Further, in the Red Cross Red Crescent Movement across the world, there are about 97 million members and volunteers worldwide. It is estimated that 20 million of these people are volunteers.

Brief History

The International Federation of Red Cross and Red Crescent (IFRC) was founded in 1919 in Paris following World War I due to the need for cooperation between Red Cross Societies in light of the European devastation. The societies were focused on providing humanitarian activities for prisoners of war and combatants. Initially, the organization was named the League of Red Cross Societies; however, it was renamed the League of Red Cross and Red Crescent Societies in October 1983, and in November 1991 the organization became known as the International Federation of Red Cross and Red Crescent Societies. The original Federation consisted of five member Societies: Britain, France, Italy, Japan, and the United States.

Main Activities

According to the IFRC Web site, the primary mission of the organization is "to improve the lives of vulnerable people by mobilizing the power of humanity." All of the organizations that compose the IFRC operate under the guidance of seven fundamental principles to ensure consistency of humanitarian assistance: humanity, impartiality, neutrality, independence, voluntary service, unity, and universality. The principles guide the Federation's activities in promotion of humanitarian principles and values, disaster response and preparedness, and health and community care.

The IFRC strives to promote humanitarian values. For example, the organization is developing initiatives to ensure that volunteers and staff working within the organization understand and act on the basis of the Fundamental Principles during their work with vulnerable populations in times of peace, disaster, or armed conflict. The IFRC, for over 80 years, has focused heavily on disaster response by providing emergency relief to refugees, victims of poverty, and victims of disaster. During emergencies, the societies provide life-saving assistance; shelter, water, food, and basic health care; and "a sense of humanity" to affected populations. The Federation also participates in reconstruction and rehabilitation efforts in the aftermath of disasters, a commitment that can continue for several years particularly in the case of refugees and socioeconomic collapse. In the past few years, the IFRC has devoted more attention to working with National Societies and communities to raise their awareness of disaster-related risks and preparedness based on the specific challenges each unique community faces. This includes working with communities to reduce their vulnerability and providing education about coping when disaster strikes. This increased focus on preparedness is a response to the increasing prevalence of natural disasters worldwide.

The IFRC also focuses on the provision of health and community care as a cornerstone activity. The main goal is to complement pre-existing national and local efforts. The Federation conceptualizes health as a critical element of development and "a cornerstone of humanitarian assistance." The IFRC focuses on "three strategic pillars" in health improvement: advocacy, including face to face and public campaigns; building capacity to "bridge the gap" between vulnerable populations and resources; and broadening interventions in crises. The global public health priorities include disease prevention, psychological support, and social welfare, in the face of challenges such as HIV/AIDS, problems with water/sanitation, malaria, tuberculosis, mother and child illness, and provision of blood. For example, in the next 10 years, the African Red Cross and Red Crescent Societies Health Initiative (ARCHI) is focusing on several large-scale public health initiatives including HIV/AIDS, preventable childhood diseases, women's and pregnancy issues, and responses to accidents and injuries.

Psychosocial Programming

Psychological support is a major element of IFRC intervention. The organization recognizes that stress-related psychological problems can accompany disaster situations. In an effort to incorporate psychological assistance into traditional disaster relief operations, the Federation developed the Reference Centre for Psychosocial Support. Since the program's inception, psychological support has been fully integrated into the Federation's model of disaster relief services.

The IFRC targets three groups for support following crisis situations: victims and others affected by the event, volunteers and staff who provide disaster response, and expatriate delegates. The IFRC seeks to provide victims with ongoing assistance to help them build feelings of security and hope, to enhance their ability to cope, to reinforce support that is received from family and friends, and to empower communities to take responsibility for their own healing. One example that illustrates the focus of these services is the Children Affected by Armed Conflict (CABAC) program. This program includes psychosocial workshops, nutritional support, and hygiene instruction, for primary school children affected by war. The goals of the program include improving the living conditions of these children, helping them to build a new life and regain trust and hope in the future, and helping them to interact with peers and teachers with skills such as conflict resolution.

The IFRC provides psychological support to volunteers and staff who respond to disasters to help them deal with feelings such as shock and powerlessness. These services advocate for strong support systems and are provided in a culturally sensitive manner utilizing local resources and professionals. Finally, regarding expatriate delegates, the IFRC places a priority of educating those involved with disaster relief work about typical reactions, stress symptoms, and stress management. Psychological debriefing is also offered in order to give the delegates a place to discuss their feelings, gain feedback, and ease the "re-entry process."

The IFRC believes that only a "reliable and long-term commitment" will ensure that psychosocial relief work will be carried out in a manner that is professional and effective in making a difference to those affected by disaster, whether they be victims or volunteers. In the spirit of this belief, the Federation works to form strong collaborative relationships with other institutions that specialize in this kind of work.

Publications

The IFRC provides an extensive list of publications that are available in their entirety, or in part, on the organization's Web site for free public use or download. Through the catalog of publications, one may order additional resources, such as works published with National Societies and the International Committee of the Red Cross. Also available on the Web site are resources which include, but are not limited to, world disaster reports, annual appeals and annual reports, quarterly reports, profiles of ICRC partners, information on Strategy 2010 (which is a project seeking to "improve the lives of vulnerable people by mobilizing the power of humanity") the code of conduct, and *The Magazine of the International Red Cross and Red Crescent Movement*. Finally, as a part of their Psychological Support Program, the IFRC and the Danish Red Cross have developed a variety of manuals that can be viewed or downloaded through the link provided below. These manuals provide a wealth of information relevant to training issues, technical practices, methodology, stress reduction methods, program guidelines, and knowledge that can be applied in specific as well as broadly defined situations. Manuals include *Community Based Psychological Support: A Training Manual, Managing Stress in the Field, Children Affected by Armed Conflict Manual, Psychological First Aid*, and *Psychological Support: Best Practices from Red Cross and Red Crescent Programs*.

Resources for Further Information

International Federation of Red Cross and Red Crescent Web site: http://www.ifrc.org

The Magazine of the International Red Cross and Red Crescent Movement: http://www.redcross.int/EN/mag/index.html

Various Downloadable Manuals: http://psp.drk.dk/sw2995.asp

Community Based Psychological Support: A Training Manual: http://psp.drk.dk/graphics/2003referencecenter/PSP_Manual_eng.pdf

Psychological Support: Best Practices from Red Cross and Red Crescent Programs: http://www.ifrc.org/what/health/psycholog/bestpractices.asp

International Society for Health and Human Rights (ISHHR)

International Base: Norway
Address: Tordenskioldsgate 6b
0160 Oslo
Norway
Domestic Base: Olympia, WA
Telephone: +47 22 47 92 00
Fax No: +47 22 47 92 01
Email: ishhr@ishhr.org

Organizational Identity

The International Society for Health and Human Rights (ISHHR) is an organization comprising individual health care workers and organizations that are committed to the treatment of survivors of human rights violations. These independent, self-contained agencies, which provide services and research of their own, use ISHHR as a forum to disseminate information about their initiatives. The organization conceptualizes the protection of mental health and psychosocial issues as a human rights issue and therefore seeks to promote the needs in affected populations. ISHHR is funded through membership fees and private financial donations. Donations may be designated to either the general assistance fund or specific projects supported by the organization.

Brief History

ISHHR is a relatively new organization, having been formally established in 1993. For years previously, a group of dedicated health professionals had been sharing their knowledge and experiences with one another through personal networks and informal channels. Currently, ISHHR has members all over the world who focus on issues relating to their respective regions and interests. ISHHR has hosted six international conferences as an opportunity for members from different regions to assemble and discuss current initiatives. A seventh conference will take place in India in early 2005.

Main Activities

ISHHR is dedicated to addressing political initiatives and petitions for advocacy from its members and affiliate organizations. Violations of human rights, including past events, ongoing problems, and possible concerns for future injustices, are considered of the utmost importance. The organization supports all efforts to bring accountability to these violations in an effort to promote effective treatment of survivors. Additionally, ISHHR works to evaluate existing methods of treatment and research new methods of treatment for survivors of organized violence. Each of the organization's psychosocial interventions focuses on strengthening coping abilities and resilience among those affected. The ISHHR models and methods of treatment center around mobilizing local resources, establishing interventions as a function of the general community action, assessing mental health needs, and ensuring assistance to vulnerable groups.

Regarding terrorism, ISHHR supports international efforts to combat and prevent terrorist attacks. The organization works to encourage governments and NGOs to strengthen their mental health support programs and assistance efforts in terrorism-affected regions as well as in communities that have been indirectly affected. In both cases, the populations may suffer from an increased susceptibility to symptoms of post-traumatic stress. ISHHR encourages ongoing discussions concerning the roots and consequences of international terrorism.

Psychosocial Programming

ISHHR conceptualizes mental health and psychosocial issues as human rights concerns and promotes advocacy in these areas. Essentially, the psychosocial activities of ISHHR are limited to those of their constituent organizations and members. For example, the International Trauma Treatment Program (United States) focuses its work on victims of torture; the Society for Psychological Assistance (Croatia) provides psychological assistance to trauma survivors; and Pharos (The Netherlands) provides health care services for refugees.

ISHHR contends that human rights violations are widespread and complex, typically receiving insufficient attention, in part because of a lack of awareness from health care workers. Many workers are uneducated about how to identify and treat these populations. This leads to a delay in appropriate services and interventions, subsequently resulting in increased symptomology and health concerns among affected individuals and communities. ISHHR hopes that its network can assist in reducing the incidence of human rights violations by facilitating the exchange of information about medical and psychosocial interventions, promoting advocacy campaigns, and examining and reforming legal standards concerning human rights.

Publications and Resources for Further Information

Listing of ISHHR Group Member Web sites: http://www.ishhr.org/links/members.php

ISHHR Forum—an electronic journal for ISHHR: http://www.ishhr.org/forum/

ISHHR Conferences: http://www.ishhr.org/conference/; http://www.ishhr2005.org/

Médecins Sans Frontières (MSF)/Doctors Without Borders

Address:	33 7th Avenue, 2nd Floor
	New York, NY 10001-5004
Phone:	(212) 679-6800
Fax:	(212) 679-7016
Email:	[via Web site] http://www.doctorswithoutborders.org/ contact.shtml

Organizational Identity

Médecins Sans Frontières (MSF), also known as Doctors Without Borders, is a multinational humanitarian organization independent of any political, economic, or religious ties. The organization is composed of volunteer medical doctors and health service workers from countless other disciplines. These professionals assist populations who lack access to proper medical care because they are living through crises such as armed conflict, natural or man-made disasters, or because they are socially and/or geographically isolated. MSF respects universal medical ethics and "claim full and unhindered freedom in the exercise of its functions." According to the official MSF Web site, over 2,500 volunteer medical professionals, logistics experts, water/sanitation engineers, and administrators provide aid annually through MSF. Most MSF operations are funded through donations from the public. Foundations, corporations, nonprofit organizations, national governments, and international agencies provide additional funding.

MSF describes a set of independent organizations with similar goals working in a cooperative alliance. MSF has sections in 18 countries around the world. Five of these sections (Belgium, France, Holland, Spain, and Switzerland) are known as the Operational Centers. These five centers directly control where MSF operations will take place and what form the response will take. The remaining 13 centers are considered to be nonoperational branch offices and are responsible for recruiting volunteers, fundraising, education, and outreach programs. These offices are located in Australia, Austria, Canada, Denmark, Germany, Hong Kong, Italy, Japan, Luxembourg, Norway, Sweden, the UK, and the United States.

Brief History

Founded in 1971, MSF comprised of a group of French doctors who believed that all people were entitled to proper medical care, regardless of race, religion, creed, or political affiliation. Their needs were considered paramount to respecting the existing national or regional borders. MSF has grown to be the largest independent medical relief agency providing service in over 80 countries annually. During the time period

1979–1986, MSF set up countless refugee programs as war and displacement crises spread through Africa and Asia. In 1979, during the Soviet invasion of Afghanistan, MSF provided clandestine assistance to Afghan resistance fighters caring for civilians. One of the largest responses occurred in 1991, when the organization provided emergency medical and sanitary relief to Kurdish refugees in Turkey, Iran, and Jordan. Currently, MSF continues to provide assistance to the Americas, Africa, Asia, Europe, the Middle East, and the Caucasus in situations involving wars and conflict, refugees, displaced persons, and disasters. Recent MSF efforts include a response to flooding in north-central Bolivia, the establishment of a center for rape survivors in South Africa, and a health campaign near Bogota, Colombia.

Main Activities

MSF begins an operation when it identifies a humanitarian crisis or when it is invited to do so by a national government or United Nations agency. The process begins with an exploratory MSF team visiting the site and assessing the medical, nutritional, and sanitary needs of the community. Considerations for the operation are also made regarding the political environment, safety issues, and transportation resources. The impression of the exploratory team is then considered by an Operations Department. This group decides if an MSF intervention is necessary and, if it is, prioritizes how the needs can be met. MSF is able to respond quickly because it has pre-packaged disaster kits available at all times, and four logistical centers where vehicles and other supplies are stored.

An average MSF field team has between 4 and 12 volunteers who serve to supervise the work of up to 200 local staff members. MSF provides a variety of services depending on the conditions and severity of the crisis. Diagnosis and treatment of affected individuals is MSF's primary mission during a response. Local medical personnel and international volunteer practitioners do most of this work. In cases where trained medical professionals have fled the affected area, MSF provides additional training to less experienced local medical personnel. The training is standardized and covers topics such as psychosocial care, drug prescription, and diagnostic work.

Psychosocial Programming

MSF began addressing mental health concerns in 1991. Since that time, mental health and psychosocial care has become a major component of many MSF emergency and long-term projects. These programs assist the affected community in dealing with traumatic events they may have witnessed, such as massacres, death of loved ones, starvation, and displacement. By addressing these issues quickly, MSF hopes to prevent ongoing physiological and psychological problems. Most mental health interventions focus on programs of psychosocial first aid, support services, and psychoeducation. When MSF workers witness rights abuses, violations of humanitarian laws, or injustice, they often speak out in an effort to bring light to the issue and increase awareness. MSF is very conscientious not to further endanger the affected community or workers by speaking out.

Publications

MSF maintains a large listing of publications on the organization's Web site. This listing includes special reports, speeches, stories from the field, annual reports, opinion articles, open-letters, and the like that are free to the public. Additionally, visitors can view *ALERT*, the MSF quarterly newsletter, free of charge, and reasonably priced MSF texts and field guides are available through the online bookstore.

Resources for Further Information

Doctors Without Borders Web site: http://www.doctorswithout borders.org

Doctors Without Borders Publication Listing: http://www.doctors without borders.org/publications/

Doctors Without Borders Quarterly Newsletter: http://www.doctors withoutborders.org/publications/alert

Oxfam International

Address: 26 West Street
               Boston, MA 02111
Telephone: (800) 776-9326
Fax: (617) 728-2594
Email: info@oxfamamerica.org

The Oxfam Organizations

Australia	Germany	The Netherlands
Belgium	Great Britain	New Zealand
Canada	Hong Kong	Spain
Quebec	Ireland	United States

Organizational Identity and Brief History

Oxfam International was established nearly a decade ago by a group of independent nongovernmental organizations. These organizations believed that by joining efforts, they could be more efficacious in their assistance efforts. This system of partnerships is active in over 100 countries, with head offices on four continents. According to Oxfam's mission statement, the partners are dedicated to fighting poverty and related injustices worldwide. Their programs seek to address the structural causes of poverty, such as unequal distribution of wealth and inadequacy of material goods. The ultimate goal of Oxfam's work is to provide individuals and communities with the abilities to exercise their rights and manage their lives.

Main Activities

Oxfam funds projects of development, provides emergency relief in times of crises, and campaigns for economic and social justice. The majority of Oxfam's work deals with food security and provision issues, sanitation, health promotion, trade, markets, and closing the gap between the rich and poor. However, in many parts of the world, Oxfam is best known for its speedy and efficient response during times of natural and man-made disasters. In the past, Oxfam has responded to situations created by earthquakes, drought, flooding, war, and famine. Emergency responses are initiated by Oxfam whenever health, lives, and livelihoods are put in jeopardy as a result of armed conflict or natural disasters. Even when the Oxfam name is not formally associated with a disaster response, it is common that one or more of the organizations that compose Oxfam supports a local resource. The Humanitarian Department of Oxfam supports disaster preparedness efforts and participates in response efforts with its own programs as well as in collaboration with partner agencies. Oxfam typically stays on after the presenting problem has been resolved in order to ensure that the affected community is able to return to an adequate level of functioning.

Oxfam International works with impoverished and disaster-affected areas in a variety of geographic areas. Oxfam's work is divided into 11 main regions: Central America/Mexico/Caribbean, South America, Central and East Africa, Horn of Africa, Southern Africa, West Africa, East Asia, South Asia, Eastern Europe and the Former Soviet Union, Maghreb and Middle East, and Pacific. In each of these regions, Oxfam strives to establish joint ventures with local providers to ensure that community-specific rights and practices are adhered to. Recent efforts by Oxfam include flood relief in Haiti; the provision of emergency water, sanitation, and health promotion for international disaster psychology programs in Western Sudan and Sudanese refugees in Chad; emergency water provision in Liberia; the provision of sanitation and health promotion for communities affected by the Bam earthquake (Iran); and the provision of relief food and other emergency food security interventions for communities affected by drought in Kenya.

Psychosocial Programming

Oxfam International does not provide mental health screening or treatment in its operational programs, although it has occasionally provided support for partner agencies providing post-disaster counseling for stress. Operational programming actively involves members of the affected communities as active participants in the response activities. Oxfam has provided facilities and supported activities that aim to reduce social tension in internally displaced persons or refugee communities. Examples of this include the provision of separate recreation tents for women and men in the Kosovo camps and long-term programs that have provided small-scale support to local partners in assisting communities affected by disasters. These programs make available services to help combat the negative psychological effects associated with traumatic events.

Oxfam has international advocacy teams in Washington, New York, Brussels, and Geneva. These offices work to link changes in policies and practices at the national level with practical changes at the grassroots level. Although their advocacy concerns are not focused solely on psychosocial issues, the effects of these campaigns have strong implications for improving the psychological state of the affected populations. Oxfam is currently working on campaigns to control arms, establish educational programs in underserved areas, and make world trade practices equitable.

Publications and Resources for Further Information

According to the Oxfam International Web site, the organization is committed to utilizing the media to campaign against poverty and injustice. For this reason the Web site contains links to many online resources and publications that explain and promote the organization. For example, the section of the Web site dedicated to Oxfam News provides articles, press releases, and policy papers regarding their work. The following list will direct the interested reader to additional resources provided by Oxfam:

> Oxfam International: http://www.oxfam.org
> Oxfam Manuals for emergency response, water treatment, disinfection, HIV/AIDS, health promotion, and water pumping: http://www.oxfam.org.uk/what_we_do/emergencies/how_we_work/manuals.htm
> Oxfam Key Papers and Reports: http://www.oxfam.org.uk/what_we_do/issues/key_papers.htm

Pan American Health Organization (PAHO)

Address: 525 23rd St. N.W.
              Washington, D.C. 20037
Telephone: (202) 974-3000
Email: leitepau@paho.org

Organizational Identity

The Pan American Health Organization (PAHO) was established over a century ago and has grown to become a leader in international public health care initiatives. PAHO is based in Washington, DC, with offices throughout Latin America. The principal goal of PAHO's work is to strengthen health care systems at the local and national levels in order to improve the livelihood of all populations residing in the Americas. Within these populations, PAHO focuses much of its efforts among vulnerable groups, including mothers and their children, workers, the poor, the elderly, and refugees or displaced persons. According to its Mission Statement, PAHO's fundamental purpose is to coordinate efforts to combat disease, lengthen life, and promote physical and mental health. As a United Nations regional office for the Americas of the World Health Organization and the health organization of the Inter-American System, PAHO is well positioned to do this.

Brief History

PAHO was formed during the Second International Conference of American States in response to a recommendation for a convention of representatives of different health organizations from American republics. This convention, initially known as the International Sanitary Conference, evolved into what is currently known as PAHO. The organization is now considered to be a fully autonomous agency with specialization in inter-American health assistance.

Main Activities

PAHO's main activities involve the promotion of primary health care strategies. These programs serve to increase efficiency of the scarce medical resources of many communities. By improving communication within the community, as well as training local providers, PAHO seeks to combat diseases such as AIDS, cholera, dengue, and tuberculosis. Additionally, PAHO is involved in establishing health care programs and serving the needs of developing communities.

PAHO is also at the forefront of disaster preparedness, creating training and technical materials (publications, videos, slides) and enhancing the efficacy of disaster preparedness and response efforts in the Americas. Hard copies of these materials are available to disaster institutions in member countries or through online download.

Following a disaster, PAHO serves the affected community by assessing the damage and identifying needs. Typical assistance projects include water and sanitation improvements, mobilizing aid from international donor communities, managing relief supplies, and organizing epidemiological surveillance systems. A Voluntary Disaster Relief Fund finances these efforts. In recent years, PAHO has been active in the relief efforts stemming from floods in Nicaragua, the Dominican Republic, and Haiti; the 2003 earthquake in Colima; volcanic eruptions in Ecuador; hurricanes in the Caribbean; and the dengue epidemic in El Salvador and Honduras. In 1990,

PAHO created the Regional Disaster Information Center (CRID), a multi-agency center to collect, classify, and distribute technical documentation concerning disaster reduction. CRID has become the leading source for disaster information dealing with Latin America and the Caribbean. Also in 1990, PAHO established the Humanitarian Supply Management System (SUMA) to direct the logistics of the influx of donations following major disasters. SUMA assists in making the disaster donation process more manageable and accountable.

Psychosocial Activities

PAHO is deeply involved in facilitating the provision of psychosocial and mental health programs, and it works to promote mental health in conjunction with human rights by providing workshops and supporting national networks in several countries. This kind of work is often done in conjunction with other organizations, such as the United Nations. PAHO's mental health program is committed to increasing awareness of, and facilitating management of, mental health issues. In striving to meet these goals, the organization promotes awareness of mental health issues, supports the development of relevant policy and legislation, and strives to implement interventions for the prevention and treatment of mental health–related difficulties. Through these activities PAHO hopes to decrease the stigma related to mental health problems, while increasing the availability of treatment and the amount of research carried out on mental health services.

PAHO has been actively involved in research projects regarding mental health issues. Projects have included, but are not limited to, examination of the prevalence of mental disorders and service utilization in several countries as a part of the World Mental Health Study; examination of mental health policy and service delivery in the ATLAS Latin American Project; and the development of mental heath information systems in conjunction with the Montreal Collaborating Center.

PAHO has been actively involved in efforts to prevent and control mental disorders such as depression and psychoses. These efforts include the development of training modules regarding treatment of these disorders and subsequent research to evaluate the training methods. PAHO is also involved in the development of programs that target the mental health needs of special populations such as children and disaster victims. PAHO is active in developing and distributing information regarding the treatment of mental disorders throughout many countries in languages appropriate to each region. In addition to training, PAHO also provides direct assistance to countries in implementing mental health policy, plans, and programs for research-based evaluation of services.

PAHO has established mental health programs in some Pan American communities in an effort to identify and treat children with pervasive mental health problems. Like many other organizations, PAHO realizes that early detection and treatment of psychological concerns is the most effective method of treatment. As a result, its programs are heavily focused on early intervention to prevent further impairment.

PAHO provides differing levels of mental health services in disaster situations. First, the organization provides emergency support to the affected countries, including a mental health component. This involves sending a task force to the affected area to determine whether a team needs to be deployed to provide further support. The mental health component includes providing support to the organization in planning how best to meet the mental health needs of affected populations, and assisting in training personnel and coordinating treatment.

In addition to responding in the event of a disaster, PAHO has more recently begun working with countries (e.g., Central American countries) to prepare plans for disaster response. These plans include mental health components. In facilitating preparation of these countries, workshops, provision of literature, and other methods of training are employed. The PAHO disaster program has a course for the Caribbean entitled SMID (stress management in disasters). Many Caribbean countries have an established team that can be deployed after disasters.

PAHO has done extensive work with disaster relief in Latin American and Caribbean countries. Historically PAHO has responded to the mental health needs of disaster victims by sending international mental health teams to the affected area; however, efforts are now also being made to have disaster plans with mental health components in place before disasters occur. Training and education for those designated to provide psychosocial and mental health care in the event of a disaster are central strategies for preparation. Illustrative of PAHO's commitment to providing such training is its sponsorship of a manual and training guidelines regarding mental health concerns for victims of disaster and organization of workshops on mental health interventions and guidelines for disaster intervention. In this way PAHO emphasizes training for experts who can intervene during disaster and provision of knowledge to build competence in handling these issues in individual countries.

Publications

PAHO actively disseminates information through publication. Specifically, the organization publishes a monthly, peer-reviewed journal titled *Pan American Journal of Public Health/Revista Panamericana de Salud Pública*, which is commonly referred to as the "Revista." This publication is the most cited journal by public health experts in the Latin American and Caribbean region. Common topics in the journal include disasters, infectious diseases, health promotion, health economics, maternal and infant health, mental health, and women's health. The journal is available free of charge to institutions in Latin America and the Caribbean and for a reasonable subscription fee to U.S. and Canadian institutions. PAHO also has a variety of textbooks, CD-ROMs, and technical papers available for order from their online bookstore.

Resources for Further Information

Pan American Health Organization (PAHO): http://www.paho.org
PAHO Publications: http://www.paho.org/english/DD/PUB/pub-Home.asp

The Refugee Studies Centre (RSC)

Address: Refugee Studies Centre
             Queen Elizabeth House
             University of Oxford
             21 St Giles
             Oxford, OX1 3LA
             United Kingdom
Telephone: +44 (1865) 270722
Fax: +44 (1865) 270721
Email: rsc@qeh.ox.ac.uk

Organizational Identity

The Refugee Studies Centre (RSC) is internationally renowned as the leading center of multidisciplinary research and education on the topic of forced migration. The Centre works with other international agencies and the United Nations in an effort to further the body of knowledge on the topic of refugee studies. This is accomplished through strong research programs and an academic program including postgraduate master's degree, summer and regional courses, and intensive short courses.

Brief History

Based in Oxford, The Refugee Studies Centre was established in 1982 as a division of the University of Oxford's Centre for Development Studies, the Queen Elizabeth House. In 2002, the RSC won the Queen's Anniversary Prize for Higher and Further Education. This prestigious award recognizes academic institutions that have contributed innovative and original work to their field.

Main Activities

The RSC seeks not only to educate others about the effects of forced migration and the lives of refugees, but also to improve the livelihood of those affected. A primary objective of the RSC is to perform detailed research. The research conducted through the RSC is policy-relevant and typically emphasizes understanding the experiences of people who have been subjected to forced migration. Recent topics of research conducted at the RSC include "Forced Migration, Global Economy and Governance," "The Experience and Management of Displacement," and "Institutional and Normative Responses to Forced Migration." The RSC has a strong focus on disseminating this information to researchers, practitioners, and the public at large in order to influence policy formation related to forced migration. The RSC is a strong advocate for the rights of refugees and internally displaced persons. In many areas, it is often difficult to deliver services to people who lack proper documentation. As a result, many of these people are denied proper accommodations, adequate access to education, adequate health care, and useful opportunities of employment. Further, the RSC is dedicated to establishing a sense of cooperation in the international community by working in joint efforts with other institutions and networks whose work focuses on refugee life. These efforts assist practitioners in developing their competence and abilities so that they may provide the best interventions and treatments possible.

Psychosocial Programming

The RSC is closely affiliated with a program known as the Psychosocial Working Group (PWG). The PWG formed in 2000 as a collaborative effort between academic institutions and humanitarian agencies with a commitment to establishing the best practices of psychosocial interventions for war-affected populations. The group has developed a series of papers that represent a range of approaches and theoretical orientations addressing various issues in psychosocial work. PWG has also outlined a research agenda that identifies areas in the body of knowledge that need to be further examined and suggests priority topics of study.

The RSC also coordinates a Web site for Forced Migration Online (FMO). This comprehensive Web site provides users with access to information resources on forced migration. The Web site contains a searchable digital library containing full-text documents that can be read online or printed, a searchable catalogue with descriptions of and links to Web-based resources, geographic and thematic research guides, and a directory of organizations conducting work related to refugee mental health. FMO assisted the PWG in constructing an "Inventory of Key Resources," which includes online versions of key papers in the field of forced migration and refugee mental health. FMO, with assistance from the RSC, has also established a psychosocial training model known as "The Refugee Experience" (www.forcedmigration.org/rfgexp). This 30-hour training program was designed to assist in the training of humanitarian assistance workers in response to the psychosocial needs specific to refugee populations, as well as planning, implementation, and evaluation of psychosocial programs. The FMO Web site is funded by The Mellon Foundation in New York and the European Union through its EuropeAid office.

Publications

The RSC, in association with the Global IDP Survey/Norwegian Refugee Council, publishes a journal called *Forced Migration Review* (*FMR*) three times a year. The publication serves as a forum for researchers, refugees, internally displaced populations, and practitioners to share ideas and information. A full-text version of the journal is available online for free download. Oxford University Press, in association with the RSC, publishes the *Journal of Refugee Studies*. This multidisciplinary journal covers all categories of forcibly displaced people and the theoretical understandings of forced migration.

Other publications made available by the RSC include a book series and list of working papers. The book series, "Studies in Forced Migration," covers refugee mental health topics related to social psychology, international law, anthropology, medicine, geography, and economics. The list of working papers includes topics such as reintegration, children affected by armed conflict, and media representation of refugees. All working papers are available for download from the RSC's official Web site.

Resources for Further Information

The Refugee Studies Center: http://www.rsc.ox.ac.uk/

Forced Migration Online: http://www.forcedmigration.org/psychosocial/

Forced Migration Review—free full-text version of journal: http://www.fmreview.org/

Save the Children

Address: 2000 M Street NW; Suite 500
               Washington, DC 20036
Telephone: (202) 293-4170 or 1-800-SAVETHECHILDREN
Email: twebster@savechildren.org

Brief History

Save the Children was initially established in the 1930s by a small group of citizens who wanted to assist rural Appalachian communities that had been affected by the Great Depression. The organization has evolved into a global child-assistance organization funded through donations and sponsorship. Its mission is to work with families in an attempt to define and solve the problems faced by their children and their communities by utilizing a broad array of strategies to ensure self-sufficiency. Like other humanitarian organizations, its goal is to provide the communities with skills to maintain long-term solutions to the oppressive problems.

The Emergencies and Protection Program of Save the Children began in Mozambique in 1988. It initially served as a means to provide for the basic needs of child soldiers of the civil war. Later, the program assisted refugee children in Malawi and Zimbabwe. The program now includes provision of care and protection of unaccompanied children, community-based psychosocial support, research to determine how children's rights are understood and practiced within society, the development of safe spaces and structured activities for children in war situations, and community response to child sex trafficking. Today, the program works with 50 partner organizations in eight countries to address special medical, behavioral, educational, legal, and social needs of affected children.

Main Activities

The Emergencies and Protection Unit of Save the Children is one of several divisions. Save the Children has sectors dealing with economic opportunity provision, education, hunger/malnutrition, health care initiatives, HIV/AIDS programs, and saving newborn lives. Collectively, these programs are active in Africa, Asia, Latin America, the Middle East/Eurasia, and the United States. With the help of local support, the Emergencies and Protection Unit of Save the Children works to guarantee rights to vulnerable children and marginalized communities. Building on its original program in Mozambique, Save the Children developed a range of innovative programs to address the needs and rights of children in crisis.

Psychosocial Programming

Save the Children believes that protection from, and treatment of, psychological trauma is one of the greatest needs in every geographic region. There is a definite need for psychosocial programs as a means to help children deal with the lingering effects of traumatic experiences. Save the Children's psychosocial interventions seek to promote healthy emotional, cognitive, and behavioral development by addressing issues such as attachment, trust, belonging, self-esteem, empowerment, and responsibility.

Save the Children's psychosocial activities are based on an inclusive community model. Rather than focusing on individual trauma counseling, they concentrate on the community as a whole. Many of the affected communities do not have access to properly trained personnel, much less resources to deal with traumatic events in a positive way. In an effort to provide for these communities, Save the Children has developed programs to combat the negative effects of trauma on children and their families. In the West Bank/Gaza Strip, they have developed a program that is based on the UN Convention of the Rights of the Child. The goals of this program focus on securing the well-being of children while meeting their basic needs during war and crises. This program also enhances their moral development and guides them toward becoming productive citizens in the community. In Africa, Save the Children is involved with The Hope for African Children Initiative (HACI). This project is a major community effort in association with other relief organizations, including CARE, Plan International, Society for Women and AIDS in Africa, World Council on Religion and Peace, and World Vision. HACI hopes to build awareness and reduce stigma associated with HIV/AIDS, extend the life of the parent-child relationship, prepare the family for transition, and ensure the child's future. In Afghanistan, a training manual has been created for teachers and health care workers who interact with affected children. Additionally, a training manual has been created for health care staff regarding response to violence, abuse, and psychosocial distress when issues of child protection are present. Psychosocial programs such as these are also present in Indonesia, Guinea, Nicaragua, Iraq, the United States, and the Philippines.

Save The Children is also involved in advocacy initiatives at the local, national, and global levels. Campaigns include "America's Forgotten Children," "Every Mother, Every Child," and "One World, One Wish." Additionally, the "Save The Children Action Network" (www.savethechildren .org/advocacy) provides users with tips for effective advocacy work and offers descriptions of current campaigns supported by Save the Children. Typically, the focal points of these campaigns are physical relief efforts and equal opportunities; however, psychosocial efforts exist within each program.

Publications

Save the Children publishes information on a regular basis through annual reports, major publications (e.g. "State of the World's Mothers," "State of the World's Newborns"), news briefs, newsletters, books, and brochures. Many documents are available for free download from the official Save the Children Web site. Additionally, transcripts of speeches and testimony on a variety of topics (e.g., children and terrorism, military effects on humanitarian response, exploitation during war) are available.

Resources for Further Information

Save the Children: http://www.savethechildren.org/emergencies/index.asp

Online Listing of Publications: http://www.savethechildren.org/publications/

Save the Children Speeches and Testimony: http://www.savethechildren.org/news/speeches.asp

United Nations Children's Fund (UNICEF)

Address: UNICEF House
                3 United Nations Plaza
                New York, NY 10017
Telephone: (212) 326-7000
Fax No.:   (212) 887-7465
Email: information@unicefusa.org

Organizational Identity and Brief History

The United Nations Children's Fund (UNICEF) is a leading advocate for the rights of children throughout the world in 158 countries and territories. Established in 1946 to assist children in postwar Europe and China, UNICEF has grown to become one of the most prominent assistance organizations in the United States and throughout the world. UNICEF is based out of New York and has regional offices in Atlanta, Boston, Chicago, Houston, and Los Angeles. Internationally, staff are located in country offices in East Asia, Africa, Latin America, the Caribbean, the Middle East, and South Asia.

Like other child assistance organizations, UNICEF supports the Convention on the Rights of the Child (CRC) as a guideline for the work necessary to provide children with resources to live happy and healthy lives. In accordance with these guidelines, UNICEF makes every effort to improve the lives of impoverished, abused, and traumatized children worldwide through programs of education and relief assistance. Typical projects of assistance include helping to meet the basic needs of children, responding to crises and emergencies, and advancing equal rights for children. UNICEF's operations are made possible through voluntary contributions from governments, intergovernmental organizations, private sector groups, and individuals.

Main Activities

UNICEF makes an effort to reach the most vulnerable populations during emergency situations such as armed conflict and natural or man-made disasters. Often, the most vulnerable persons during these times are women and children who lack access to the items needed for basic survival. When safe access is available, UNICEF will seek out these populations so that they may provide basic health services, clean water, adequate sanitation, and food. UNICEF is active in disaster relief operations worldwide, providing food, vaccines, and health supplies.

UNICEF realizes that helping children to thrive in their early years increases their chances of achieving a lifetime of health and happiness. Annually, UNICEF invests approximately $440 million in comprehensive care for youth populations worldwide. Programs in emergency obstetrics care, prenatal care, birth registration, parental education, water sanitation, nutrition, and psychosocial stimulation have been established in many countries as a result of UNICEF's assistance.

The HIV/AIDS pandemic is a primary focus of UNICEF's relief efforts, particularly regarding children who have been orphaned because of the disease. In 2003, UNICEF offices in 36 countries reported that they had established programs to protect and care for these orphans, with another 32 offices developing programs of their own. Also in 2003, UNICEF convened the Global Partners Forum on orphans and vulnerable children, where over 50 organizations met to discuss how to increase the efficacy of a worldwide response. UNICEF's efforts are visible in many forums, both social and religious. Until a cure is developed, UNICEF will continue to be a major force in the fight against HIV/AIDS.

UNICEF works hard to combat all forms of child exploitation, including child labor, child pornography, trafficking, and the use of children as soldiers. With the assistance of faith-based organizations, nongovernmental agencies, and exploited children themselves, UNICEF seeks to correct unjust practices throughout the world. By encouraging governments to establish laws, guidelines, and acceptable standards for the treatment of children, the organization hopes to reduce the number of occurrences of exploitation. One way UNICEF has advocated for children's rights is by endorsing the ratification of the 1999 International Labor Organization Convention No. 182 on the Worst Forms of Child Labor. Already, this convention has made great strides in increasing government awareness of, and response to, child exploitation. Other efforts by UNICEF include establishing increased security at borders to identify people traveling with unrelated children, educating parents about how to protect their children, and encouraging governments to prosecute the perpetrators of the child sex trade.

In many countries, the quality of health care is either poor or nonexistent; therefore, over 30 million children are not properly immunized. UNICEF has established a program calling for "immunization plus" in order to reduce child mortality rates. These efforts provide millions of children in developing countries with protection from diseases such as measles, polio, diphtheria, pertussis, tetanus, tuberculosis, yellow fever, and hepatitis B. The "plus" in this program refers to providing children with micronutrients and other protective items in addition to vaccines. By providing children with a supplement, such as Vitamin A, UNICEF seeks to strengthen the immune systems in these children, thus increasing their chances of survival.

UNICEF has given over $233 million to increase the number of children, particularly females, in school. The goal is for gender parity to be present in the classroom by 2005 and for all children to have at the very least a primary education by 2015. Additionally, UNICEF is involved the

"25 by 2005" campaign to accelerate the progress of gender equality in 25 countries. Another factor that UNICEF has addressed with regard to education is that of school fees. In many countries, families are simply unable to pay the high fees that are required to send a child to school and are less likely to pay for their female children. UNICEF has encouraged eliminating school fees in certain countries to increase enrollment.

Psychosocial Programming

UNICEF considers mental health to be a key consideration for primary health care services. During relief operations, the organization provides its workers with the necessary supplies and training so that they are well equipped to offer appropriate services to the communities they are assisting. UNICEF's psychosocial programs during times of crisis are focused on meeting the current needs of the child while strengthening their coping abilities and resilience. The overriding goal is to improve the well-being of the child as well as the family. This is accomplished through direct psychosocial interventions, supportive counseling opportunities, mentoring programs, and recreational/expressive activities. Children with healthy psychosocial development can more easily function and thrive in the world as they grow. As a result, UNICEF seeks to establish environments that are conducive to positive psychosocial development for children during their formative years.

Publications

UNICEF publishes an annual review of statistical data, analyses, and country profiles in a report called *The State of the World's Children*. This publication is considered to be one of the foremost reports on children's well-being throughout the world. Recent editions have focused on issues such as "Girls, Education, and Development," "Child Participation," "Leadership," "Early Childhood," and "Child Labor." UNICEF also publishes literature on a wide variety of other topics, such as HIV/AIDS, the impact of war on children, and child development. Most publications are available in English, French, and Spanish and can be ordered from an online bookstore on the official UNICEF Web site.

Resources for Further Information

The United Nations Children's Fund (UNICEF): http://www.unicef.org
UNICEF Emergency–Countries in crisis: http://www.unicef.org/emerg/index_role.html
UNICEF Publications: http://www.unicef.org/publications/index.html

United Nations High Commissioner for Human Rights (UNHCHR) recently renamed Office of the United Nations High Commissioner for Human Rights (OHCHR)

Address: United Nations Office at Geneva
              1211 Geneva 10, Switzerland
Fax: 41 22 917 9011
Email: 1503@ohchr.org

Organizational Identity

Based in Geneva, the United Nations High Commissioner for Human Rights (UNHCHR) seeks to identify violations of human rights and subsequently alert national governments and the world community. The High Commissioner participates in active dialogue with governments in order to strengthen human rights protection efforts. By doing so, the organization plays a key role in leading the world toward global peace. The High Commissioner keeps a vision of equality and peace at the forefront. This is accomplished by constantly encouraging the international community to uphold the universally agreed-upon paradigm for all human rights as set forth in the Charter of the United Nations and the Universal Declaration of Human Rights.

Main Activities

In many countries, UNHCHR has established field offices to ensure that human rights standards are upheld and protected at the national level. The presence of these field workers helps local agencies to strengthen and uphold national human rights capacities and institutions, follow up on guidelines and recommendations of treaties, and bolster a culture of human rights. Currently, field offices are active in over 30 countries in Africa, Asia, Europe, North America, and Latin America/Caribbean.

UNHCHR's Technical Cooperation Program conducts assessments of human rights needs with broad national participation, including courts and civil society. Much of this program's work occurs in societies recovering from conflict or otherwise lacking resources to implement human rights standards. As a result of such assessments, communities may identify the areas in need of improvement and subsequently set forth a plan of action including policy formation, education, and formation of national human rights institutions.

UNHCHR is actively involved in educating communities about their human rights. The human rights education programs promote values, beliefs, and attitudes that encourage individuals to recognize the importance of defending their own human rights as well as the rights of others. These long-term programs help foster a sense of unity within the community and are essential to achieving a society where all are valued.

UNHCHR programs cover a wide variety of human rights issues, including health, housing, disabilities, internal displacement, migration, poverty, and racism. A current focus lies with terrorism and counter-terrorist measures. UNHCHR unequivocally condemns acts of terrorism and recognizes the duty of the states to protect individuals living within their province. It encourages all governments to place a high priority on protecting their communities during counter-terrorist actions while respecting human rights and fundamental freedoms.

Psychosocial Programming

UNHCHR focuses on the interconnection of social issues and with human rights issues. The guiding principle of this organization is that human rights are universal, indivisible, interdependent, and interrelated. The organization also strives to protect and emphasize the equality of all human rights, for both men and women, whether they be civil, cultural, economic, political, or social. An example of this kind of work is the UNHCHR appointment, in accordance with Resolution 2002/31, of a Special Rapporteur to focus on the right of everyone to attain the highest standard of physical and mental health. The duties of the Special Rapporteur include gathering, requesting, receiving, and exchanging right-to-health information; discussing possible areas of cooperation with relevant parties (governments, United Nations bodies, nongovernmental organizations, etc.); reporting on the worldwide status of the right to health including, but not limited to, laws, policies, obstacles, and good practices; and making recommendations for improving the practices aimed at promoting and protecting the right to health.

Publications

Fact sheets, educational literature, reference materials, and promotional items are available by request from UNHCHR. Many documents are available for free download and others are available for order. The UNHCHR Web site has a listing of existing items and the languages in which they are printed. Most publications are available in all the official languages of the UN: Arabic, Chinese, English, French, Russian, and Spanish. UNHCHR ships these materials free of charge to the requesting institution.

Resources for Further Information

OHCHR Web site—contains links to highlights of recent UNHCHR activities, the media center, the Universal Declaration of Human

Rights (in 300 languages), a link to a searchable UN human rights document database, and downloadable reports relevant to the UNHCHR: http://www.ohchr.org

OHCHR Media Center—this section of the OHCHR Web site offers highlights of current organization activities, links to notable speeches and news releases, and a link to the OHCHR Newsletter: http://www.ohchr.org/english/press/index2.htm

OHCHR Issues—this section of the OHCHR Web site provides information about the various issues and committees that are the focus of the organization: http://www.ohchr.org/english/issues/index.htm

United Nations High Commissioner for Refugees (UNHCR)

Address: United Nations High Commissioner for Refugees
              Case Postale 2500
              CH-1211 Genève 2 Dépôt
              Switzerland
Telephone: +41 22 739 8111
Email: http://www.unhcr.ch/cgi-bin/texis/vtx/contact

Organizational Identity

Based in Geneva, Switzerland, UNHCR is the primary refugee agency for the United Nations, with an annual operating budget of nearly 1 billion dollars. Its humanitarian activities are guided by the 1951 UN Convention on the Status of Refugees, as well as its 1967 Protocol. UNHCR provides assistance to all refugees regardless of race, religion, creed, or political affiliation. Its mission is to safeguard the rights and well-being of refugee populations by reducing the occurrence of situations of forced displacement. UNHCR encourages states and institutions to provide for peaceful resolutions to disputes. Additionally, the agency advocates for reintegration of returning refugees to their country of origin. To accomplish its mission, the agency works closely with other humanitarian organizations such as UNICEF and WHO, as well as with international governments and regional organizations.

Brief History

Refugees are legally defined as people who are outside their countries because of a well-founded fear of persecution based on their race, religion, nationality, political opinion, or membership in a particular social group, and who cannot or do not want to return home. In an effort to help these individuals, UNHCR was established on December 14, 1950, by the United Nations General Assembly. The agency helps people restart their lives by resettling in other countries or by returning to their countries of origin. Currently, UNHCR has approximately 6,000 staff members who are active in over 100 countries, assisting more than 17 million individuals. UNHCR has received two Nobel Peace Prizes (1954, 1981) in recognition of its significant contribution to refugee assistance.

Main Activities

When emergency relief is necessary, UNHCR provides water, food, shelter, sanitation, and medical care services. Specific attention is paid to vulnerable populations such as women, children, and elderly. UNHCR is committed to facilitating the participation of refugees in decisions that affect their lives in ways that are consistent with the principles of the United Nations Charter. For example, in an effort to integrate humanitarian relief and longer-term development that would provide repatriating refugees with sustainable solutions, the High Commissioner put the 4R initiative into effect. The four R's are repatriation, reintegration, rehabilitation, and reconstruction. Further, the UNHCR seeks to ensure that refugees are involved in planning and programming within the Framework for Durable Solutions. In this way, the organization emphasizes the importance of participation and continues to be active in the elimination of poverty and global development.

Psychosocial Programming

UNHCR is committed to the recognition and management of mental health and psychosocial issues among refugee populations. Specifically, the organization believes that, because of past experiences, issues in adjustment and/or resettlement, and the impact of trauma and/or torture, refugees are at a risk of developing mental health problems. UNHCR is committed to implementing integration programs that provide resources for the emotional support and personal rebuilding of refugees in order to promote well-being and prevent the development of serious mental health problems.

Integration program components include considerations of placement, settlement, and social support; income support; language training; housing; employment; health care; and promotion of hospitable communities. Additionally, issues such as professional development and debriefing for support personnel, as well as development of support provider networks for the purposes of information exchange and support coordination, are considered.

The goals for integration programs include restoring feelings of security, control, and independence by meeting refugee needs and facilitating communication within the receiving society; promoting capacity to rebuild; promoting family reunification and relationships with helping professionals; restoring confidence in the political system; promoting cultural integrity; countering racism and discrimination in receiving communities; supporting the development of refugee communities; and fostering support and potential in light of diversity issues such as age, gender, family status, and past experiences.

UNHCR believes that the optimal approach to treating refugee-related trauma/mental health issues combines the following: individual, family, or group therapy; support in the face of adverse environmental conditions; and pharmacological therapy. This support is most often provided by a multidisciplinary team including, but not limited to, counselors, social support providers, psychiatrists, general medical practitioners, natural therapists, and physiotherapists. In addition, many countries have implemented culturally sensitive alternative therapies that are developed in consultation with the refugee communities. UNHCR also believes that it is essential to develop the capacity of existing psychological support resources within the refugee community. For example, the organization works to develop networks of professionals to offer affordable services to refugees within their developing communities.

UNHCR also strives to enhance the ability of refugees to make use of psychological health services. Several strategies are utilized to meet this goal, including, but not limited to, incorporating bilingualism into the support staff workforce, providing language assistance, educating refugees about mental health issues, and exploring alternative methods of healing in consultation with the refugee community. Further, UNHCR recognizes the emotional effects of working with traumatized populations and believes professional debriefing to be one way of helping those who provide support to refugee populations deal with the stress.

UNHCR is committed to advocacy initiatives on behalf of refugee populations in many areas, including, but not limited to, education. Further, the organization is committed to policy formation relevant to refugee issues. For example, UNHCR plans to strengthen the implementation of policy priorities for refugee women and children, gender equality, and older persons through community development in 2005. UNHCR will approach this task by encouraging staff worldwide to emphasize refugee protection strategies and programming in their work.

UNHCR, in addition to various publications available on the organization's Web site, provides a listing of new issues in refugee research. This listing includes working papers that are produced and published by UNHCR's Evaluation and Policy Analysis Unit. The papers address such issues as unwanted migration, refugee integration, refugee livelihoods, and methodological issues regarding research and evaluation in refugee populations.

Publications

UNHCR publishes a wide variety of literature on all aspects of refugee health and service. The official Web site for UNHCR contains a link to publications that are available for free online download. Key documents such as the *1951 Geneva Refugee Convention* and *The State of the World's Refugees 2000* are available in full. Additionally, the site provides access to a map library, graphics, photo archives, a video unit, and reports on specialized subjects.

Resources for Further Information

UNHCR: http://www.unhcr.ch
UNHCR Publications: http://www.unhcr.ch/cgi-bin/texis/vtx/publ

U.S. Agency for International Development (USAID)

Address: Information Center
                  U.S. Agency for International Development
                  Ronald Reagan Building
                  Washington, DC 20523-1000
Telephone: (202) 712-0000 (main switchboard)
Fax No.:   (202) 216-3524
Email: pinquiries@usaid.gov.

Organizational Identity

The U.S. Agency for International Development (USAID) is an independent government agency that assists in providing economic, humanitarian, and developmental assistance to countries around the world. Based in Washington, DC, USAID also has field offices around the world and works closely with universities, other humanitarian organizations, indigenous groups, and businesses. USAID provides assistance programs in four parts of the world: Sub-Saharan Africa, Asia and the Near East, Europe and Eurasia, and Latin America/Caribbean.

Brief History

USAID was established in 1961 as the principal responding organization to crises and reforms throughout the world. This assistance work helps the United States further develop its foreign policy interests while improving the lives of individuals in developing or disadvantaged countries.

Main Activities

USAID responds to a disaster when it is severe enough to satisfy the following three conditions: the affected country is unable to respond adequately; the affected country is willing to accept such assistance; and it is in the best interest of the United States to respond. Funds for immediate relief assistance projects are provided when lives are at risk, when there is a large degree of human suffering, or when there is a severe economic impact. During initial response efforts, USAID sends an assessment team composed of specialists in USAID policy, health concerns, nutrition, agriculture, water sanitation, geohazards, protection, and disaster management. This team assesses the severity and magnitude of the disaster. If necessary, a Disaster Assistance Response Team (DART) may be deployed. This team is composed of members with expertise in management, logistics, planning operations, liaising, and contracting. The role of the DART is to expedite the disaster relief efforts by assessing the effectiveness of the current program, identifying unmet needs in the population, and assisting with operation management.

USAID works in conjunction with other humanitarian organizations, both domestic and abroad, to supply services to areas affected by crisis or disaster. The amount of assistance from USAID is dependent on the magnitude of the disaster as well as the affected country's own response capacity. USAID's key partner is the U.S. Office of Foreign Disaster Assistance (OFDA), the primary facilitator of U.S. relief assistance abroad. Through this program, the United States and its partner agencies are able to help communities meet their basic needs, as well as foster economic and social recovery. USAID is also involved with programs that provide food commodities. USAID's Office of Food for Peace has also established a variety of funds to assist families who have been affected by war or other traumatic events. The Victims of Torture Fund assists in programs for rehabilitating individuals who have lasting physical or psychological effects following tortuous experiences. The programs work not only with individuals, but also with their families and their communities.

Psychosocial Programming

USAID does not directly provide psychosocial services; however, it operates as a conduit for financial assistance from the United States federal government to countries around the world. This organization funds a wide variety of programs that include psychosocial components. For example, USAID assisted in the aftermath of the terrorist bombing of the U.S. embassy in Nairobi, and is actively involved in many children's health initiatives.

Publications

USAID has produced many publications. For example, USAID/OFDA has published the *Field Operations Guide*, a pocket-sized text containing methodology and information relating to conducting assessments of disasters. Additionally, there are many downloadable documents located on the USAID Web site that are available to the public.

Resources for Further Information

USAID Web site: http://www.usaid.gov
USAID Press Page: http://www.usaid.gov/press/

USAID Humanitarian Assistance/Disaster Assistance page—this section of the Web site contains information about recent disaster-related publications, annual reports, evaluations of humanitarian information centers, guidelines for grant proposals, and how to contribute to USAID disaster services: http://www.usaid.gov/our_work/humanitarian_assistance/disaster_assistance

Development Experience Clearinghouse: http://www.dec.org/default.cfm?CFID=658522&CFTOKEN=87540754

World Health Organization (WHO)

Address: Avenue Appia 20
              1211 Geneva 27
              Switzerland
Telephone: +41 22 791 2111
Fax No.:   +41 22 791 3111
Email: info@who.int

Brief History

Based in Geneva, Switzerland, the World Health Organization (WHO) was established in 1948 as a specialized health agency for the United Nations. WHO is governed by the World Health Assembly, which is composed of members from 192 member states. According to WHO's constitution, its guiding principle is to assist all people in achieving their highest possible level of health. WHO defines health as "a state of complete physical, mental and social well-being and not merely the absence of disease or infirmity."

Main Activities

The core activities of WHO revolve around assisting countries in reducing excess mortality and morbidity. Activities related to mental health and conflict/disaster are led by the Department of Mental Health and Substance Abuse in close collaboration with Regional Mental Health Advisors and the Department of Health Action in Crises. The latter is the WHO department generally responsible for health activities whenever disaster-affected systems become unable to respond to people's most basic needs. The subregional office of WHO/PAHO in Panama specializes in disaster mental health preparation.

The Department of Mental Health and Substance Abuse recently summarized its position with respect to principles and intervention strategies during and after emergencies. The selection of principles and strategies was informed by a range of existing consensus statements and guidelines by a variety of international organizations and by a postal survey of expert opinion. The WHO position on mental health in emergencies is contained in the "mental and social aspects of health" standard of the *2004 Sphere Handbook*. The Sphere Project was initiated in 1997 by a group of humanitarian organizations and the Red Cross and Red Crescent Movement in order to satisfy the need for a humanitarian charter and minimum standards in disaster response. Further, the WHO document "Mental Health in Emergencies" outlines general principles and intervention strategies that the organization advises in emergency situations. WHO advocates strongly for social interventions (e.g., adequate risk communication in emergencies) to address some of the determinants of mental sequelae after disaster.

WHO is concerned with the promotion of access to mental health care in all countries. In the *World Health Report 2001* on mental health, WHO strongly advocates for a community-based approach, emphasizing the inefficiencies and potential harmful effects of institutional care. The organization seeks to address care of all groups—including marginalized populations such as disaster victims, refugees, the elderly, and the poor—within the general mental health system, which is integrated into the general health system. To reduce fragmentation, the organization cautions against vertical programs that focus on specific disorders and problems *in the absence of* a strong link to existing systems (e.g., general health services, general mental health services, the school system). The development of national-level plans for the organization of mental health services is also an increasingly important focus of field work by WHO.

Publications

WHO publishes a monthly peer-reviewed scientific journal titled *Bulletin of the World Health Organization*. This publication serves to disseminate scientific public health information to researchers and policy makers in the field. The journal may be accessed gratis online. Most WHO publications on mental health may be downloaded from the Web site listed below.

Resources for Further Information

WHO Web site: http://www.who.int/en/
WHO Mental Health in Emergencies: http://www.who.int/mental_health/prevention/mnhemergencies/en/
Downloadable WHO Publications: http://www.who.int/mental_health/resources/publications/en/

World Vision International (WV)

Address: 800 West Chestnut Avenue
             Monrovia, CA 91016-3198
Email: newsvision@wvi.org

World Vision Partners' Offices

USA	Monrovia, CA
International Liaison Office	Geneva, Switzerland
Africa	Nairobi, Kenya
Asia-Pacific	Bangkok, Thailand
Latin America and Caribbean	San Jose, Costa Rica
Middle East and Eastern Europe	Nicosia, Cyprus

Organizational Identity

World Vision (WV) is an international, faith-based, Christian organization whose primary mission is to assist poor and oppressed populations to promote human transformation, seek justice, and bear witness to the good news of the Kingdom of God. The guiding philosophy is "Our vision for every child, life in all its fullness; Our prayer for every heart, the will to make it so." WV operates as a partnership of autonomous national entities, governed by common core values and principles. The international board comprises 25 members from 19 nations.

Brief History

Child sponsorship began over 50 years ago when a Christian minister, Rev. Bob Pierce, witnessed severe poverty and hunger in Asia. He soon established a child sponsorship program to assist children who had been orphaned by the Korean War. The money gathered in this program provided children with food, educational opportunities, health care, and vocational training. The program eventually expanded through Asia, and into Latin America and Africa. An emergency relief division that focused on addressing community needs, including water sanitation, education, leadership training, and income generation, was added to WV's functions in the 1970s.

Over 70 percent of WV's funding comes from private sources, including individuals, corporations, and foundations. The remainder comes from governments and multilateral agencies. WV accepts cash contributions and gifts-in-kind such as food supplies, medicine, and clothing donated by corporations or government agencies. Approximately half of WV's programs are funded through child sponsorship. Individuals, families, churches, and other groups are linked with specific children and community projects in their own country or abroad. Sponsorship money is applied directly to the support of the child or community on a monthly basis with the purpose of addressing the root causes of poverty and suffering so that a child can enjoy as full a life as possible.

Main Activities

In 2003, WV was active in nearly 100 countries throughout Africa, Asia, Central Asia, Europe, Latin America, the Middle East, North America, and Oceania. The organization's projects may be grouped into two major areas: long-term development and short-term emergency relief. Long-term sustainable community development programs focus on meeting the basic needs identified by the community, such as provision of clean water, educational opportunities, health care, agricultural improvements, and public hygiene. With WV's assistance, the communities can recognize their resources and work to maintain the new programs. Short-term emergency relief programs are established in the wake of natural or man-made disasters. WV is committed to respond to major emergencies around the world through its own programs or in cooperation with partner agencies. Many of the relief programs are structured so that they can easily evolve into more sustainable development programs. The fundamental aim of the emergency programs is meeting basic survival needs of the affected populations, such as providing shelter, medical care, and food, and working toward economic recovery. In 2003, WV was the largest food aid handler in the world, and currently its response to HIV/AIDS, the Hope Initiative, is active in every country with a high prevalence of HIV.

Psychosocial Programming

In addition to physical response efforts, WV assists communities in the psychosocial recovery process. Programs have been implemented in postconflict/disaster areas where depression and other psychological issues are prevalent. This process is necessary since community development may be impaired if a large number of individuals within the community are affected by mental health issues.

The Psychosocial Sector of WV realizes the importance of assessing the needs of affected communities before interventions are applied; therefore, in collaboration with other mental health institutions, they have worked to develop culturally relevant ethnographic assessments and measures of symptoms and needs. This work on needs assessment, and a process that allows communities to express their perception of their mental health issues, prompted the implementation of a community-based therapy program. This program is sustainable and easily applied in areas where clinical and medical approaches were previously unavailable. Specifically, WV found that a program of Interpersonal Psychotherapy for Groups is an effective short-term therapy that locally trained staff can easily replicate. The organization is working to implement this community-based model in other areas and cultures, and to implement a program to help equip staff with appropriate coping skills when dealing with high levels of occupational stress and personal safety issues.

Advocacy: WV defines advocacy as activities aimed at achieving specific and defined policy changes. Advocacy is generally aimed at decision makers at the local, regional, national, and/or international levels. WV is also often involved in advocacy campaigns aimed at persuading the public to apply pressure to decision makers. Priority areas of focus are children, poverty, conflict, and HIV/AIDS.

Advocacy for Children: WV seeks to assist children who are most vulnerable, including street children, child laborers, sexually exploited and abused children, children with disabilities, female children, children who are orphaned, refugee children, and children affected by armed conflict. WV advocates a multi-pronged approach to address these issues through representations at local, national, and international levels. Regarding child trafficking, for example, WV Malaysia has advocated for, and secured, a stricter sentencing regime for pedophiles; simultaneously, WVUK successfully lobbied for a change in regulations relating to overseas travel by pedophiles. WV offices have also been active in seeking new legislation, codes of practice, or national policy guidelines regarding children.

WV endorses the United Nations Convention on the Rights of the Child (CRC), which calls for national governments to legislate for child protection, properly train law enforcement agencies about children's rights, and invite children to be participants in discussions that will foster their development and guarantee their rights. WV considers this a written commitment to children's issues and promotes the principles of the Convention as a basis for action. WV also supports The Global Movement for Children (Chair), the NGO Group on the Rights of the Child (Steering Committee) and its Sub-Group on Sexual Exploitation (Chair), the NGO Committee on UNICEF (co-Chair), ECPAT (End Child Prostitution and Trafficking), the Child Rights Caucus for the UN General Assembly Special Session on Children, the Coalition to Stop the Use of Child Soldiers (Steering Committee), the Children and Violence Caucus for the Special Session (Chair), and the Global Campaign for Education.

Advocacy Amid Poverty: WV International is concerned with poverty and economic justice. In this arena some of WV's achievements will have dramatic effects on the communities involved. WV also influences the content and implementation of national strategies for poverty reduction that govern all aspects of local social policy, such as education and health.

Advocacy amid Conflict: WV advocates for an end to violent conflict and for promotion of a culture of peace to prevent conflict among the international community and other stakeholders. WV is also active in advocacy regarding resourcing and planning postconflict reconstruction, and in lobbying for a legally enforceable policy framework to prevent proliferation of small arms and light weapons.

Advocacy Regarding HIV/AIDS: WV is active in advocacy specific to the HIV/AIDS epidemic. Specifically, the organization focuses on four main advocacy messages related to HIV/AIDS:

1. Strengthen care for orphans and vulnerable children, including incorporating psychosocial care
2. Reduce the vulnerability of girls and women to HIV
3. Increase access to treatment and care
4. Mobilize resources for expanded HIV/AIDS response

WV has made considerable strides in this area of advocacy. For example, in 2004, World Vision UK gained the inclusion of OVC issues in DFID's new HIV/AIDS strategy, and work by WV Australia resulted in $70 million in pledges to the Global Fund. Further, regarding programming, WV secured a considerable loosening of national policy on AIDS education in Mauritania, including open discussion of controversial issues such as condoms.

Publications

WV has produced the *Stress and Trauma Handbook*, a text that focuses on the effects of stress on international aid workers. WV also offers readings on a variety of topics in downloadable format from its Web site. Topics include Peace and Conflict, Gender and Development, Child Rights, Global Economics and Trade, HIV/AIDS, Human Rights, Reducing Poverty, and Violence in the Home. Additionally, WV offers an online store (http://www.worldvisionresources.com) where visitors can purchase books, CD-ROMs, maps, and videos.

Resources for Further Information

A listing of documents available for public use can be found at the following URLs:

World Vision Publications: http://www.wvi.org/wvi/publications/publications.htm
World Vision International: http://www.wvi.org
World Vision Advocacy Initiatives: http://www.globalempowerment.org/

INDEX

ABOUT THE VOLUME EDITORS

GILBERT REYES, PhD, is a licensed clinical psychologist and the Associate Dean for Clinical Training at Fielding Graduate University in Santa Barbara, California. He has responded to several major disasters in the United States, including the September 11, 2001, attack on the World Trade Center. Reyes has also consulted with the International Federation of Red Cross and Red Crescent Societies on various projects and in 2002 co-authored that organization's training manual for community-based psychological support. He recently co-authored a training course for the American Red Cross on children's disaster mental health needs and is now collaborating with the Terrorism and Disaster Center of the National Child Traumatic Stress Network on the development of interventions for children in disasters.

GERARD A. (JERRY) JACOBS, PhD, is Director of the Disaster Mental Health Institute (DMHI) and a Professor at the University of South Dakota. He is active in field work, training, program development, and consultation nationally and internationally for the Red Cross movement and the American Psychological Association. He is a co-author of the WHO Tool for the Rapid Assessment of Mental Health and served on the Institute of Medicine Committee on Responding to the Psychological Consequences of Terrorism. He also works with the Asian Disaster Preparedness Center in psychological support training and program development.

About the Contributors

PETER BERLINER is Associate Professor at the University of Copenhagen and Consultant Psychologist at the Rehabilitations and Research Centre for Torture Victims (RCT), Copenhagen, Denmark.

JO BOYDEN is a social anthropologist who has specialized in policy and research on children, childhood, and child development. She has worked for many years as a consultant to a wide range of humanitarian and development agencies in South and Southeast Asia, parts of Africa, and the Andean Region. As Senior Research Officer at the University of Oxford, she is developing a research program on children affected by forced migration and armed conflict.

YAEL DANIELI, PhD, is a clinical psychologist in private practice in New York City, a traumatologist, and victimologist. She is also Co-founder and Director, Group Project for Holocaust Survivors and Their Children; Founding President, International Network for Holocaust and Genocide Survivors and their Friends; and Co-founder, past-President, Senior United Nations Representative, International Society for Traumatic Stress Studies (ISTSS). Dr. Danieli integrates treatment, worldwide study, teaching/training, publishing, expert advocacy, and consulting to numerous governments, news, international and national organizations, and institutions on victims rights and optimal care, including for their protectors and providers. Most recently she received the ISTSS Lifetime Achievement Award.

JOANNA DE BERRY has a background in anthropology. She specializes in research, policy development, and programming for conflict-affected young people. She has worked extensively in Afghanistan, across South Asia, and in Uganda for organizations including UNICEF and Save the Children. She is currently working with local government in South London promoting young people's participation and conflict resolution.

ERIK L. J. L. DE SOIR, MAJOR, is a Psychologist, Senior Lecturer, and Researcher at the Stress & Trauma Research Center in the Royal Military Academy, Brussels. He is the author of more than 50 articles on traumatic stress in fire, emergency, and police services, and books including *Traumatische stress en politie* (*Traumatic Stress and Police*) and *Op het netvlies gebrand . . . ! Traumatische stress bij hulpverleners* (*Burned on the Retina . . . ! Traumatic Stress in Caregivers*). He provided special training seminars for trauma counselors and crisis responders in Russia, Norway, the Czech Republic, Switzerland, Bulgaria, the Netherlands, New Zealand, Australia, the United States of America, France, Germany, Luxembourg, and Italy. De Soir is a Board Certified Expert of the American Academy of Experts in Traumatic Stress, an International Advisor for several risk organizations, and a member of several international societies for traumatic stress, including the Australasian Critical Incident Stress Association. He is currently Vice-President of the Association de Langue Française pour l'Etude du Stress et du Traumatisme, and Co-Chair of the International Structure & Affiliations Committee of the International Society for Traumatic Stress Studies. He is a founding member of the Belgian Society for Psychotraumatology and the new French scientific trauma journal *La Revue francophone pour le Stress et le Trauma*.

JOHN H. EHRENREICH is Professor of Psychology at the State University of New York, College at Old Westbury. He is the author of *The Humanitarian Companion: A Guide for International Aid, Development and Human Rights Workers* (2005) and *Coping with Disaster: A Guide to Psychosocial Intervention* (2001). He co-chaired the panel of experts, convened by the Antares Foundation (Amsterdam), that developed the "Guidelines for Good Practice: Managing Stress in Humanitarian Workers" (2005).

THOMAS FEENY has specialized in child protection issues for the last six years. Since graduating with a BA from Cambridge University and an MA in Social Anthropology from The School of Oriental & African Studies, University of London, he has worked as a consultant for a number of charities, including UNICEF, Save the Children, Christian Children's Fund, and Plan. In 2003–2004 he worked as Advocacy Officer for The Consortium for Street Children UK and has since emigrated to Australia, where he is Senior Research Officer for The Smith Family, one of the largest charities working with disadvantaged children and families around the country.

JASON HART is a research officer at the Refugee Studies Centre, University of Oxford, and, during 2004–2005, a research fellow in the Department of Anthropology, Johns Hopkins University. His work focuses principally on children and adolescents living amid political violence. A social anthropologist whose doctoral research was conducted with refugee children in Jordan, he has worked as a researcher and trainer for aid and development agencies in Africa, the Middle East, and South Asia.

AMY C. HUDNALL was educated in history (MA) and history and German studies (BA) at Appalachian State University. She studied at the Goethe Institute and the Bayerische Julius-Maximilians-Universität, Germany. She is a lecturer in the History and Women's Studies Departments, Appalachian State University, and a Research Assistant Professor at the Institute of Rural Health, Idaho State University. Her work focuses on cross-cultural trauma and genocide from psychological and historical references, and she teaches courses on peace and conflict. She has presented and published on captivity trauma, human rights, secondary trauma, cultural relativism, and cross-cultural conflict.

EVELIN GERDA LINDNER is a social scientist with an interdisciplinary orientation, holding PhDs in social medicine and in social psychology. In 1996–2001, she designed and carried out a research project on the concept of humiliation and its role in genocide and war in Rwanda, Somalia, and Germany. Her research indicates that the dynamics of humiliation may be at the core of war and genocides as well as issues like the "war on terror," and it explores whether combating poverty might reduce terror. Lindner has written multiple books and articles on humiliation and established the Human Dignity and Humiliation Studies.

SUSAN McKAY, PhD, is a psychologist, nurse, and Professor of Women's Studies and Adjunct Professor of International Studies and Nursing at the University of Wyoming in Laramie, Wyoming. For 15 years she has taught and researched issues focused upon women, girls, and armed conflict; women and peacebuilding; and feminist issues in peace psychology. She has published over 70 books, chapters, and articles. Recent books include *Where Are the Girls? Girls in Fighting Forces in Northern Uganda, Sierra Leone, and Mozambique, Their Lives during and after War* (2004), *The Courage Our Stories Tell: The Daily Lives and Maternal Child Health Care of Japanese-American Women at Heart Mountain* (2002), and *Raising Women's Voices for Peacebuilding: Vision, Impact, and Limitations of Media Technologies* (2001). She is past President of the Division of Peace Psychology of the American Psychological Association. Recent awards include designation as a fellow of the American Psychological Association (2002), Extraordinary Merit in Research (2003), and selection as Seibold Professor in the College of Arts and Sciences at the University of Wyoming (2003–2004).

ELISABETH NAIMA MIKKELSEN is a postgraduate student in Psychology and International Development Studies, Roskilde University, and Research Assistant at the Rehabilitations and Research Centre for Torture Victims (RCT), Copenhagen, Denmark.

ELANA NEWMAN is an Associate Professor of Psychology at the University of Tulsa. Her recent work has focused upon understanding the effects of trauma reporting on journalists, and teaching journalists about traumatic stress. Newman co-directed the New York Office of the Dart Center for Journalism and Trauma after the 9/11 attacks, and she acts as research director of the Dart Center for Journalism and Trauma. Other areas of interest include bioterrorism preparedness, dissemination of best trauma-focused practice, assessment of adults and children, and the ethics of conducting research with trauma survivors.

CHEN REIS, MPH, JD, is a human rights researcher specializing in health and human rights with a focus on gender-based violence, health in conflicts, women's rights, children's rights, and HIV/AIDS. Until recently, she was a Senior Researcher with Physicians for Human Rights (USA). She holds a master's degree in public health and a bachelor's degree in social and cultural anthropology from Johns Hopkins University and law degree from Columbia University.

BENEDETTO SARACENO, MD, an internationally admired psychiatrist, is the Director of the Department of Mental Health in the World Health Organization (WHO). He has been a committed mental health reformer for over three decades, both in Italy and in the global arena. As a progressive voice for patients' rights and de-institutionalization, he has contributed to the reduction of the stigma associated with mental illnesses. Dr. Saraceno works closely with nongovernmental humanitarian organizations to promote greater awareness of the growing burden of mental illness around the world. He has recently worked tirelessly to ensure adequate and appropriate psychosocial support for victims of the Indian Ocean tsunamis.

BRUCE SHAPIRO is Field Director of the Dart Center for Journalism and Trauma and Lecturer at Yale College, where he teaches investigative journalism. His books include *Shaking the Foundations: 200 Years of Investigative Journalism in America* (2003) and *Legal Lynching: The Death Penalty and America's Future* (with Rev. Jesse Jackson and U.S. Rep. Jesse Jackson, Jr.) (2001).

CHARLES D. SPIELBERGER is Distinguished Research Professor of Psychology and Director of the Center for Research in Behavioral Medicine and Health Psychology at the University of South Florida. He previously directed the USF Doctoral Program in Clinical Psychology. An ABPP Diplomate in Clinical Psychology and Distinguished Practitioner of the National Academies of Practice, Spielberger focuses his current research on anxiety, curiosity, and the experience, expression, and control of anger; job stress and stress management; and the effects of stress, emotions, and lifestyle factors on hypertension, cardiovascular disorders, and cancer. During 1991–1992, Spielberger served as the 100th president of the American Psychological Association.

BETH VANN, MSW, Global Gender-Based Violence Technical Advisor, specializes in projects that address violence against women in populations affected by armed conflict. Since 1998, her work has focused on GBV technical advising, training, and research with displaced communities, NGOs, UN agencies, and host governments. Ms. Vann has 20 years of experience in development and management of health and social services programs, and has worked in 17 countries. She holds a master's degree in social work and a bachelor's degree in psychology. Vann is currently employed by the GBV Global Technical Support Project at JSI Research and Training Institute and on behalf of the Reproductive Health Response in Conflict (RHRC) Consortium.

ABOUT THE SERIES

As this new millennium dawns, humankind has evolved—some would argue has developed—exhibiting new and old behaviors that fascinate, infuriate, delight or fully perplex those of us seeking answers to the question, "Why?" In this series, experts from various disciplines peer through the lens of psychology telling us answers they see for questions of human behavior. Their topics may range from humanity's psychological ills—addictions, abuse, suicide, murder, and terrorism among them—to works focused on positive subjects including intelligence, creativity, athleticism, and resilience. Regardless of the topic, the goal of this series remains constant—to offer innovative ideas, provocative considerations, and useful beginnings to better understand human behavior.

Chris E. Stout
Series Editor

ABOUT THE SERIES EDITOR AND ADVISORY BOARD

CHRIS E. STOUT, PsyD, MBA, is a licensed clinical psychologist and is a Clinical Full Professor at the University of Illinois College of Medicine's Department of Psychiatry. He served as an NGO Special Representative to the United Nations, was appointed to the World Economic Forum's Global Leaders of Tomorrow, and has served as an Invited Faculty at the Annual Meeting in Davos. He is the Founding Director of the Center for Global Initiatives. Dr. Stout is a Fellow of the American Psychological Association, past-President of the Illinois Psychological Association, and a Distinguished Practitioner in the National Academies of Practice. Dr. Stout has published or presented over 300 papers and 30 books/manuals on various topics in psychology, and his works have been translated into six languages. He has lectured across the nation and internationally in 19 countries, visited 6 continents, and almost 70 countries. He was noted as being "one of the most frequently cited psychologists in the scientific literature" in a study by Hartwick College. He is the recipient of the American Psychological Association's International Humanitarian Award.

BRUCE BONECUTTER, PhD, is Director of Behavioral Services at the Elgin Community Mental Health Center, the Illinois Department of Human Services state hospital serving adults in greater Chicago. He is also a Clinical Assistant Professor of Psychology at the University of Illinois at Chicago. A clinical psychologist specializing in health, consulting, and forensic psychology, Mr. Bonecutter is also a longtime member of the American Psychological Association Taskforce on Children & the Family. He is a member of organizations including the Association for the Treatment of Sexual Abusers, International; the Alliance for the Mentally Ill; and the Mental Health Association of Illinois.

JOSEPH FLAHERTY, MD, is Chief of Psychiatry at the University of Illinois Hospital, a Professor of Psychiatry at the University of Illinois College of Medicine, and a Professor of Community Health Science at the UIC College of Public Health. He is a Founding Member of the Society for the Study of Culture and Psychiatry. Dr. Flaherty has been a consultant to the World Health Organization, the National Institutes of Mental Health, and also the Falk Institute in Jerusalem. He has been Director of Undergraduate Education and Graduate Education in the Department of Psychiatry at the University of Illinois. Dr. Flaherty has also been Staff Psychiatrist and Chief of Psychiatry at Veterans Administration West Side Hospital in Chicago.

MICHAEL HOROWITZ, PhD, is President and Professor of Clinical Psychology at the Chicago School of Professional Psychology, one of the nation's leading not-for-profit graduate schools of psychology. Earlier, he served as Dean and Professor of the Arizona School of Professional Psychology. A clinical psychologist practicing independently since 1987, he has focused his work on psychoanalysis, intensive individual therapy, and couples therapy. He has provided Disaster Mental Health Services to the American Red Cross. Mr. Horowitz's special interests include the study of fatherhood.

SHELDON I. MILLER, MD, is a Professor of Psychiatry at Northwestern University, and Director of the Stone Institute of Psychiatry at Northwestern Memorial Hospital. He is also Director of the American Board of Psychiatry and Neurology, Director of the American Board of Emergency Medicine, and Director of the Accreditation Council for Graduate Medical Education. Dr. Miller is also an Examiner for the American Board of Psychiatry and Neurology. He is Founding Editor of the American Journal of Addictions, and Founding Chairman of the American Psychiatric Association's Committee on Alcoholism. Dr. Miller has also been a Lieutenant Commander in the U.S. Public Health Service, serving as psychiatric consultant to the Navajo Area Indian Health Service at Window Rock, Arizona. He is a member and Past President of the Executive Committee for the American Academy of Psychiatrists in Alcoholism and Addictions.

DENNIS P. MORRISON, PhD, is Chief Executive Officer at the Center for Behavioral Health in Indiana, the first behavioral health company ever to win the JCAHO Codman Award for excellence in the use of outcomes management to achieve health care quality improvement. He is President of the Board of Directors for the Community Healthcare Foundation in Bloomington, and has been a member of the Board of Directors for the American College of Sports Psychology. He has served as a consultant to agencies including the Ohio Department of Mental Health, Tennessee Association of Mental Health Organizations, Oklahoma Psychological Association, the North Carolina Council of Community Mental Health Centers, and the National Center for Health Promotion in Michigan. Dr. Morrison served across 10 years as a Medical Service Corp Officer in the U.S. Navy.

WILLIAM H. REID, MD, is a clinical and forensic psychiatrist, and consultant to attorneys and courts throughout the United States. He is Clinical Professor of Psychiatry at the University of Texas Health Science Center. Dr. Miller is also an Adjunct Professor of Psychiatry at Texas A&M College of Medicine and Texas Tech University School of Medicine, as well as a Clinical Faculty member at the Austin Psychiatry Residency Program. He is Chairman of the Scientific Advisory Board and Medical Advisor to the Texas Depressive & Manic-Depressive Association, as well as an Examiner for the American Board of Psychiatry & Neurology. He has served as President of the American Academy of Psychiatry and the Law, as Chairman of the Research Section for an International Conference on the Psychiatric Aspects of Terrorism, and as Medical Director for the Texas Department of Mental Health and Mental Retardation. Dr. Reid earned an Exemplary Psychiatrist Award from the National Alliance for the Mentally Ill. He has been cited on the Best Doctors in America listing since 1998.